Globalisation and Economic Development

Globalisation and Economic Development

B.K.Panda

Sukanta Sarkar

KALPAZ

ISBN: 978-93-5128-126-9

Price: ₹ 990

First Published, 2015

Published by

Kalpaz Publications
C-30, Satyawati Nagar,
Delhi-110052
Ph. : 9212142040
E-mail: kalpaz@hotmail.com

Printed at : G. Print Process, Delhi

Cataloging in Publication Data—DK
Courtesy: D.K. Agencies (P) Ltd. <docinfo@dkagencies.com>

Globalisation and economic development / B.K.Panda, Sukanta Sarkar.
pages cm
Contributed articles.
Includes bibliographical references (pages).
ISBN 9789351281269

1. Globalisation—Economic aspects—India. 2. Economic development—India. 3. India—Economic policy—1991- 4. Poverty—Government policy—India. 5. Women in development—Government policy—India. I. Panda, B.K., editor. II. Sarkar, Sukanta, editor.

DDC 338.954 23

Contents

Preface

The economic reforms were introduced in India since the middle of 1991 which have received wide attention globally. Specifically, structural reforms were introduced in manufacturing, trade and financial sectors to increase productivity by improving efficiency and to increase the competitiveness of the Indian manufacturing sector. India, which is one of the largest agricultural-based economies, remained closed until the early 1990s. By 1991, there was growing awareness that the inward-looking import substitution and overvalued exchange rate policy coupled with various domestic policies pursued during the past four decades. Limited entrepreneurial decision making in many areas and resulted in a high cost domestic industrial structure that was out of line with world prices. The new government by Shri Narasimha Rao, which took office in June 1991, announced a package of liberalisation measures under its Industrial Policy on July 24, 1991. The New Industrial Policy,1991 seeks to liberate the industry from the shackles of licensing system Drastically reduce the role of public sector and encourage foreign participation in India's industrial development.

This book consists of 18 papers prepared on a variety of topics by eminent personalities. The issue covered in the book has a practical and policy significance in India. The theme have deeply and intensively discussed by the paper writers. All the articles in this book have been reviewed. We have made an earnest attempt to make the articles error free and reader friendly as much as possible. However, we believe that perfection is achievable, but not an achieved one. We invite your comments and constructive suggestions, if any.

Thanks are due to Dr. K.B.Das, Professor, P.G. Dept. of Commerce, Prof. P.K.Sahoo, Vice Chancellor, Utkal University, Bhubaneswar, Dr.D.P.Mishra, Professor, Dept. of MBA, F.M. University, Balasore, Dr.Hitesh Shukla, Professor, Dept. of MBA, Shaurastra University, Dr.R.P.Dash, Professor, Pt.Ravisankar Shukla University, Raipur, Dr.P.K.Padhy, Professor, Dept. of MBA, Berhampur University, Dr.P.C.Mishra, P.G. Dept. of Commerce, Berhampur University, Dr. R.Prasad, Professor, Pt.Ravisankar Shukla University, Raipur, Dr. N.G.Pendse, Professor, Rani Durgabati University, Jabalpur, Dr. D.Pulla. Rao, Professor, Andhra University for constant encouragement, advice and help extended to us. Further, we express our heartily thankfulness to each and every person who directly/ indirectly helped us in preparing this work.

We wish to record our heartfelt gratitude to all the esteemed contributors for having made their articles, completely research related in the choice of the topics and the substances put inside them for worth reading. Further, we express our heartily thankfulness to each and every person who directly/indirectly helped us in preparing this work. It is hoped that this book will be very useful society in general and students of economics/finance in particular.

Dr B.K.Panda

Dr Sukanta Sarkar

About the Contributors

Dr B.K Panda, Professor, P.G.Department of Economics, Berhampur University, Odisha.

Dr D. Pulla Rao, Professor, Department of Economics, Andhra University, Visakhapatnam, Andhra Pradesh, India.

Dr Farzana Alim, Professor, Department of Home Science, Faculty of Agricultural Sciences, Aligarh Muslim University Aligarh, Uttar Pradesh

Dr Md. Momtazur Rahman, Associate Professor and Coordinator, Department of Languages, College of Arts and Sciences, International University of Business, Agriculture and Technology-IUBAT, Uttara, Sector, Dhaka, Bangladesh.

Dr Mohammed Ataur Rahman, Director, Centre for Global Environmental Culture (CGEC), IUBAT-International University of Business Agriculture and Technology, Uttara Model Town, Dhaka, Bangladesh.

Dr N.G. Pendse, Professor, Department of Economics, Rani Durgabati University, Jabalpur, Madhya Pradesh.

Dr P.K. Pandey, Assistant Professor, Centre of Juridical Studies, Dibrugarh University, Assam.

Dr R. Prasad, Professor, Department of Economics, Pandit Ravishankar Shukla University, Raipur, Chhattisgarh.

Dr Rakesh Joshi, Associate Professor, Department of Economics, Saurashtra University, Rajkot, Gujarat.

Dr S. K.Chaudhury, Faculty Member, Department of Business Administration, Berhampur University, Odisha.

Dr Deepali Singh, Associate Professor, Department of Political Science, NIMS University, Jaipur, Rajasthan.

Dr Sangeeta Solanki, Assistant Professor, Institute of Professional Excellence and Management, Ghaziabad, Uttar Pradesh.

Krupa D. Bhatt, Assistant Professor, A.A.Patel Commerce College, Gandhinagar, Gujarat

Mariyam Fatima, Assistant professor, Department of Home Science AMU, Aligarh, Uttar Pradesh.

Moulaey Zainab, Research Scholar, Department of Home Science, Faculty of Agricultural Sciences, Aligarh Muslim University Aligarh, Uttar Pradesh

Ms. Ritu Sharma, Assistant Professor, Institute of Professional Excellence and Management, Ghaziabad, Uttar Pradesh

P. Prabhuswamy, Research Analyst, Population Research Centre, Institute for Social and Economic Change (ISEC), Bangalore, Karnataka.

Patil Vijay Ramchandra, Assistant Professor, Department of Sociology, D D. Shinde Sarkar College, Kolhapur, Maharashtra.

Shikha Chantia, Assistant Professor, Amity School of Fashion Technology, Amity University, Lucknow Campus (U.P.), India.

Abbreviations

BIFR	:	Board for Industrial and Financial Reconstruction
CEDAW	:	Convention on Elimination of All Forms of Discrimination against Women
CSD	:	Commission on Sustainable Development
CSO	:	Central Statistics Office
CSWI	:	Committee on the Status of Women in India
DIPP	:	Department of Industrial Policy and Promotion
ELC	:	European Landscape Convention
EPCH	:	Export Promotion Council of Handicrafts
EU	:	European Union
FAO	:	Food and Agriculture Organisation
FDI	:	Foreign Direct Investment
FYPs	:	Five-Year Plans
GATT	:	General Agreement on Tariffs and Trade
GDP	:	Gross Domestic Product
GEM	:	Gender Empowerment Measure
GST	:	Goods and Service Tax
IDA	:	International Development Agency
IIT	:	Indian Institutes of Technology
ILO	:	International Labour Organisation
IMF	:	International Monetary Fund

IRBD	:	International Bank for Reconstruction and Development
LDCs	:	Less-Developed Countries
LED	:	Local Economic Development
LPG	:	Liberalisation, Privatization and Globalisation
MDG	:	Millennium Development Goals
MFIs	:	Micro Finance Institutions
MGNREGS	:	Mahatma Gandhi National Rural Employment Guarantee Scheme
MNC	:	Multinational Company
MPI	:	Microfinance Penetration Index
MSME	:	Micro, Small and Medium Enterprise
MT	:	Million Tonnes
NABARD	:	National Bank for Agricultural and Rural Development
NBFCs	:	Non-Banking Finance Companies
NCAER	:	National Council of Applied Economic Research
NCU	:	National Commission on Urbanisation
NDC	:	National Development Council
NEP	:	New Economic Policy
NFHS	:	National Family Health Survey
NGOs	:	Non-Government Organisations
NRHM	:	National Rural Health Mission
NRI	:	Non-Resident Indians
OGL	:	Open General License
PRIs	:	Panchayati Raj Institutions
PSA	:	Present Situation Analysis
QRs	:	Quantitative Restrictions
RBI	:	Reserve Bank of India

SCs	:	Scheduled Castes
SD	:	Standard Deviation
SHGs	:	Self Help Groups
SICA	:	Sick Industrial Companies (Special Provisions) Act
STs	:	Scheduled Tribes
TBT	:	Technical Barriers to Trade
TEEB	:	The Economics of Ecosystems and Biodiversity
TFC	:	Twelfth Finance Commission
TRIMs	:	Trade Related Investment Measures
TRIPs	:	Trade Related Intellectual Property Right
TSA	:	Target Situation Analysis
UGC	:	University Grant Commission
UNDP	:	United Nations Development Program
UNICEF	:	United Nations International Children's Fund
US	:	United States
USSR	:	Union of Soviet Socialist Republics
WCED	:	World Commission on Environment and Development
WTO	:	World Trade Organisation

GLOBALISATION

1

Globalisation: A Reality in 21st Century

S. K. Chaudhury & Sukanta Sarkar

"Where globalisation means, as it so often does, that the rich and powerful now have new means to further enrich and empower themselves at the cost of the poorer and weaker, we have a responsibility to protest in the name of universal freedom."

–Nelson Mandela

Introduction

Innovation remains a crucial source of competitive advantage as mass customisation has assumed greater importance in virtually all industrial sectors. The demand for constant innovation has been fuelled by rapid technological advance and change in consumer tastes. The globalisation of high-skilled work is not only a question of how far off shoring will lead to a decline in demand for middle class managers, professionals, or technically trained workers in the West, but it is likely to have an impact on job quality, including compensation packages. As differences in productivity narrow between operations in different parts of the world, the cost and working conditions of Western employees are no longer the global benchmark. The benchmark will gravitate towards high-skilled but lower-waged economies rather than those in Western Europe and North America.

Alternatively, globalisation might be characterised functionally by an intrinsically related series of economic phenomena. These include the liberalisation and deregulation of markets, privatisation of assets, retreat of state functions (particularly welfare ones), diffusion of technology, cross-national distribution of manufacturing production (foreign direct investment), and the integration of capital markets. In its narrowest formulation, the term refers to the worldwide spread of sales, production facilities, and manufacturing processes, all of which reconstitute the international division of labour.

The combination of technological progress, lower transport costs and policy liberalisation in the European Union and elsewhere has led to increasing trade and financial flows between countries. This has important consequences for the functioning of the EU economy. While globalisation brings huge benefits and opportunities, it also means that Europe has to face increased competition in all traded goods and services. The European Globalisation Adjustment Fund provides support to people losing their jobs as a result of major structural changes in world trade patterns due to globalisation, e.g. when a large company shuts down or production is moved outside the EU, or as a result of the global economic and financial crisis.

In the past two decades, workers' remittances from developed countries, but also from developing countries with higher levels of per-capita income, have become an increasingly important source of external development finance, both in absolute terms and relative to other sources of external finance. The importance of workers' remittances as a source of foreign exchange income differs considerably among developing countries. India, Mexico and the Philippines receive the largest amounts of workers' remittances. In absolute terms, the United States is the most important country of origin of workers' remittances to developing and other countries, but these flows constitute only a small item in that country's balance of payments. Expressed as a percentage of total imports, the outflow of remittances is particularly large in Saudi Arabia, where they correspond to almost 30 percent of the total import bill, and some other resource-rich countries in the Middle East.

What is Globalisation?

Globalisation is the process of international integration arising from the interchange of world views, products, ideas and other aspects of culture. The term globalisation has been increasingly used since the mid-1980s and especially since the mid-1990s. The term globalisation is derived from the word globalise, which refers to the emergence of an international network of economic systems. It refers to the growing interdependence of countries resulting from the increasing integration of trade, finance, people, and ideas in one global marketplace. International trade and cross-border investment flows are the main elements of this integration.

Globalisation is currently a popular and controversial issue, though often remaining a loose and poorly-defined concept. Sometimes too comprehensively, the term is used to encompass increases in trade and liberalisation policies as well as reductions in transportation costs and technology transfer. An ex-post measurable and objective definition of globalisation has been used, namely increasing trade openness and FDI. Sectoral vulnerability can be apprehended through the concepts of product cycle and space-time diffusion: new products and technologies appear in the most developed parts of the world. Globalisation is much more than an economic phenomenon. The technological and political changes that drive the process of economic globalisation have massive noneconomic consequences

History of Globalisation

There are both distal and proximate causes which can be traced in the historical factors affecting globalisation. Large-scale globalisation began in the 19th centure. During the 19th century, globalisation approached its modern form as a result of the industrial revolution. Globalisation started after World War II but has accelerated considerably since the mid-1980s, driven by two main factors. One involves technological advances that have lowered the costs of transportation, communication, and computation to the extent that it is often economically feasible for a firm to locate different phases of production in different countries.

In the 19th century, steamships reduced the cost of international transport significantly and railroads made inland transport cheaper. The transport revolution occurred some time between 1820 and 1850, more nations' embraced international trade. Globalisation in this period was decisively shaped by nineteenth-century imperialism such as in Africa and Asia. With improvements in transportation and communication, international business grew rapidly after the beginning of the 20th century. International business arrangements have led to the formation of multinational enterprises (MNE). It is companies that have a worldwide approach to markets and production or one with operations in more than one country. Establishment of free trade areas has become an essential feature of modern governments to handle preferential trading arrangements with foreign and multinational entities. A free trade area is a trade bloc whose member countries have signed a free-trade agreement, which eliminates tariffs, import quotas, and preferences on most (if not all) goods and services traded between them.

Economic globalisation, the ongoing process of greater economic interdependence among countries, is reflected in the increasing amount of cross-border trade in goods and services, the increasing volume of international financial flows, and increasing flows of labour. While the founders of the Bretton Woods system saw the restoration of trade in goods and services as essential to the recovery of the global economy, they did not have the same benign view of capital flows. Nonetheless, capital flows among the industrialised countries did recover during the 1950s, and intensified in the 1960s. Capital flows to developing countries grew more slowly. In the late 1970s and early 1980s they consisted mainly of bank loans; by the 1990s they took the form mainly of foreign direct investment and purchases of marketable securities.

Significance of Globalisation

There is a shared sense that globalisation is a powerful engine that has already contributed to lifting many out of poverty and that, if properly harnessed, could further promote growth and development to the benefit of all. For many years, concerns have been raised regarding certain effects of globalisation on jobs, wages, and job insecurity. Recent survey evidence in European countries, for instance, indicates that in most countries a majority of respondents believe that globalisation provides opportunities for economic growth but increases social inequalities. It potentially plays a key role in these dynamics and in the ensuing effects on workers' earnings and employment. Empirical evidence shows that in countries that open their markets, less-productive businesses are more likely to exit and more productive businesses are more likely to survive. This improved market selection contributes positively and substantially to productivity growth.

The term globalisation means International Integration. Opening up of world trade, development of advanced means of communication, internationalisation of financial markets, growing importance of MNC's, population migrations and more generally increased mobility of persons, goods, capital, data and ideas. It is a process through which the diverse world is unified into a single society.

Measurement of Globalisation

Measurement of economic globalisation focuses on variables such as trade, Foreign Direct Investment, portfolio investment, and income. However, newer indices attempt to measure globalisation in more general terms, including variables related to political, social, cultural, and even environmental aspects of globalisation. One index of globalisation is the KOF Index, which measures three important dimensions of globalisation: economic, social, and political. Another is the A.T. Kearney / Foreign Policy Magazine Globalisation Index. The Enabling Trade Index measures the factors, policies and services that facilitate the trade in goods across borders and to destinations. The Good Country Index is a composite statistic of 35 data points which are mostly generated by the United Nations. These data points are combined into a common measure which gives an overall ranking and a ranking in seven categories such as Science and Technology, Culture, International Peace and Security, World Order, Planet and Climate, Prosperity and Equality, Health and Wellbeing.

Components of Globalisation

Broadly speaking, the term 'globalisation' means integration of economies and societies through cross country flows of information, ideas, technologies, goods, services, capital, finance and people. Cross border integration can have several dimensions – cultural, social, political and economic. In fact, some people fear cultural and social integration even more than economic integration. The fear of "cultural hegemony" haunts many. Limiting ourselves to economic integration, one can see this happen through the three channels of (a) trade in goods and services, (b) movement of capital and (c) flow of finance. Besides, there is also the channel through movement of people. Indian economy had experienced major policy changes in early 1990s. The new economic reform, popularly known as, Liberalisation, Privatisation and Globalisation (LPG model) aimed at making the Indian economy as fastest growing economy and globally competitive. The series of reforms undertaken with respect to industrial sector, trade as well as financial sector aimed at making the economy more efficient.

Globalisation in India

India, which is one of the largest agricultural-based economies, remained closed until the early 1990s. By 1991, there was growing awareness that the inward-looking import substitution and overvalued exchange rate policy coupled with various domestic policies pursued during the past four decades, limited entrepreneurial decision making in many areas and resulted in a high cost domestic industrial structure that was out of line with world prices. After Independence, the managers of the Indian economy took very cautious steps. They found the world sharply divided into two blocs: the one led by the capitalist economies (the US in particular) and other led by the communist economies, primarily the then USSR. There was a cold war between these two blocs. Less developed economies had no option than to join either of the two and invite the ire of the opposite bloc. Especially those economies that were under the British Empire and won freedom in the near past faced a difficult choice. India chose to keep a safe distance from both the blocs by inventing the idea of a mixed economy. The agriculture sector performed miserably in 1987-89. Following the assassination of Rajiv Gandhi, P.V. Narsinmha Rao came to power in June 1991. At that time, India's condition on foreign exchange reserves was poor and precarious. India made a proposal for a loan of US$ 2.26 billion from the IMF. In view of the destitution that the country was in, it had no alternative than to succumb to the World Bank-IMF prescription in embarking on the so-called stabilisation and structural adjustment programmes as a precondition to loan. The World Bank was ready with its proposed 'Strategy for Trade Reform'. As a result, thus, India introduced the New Economic Policy (NEP) in 1991.

India is a founding-member of General Agreement on Tariffs and Trade (GATT) since 1947 and its successor, the World Trade Organisation. While participating actively in its general council meetings, India has been crucial in voicing the concerns of the developing world. Since independence, India's balance of payments on its current account has been negative. Since liberalisation in the 1990s, India's exports have been consistently rising, covering 80.3 percent of its imports in 2002–03, up from 66.2 percent in 1990–91. India's reliance on external assistance and commercial borrowings has decreased since 1991–92, and since 2002–03, it has gradually been repaying these debts. Declining interest rates and reduced borrowings decreased India's debt service ratio to 4.5 percent in 2007. Indian economy was in deep crisis in July 1991, when foreign currency reserves had plummeted to almost $1 billion; Inflation had roared to an annual rate of 17 percent; fiscal deficit was very high and had become unsustainable; foreign investors and NRIs had lost confidence in Indian Economy. Capital was flying out of the country and we were close to defaulting on loans. Along with these bottlenecks at home, many unforeseeable changes swept the economies of nations in Western and Eastern Europe, South East Asia, Latin America and elsewhere, around the same time. These were the economic compulsions at home and abroad that called for a complete overhauling of our economic policies and programs.

The wave of globalisation hitted India at the end of the last century and still the country is flowing with the current of global changes. Globalisation with respect to India has been seen mostly in terms of how freely the GOI has allowed the foreign business entities to operate in India and how much of foreign direct investments have entered India. However, seeing globalisation on these lines is only seeing globalisation as a one-way process. Globalisation process in India is generally perceived as a phenomenon of post 1991. The trends in the changes in the policies of the GOI again reveal a different reality. According to Section (2) of FERA, 1973, all foreign companies that owned more than 40 percent equity in their Indian operations were required to get the permission of Reserve Bank of India to continue their business in India. The law required the foreign firms to include local participation in the equity of foreign companies in India. Depending on the nature of business, some companies were allowed to own 51 percent of equity and others were allowed to own 74 percent of equity.

The Industrial Policy Statement, 1977 had announced the relaxation in remittances of profits, royalties, dividends and repatriation of capital of foreign companies, the Industrial Policy 1980 set the tone of liberalisation in a slow but steady pace. Industrial licensing was streamlined and made easier. Provisions in MRTP Acts were modified to simplify business transactions. In the Uruguay round of negotiations of GATT 1994, India signed the agreement on trade related investment measures that has forced India to do away with protection of Indian industry from severe global competitions within five years. FEMA, 1999 replaced the FERA, 1973 that regulated all foreign exchange transactions. The objectives of FEMA have been to facilitate external trade and payments and to promote orderly development and maintenance of foreign exchange market. The World Bank that is largely financed by the industrially advanced countries is also known to have provided loans to various development projects in India. In reality, the highly talked about loans from the World Bank Group concerns like International Development Agency (IDA) and International Bank for Reconstruction and Development (IBRD) are only a small component of the total project cost. India has adopted several trade related investment measures to reduce its Balance of Payment (BOP) problem to improve productivity and competitiveness in the Indian industry, and to facilitate the local ownership of Indian public.

Following the discursive principles of globalisation, India systematically started liberalising its economy from 1991 by adopting the primary policy instrument of the neo-liberal economic agenda, i.e., structural adjustment programme. Consequently, important domestic regulatory measures were either removed or slackened in the name of liberalisation or economic reforms accompanied by an encouragement for free trade, technology imports and foreign direct investment

Effects of Globalisation

The process of globalisation has both positive and negative effects to different category of economies of the world. Competition among firms to get a good a share of the large world market leads to; specialisation and efficiency; better quality products at reduced prices; economies of scale in production; technological and managerial improvements. Globalisation means linking the national economy with world economy as an outcome of new economic policy which has been adopted in 1991, to accelerate the rate of economic growth. The globalisation emphasised the removal of restrictions of licensing, quota and tariffs on the export and import of goods across the country. It has brought with it new technologies, quality and quantity of goods, improved and advanced methods of production and increased scope of private sectors, especially the multinational corporations in the country, competitive environment in the national economy as a mean to improve the productivity and efficiency of the system. It has introduced structural adjustment programmes, government controls have been removed over the flow of goods, services, capital, technology and investments. As a result, government interference in the economic activities has been reducing.

Globalisation has been increasing efficiency, productivity and customer orientation in Indian administration and liberalisation has enforced for transparency, ethical values and responsiveness. It has encouraged market oriented policies and structure of administration and liberalisation has encouraged flattening of hierarchy, downsizing of bureaucracy, and decentralisation of policy formulation. It has emphasised on reducing restrictions and controls on economic activities of administration and liberalisation has emphasised self-controls in administration. It has brought advanced technologies, IT advancements in administration and liberalisation has brought right to information, e-governance and transparency in administration. It has introduced competition with private sector for quality and price and liberalisation has introduced administrative effectiveness and efficiency in administration.

Globalisation gives rise to the creation, production, distribution and consumption of goods and services on an unprecedented scale. That process is meant to increase economic activity for people, enterprises and countries through free international trade, direct foreign investment, and capital market flows. For a capital deficient economy it means opining up new avenues of investment and utilisation of untapped natural resources and latent energies. Poverty has fallen in regions where exports or foreign investment is growing. In India, opening up to foreign investment has been associated with a decline in poverty. The rapid development of the capital market has been one of the important features of the current process of globalisation. Assessing the impact of globalisation on employment in the formal and informal sectors would require establishing the position and trends prior to liberalisation, i.e. upto 1991. Legal rights in the two sectors could hardly be more different if they belonged to different countries. The bulk of labour legislation deliberately excludes the informal sector. For example, the Factories Act, 1948, which covers working conditions, health and safety, basic amenities like toilets, working hours, prohibition of child labour and night work for women, workplace creches, and much more, does not apply to informal workers; similarly the Employees' State Insurance Act, 1948, providing for accident compensation and sickness and maternity benefits, does not apply to workplaces with less than twenty workers without power.

Free trade is a way for countries to exchange goods and resources. This means countries can specialise in producing goods where they have a comparative advantage. Increased labour migration gives advantages to both workers and recipient countries. If a country experiences high unemployment, there are increased opportunities to look for work elsewhere. This process of labour migration also helps reduce geographical inequality. Globalisation enables goods to be produced in different parts of the world. This greater specialisation enables lower average costs and lower prices for consumers. Domestic monopolies used to be protected by lack of competition. However, globalisation means that firms face greater competition from foreign firms. It has enabled increased levels of investment. It has made it easier for countries to attract short term and long term investment. Investment by multinational companies can play a big role in improving the economies of developing countries.

Globalisation lets countries move closer to each other. People, companies and organisations in different countries can live and work together. It has possible to exchange goods, money and ideas faster and cheaper than ever before. Modern communication and technology, like the Internet, cell phones or satellite TV help in daily lives. Many experts say that we need a different kind of globalisation in our world today. There must be ways to make sure that all countries profit from the good sides of globalisation. We should help poorer countries by giving them better education and showing them how new technology works. Every year, leaders of the world's biggest industrial countries are get together to discuss economic problems. This meeting is called the G8 summit. In the last few years groups against globalisation have organised protest marches and demonstrations to point out that not everyone is happy with how the world's economy is developing.

Problems of Globalisation

Globalisation seems to be looked on as an unmitigated "good" by economists. Unfortunately, economists seem to be guided by their badly flawed models; they miss real-world problems. Economists also tend to look at results too narrowly from the point of view of a business that can expand, or a worker who has plenty of money, even though these users are not typical. In real life, the businesses are facing increased competition, and the worker may be laid off because of greater competition. Globalisation increases world carbon dioxide emissions. If the world burns its coal more quickly, and does not cut back on other fossil fuel use, carbon dioxide emissions increase. Globalisation makes virtually impossible for regulators in one country to foresee the worldwide implications of their actions. Actions which would seem to reduce emissions for an individual country may indirectly encourage world trade, ramp up manufacturing in coal-producing areas, and increase emissions over all.

Globalisation transfers consumption of limited oil supply from developed countries to developing countries. If world oil supply is not growing by very much, and demand is growing rapidly in developing countries, oil to meet this rising demand must come from somewhere. Globalisation transfers jobs from developed countries to less developed countries. Globalisation levels the playing field, in a way that makes it hard for developed countries to compete. It transfers investment spending from developed countries to less developed countries. It tends to move taxation away from corporations, and onto individual citizens. It sets up a currency race to the bottom, with each country trying to get an export advantage by dropping the value of its currency. It encourages dependence on other countries for essential goods and services. With globalisation, goods can often be obtained cheaply from elsewhere. A country may come to believe that there is no point in producing its own food or clothing.

One problem of globalisation is that it has increased the use of non renewable resources. It has also contributed to increased pollution and global warming. Globalisation enables workers to move more freely. Some countries find it difficult to hold onto their best skilled workers, who are attracted by higher wages elsewhere. It has led to increased economic and cultural hegemony. With globalisation there is arguably less cultural diversity, however it is also led to more options for some people. Developing countries often struggle to compete with developed countries; therefore it is argued free trade benefits developed countries more. There is an infant industry argument which says industries in developing countries need protection from free trade to be able to develop.

Small Scale Industry and Globalisation

SSI means small scale industries, which is an industrial undertaking with the investment not exceeding Rs. 100 lakhs in plant and machinery. The small-scale industries sector plays a vital role in the growth of the country. Worldwide, the micro small and medium enterprises (MSMEs) have been accepted as the engine of economic growth and for promoting equitable development. The micro, small and medium enterprises sector contributes significantly to the manufacturing output, employment and exports of India. It is estimated that in terms of value, the sector accounts for about 45 per cent of the manufacturing output and 40 per cent of the total exports. Small scale industry development has been one of the major planks of India's economic development strategy since independence. Today, small scale industry occupies a place of strategic importance in Indian economic structure due to its considerable contribution in terms of output, exports and employment. In the globalised regime, the industrially advanced countries planned to dominate the world market by making use of labour and other resources available in the developing countries through collaborations, agreements or direct investments. On the other hand, for developing nations, globalisation is a means to invite foreign investment and to restructure the existing organisations so that they could enter the world market and survive. The industrial production in developed countries is decreasing due to the outsourcing of industries to other countries that possess favourable conditions for factors such as labour costs etc.

The development of small scale industrial sector has been one of the major planks of India's economic development strategy since independence. Despite numerous protection and policy measures for the past so many years Indian small scale units have remained mostly small, technologically backward and uncompetitive. It has been observed that small scale industrial sector in India has been facing an increasingly competitive environment due to: (1) liberalisation of the investment regime in the 1990s, favouring foreign direct investment; (2) the formation of the World Trade Organisation (WTO) in 1995, forcing its member countries (including India) to drastically scale down quantitative and non-quantitative restrictions on imports; and (3) domestic economic reforms. Article XVII of GATT provides for imposition of Quantitative Restrictions (QRs) on imports for balance of payments reasons. India has built up a large foreign exchange reserve in relation to imports and is under pressure to remove all QRs at the earliest. India has already removed QRs by brining more and more items in the Open General License (OGL) category. While the domestic market is going to be fully exposed to external competition, the small enterprises may have to be cautious against possible dumping by their competitors from abroad.

The small enterprises would have to take note of growing Technical Barriers to Trade (TBT) in view of high technical standards, set by the developed countries. Another area of concern for the small enterprises is the agreement on Trade Related Investment Measures (TRIMs) as its enforcement will intensify the competition further in the domestic market. The agreement on TRIMs does not allow the imposition of local content requirements, trade balancing requirements and foreign exchange neutrality. The enforcement of the Agreement on Trade Related Intellectual Property Right (TRIPs) will threaten the survival of several small enterprises in the country. Indian small enterprises must brace themselves against the issue of child labour which of late is attracting a lot of global attention. Globalisation had a negative impact on Small Scale Industries. SSIs were not in fashion as they produced goods on small scale and their markets too were little. They are less priced. But with coming the wave of globalisation, the entire scenario changed. Globalisation has ultimately led to the demise of the SSI in India. Large factories produced the goods on much larger scale to get economies of scale and made the prices much cheaper or reasonable and as a result, small scale industries started shutting down because they could have the capability to face competition by the large producers.

In the wake of sickness in the country's industrial climate prevailing in the eighties, the Government of India enacted a special legislation namely, the Sick Industrial Companies (Special Provisions) Act, 1985 commonly known as the SICA. The main objective of SICA is to determine sickness and expedite the revival of potentially viable units or closure of unviable units. It was expected that by revival, idle investments in sick units will become productive and by closure, the locked up investments in unviable units would get released for productive use elsewhere. Later on in January 1987, under the provisions of SICA, the Central Government established Board for Industrial and Financial Reconstruction (BIFR) consisting of experts for timely detection of sick and potentially sick companies, speedy determination of remedial and other measures with respect to such companies and for expeditious implementation of these measures.

Conclusion

Globalisation is the process where the economies of various countries in the world become more and more connected to one another. In a globalised economy, people from one country can buy goods quite easily from other countries. This integration occurs as technological advances expedite the trade of goods and services, the flow of capital, and the migration of people across international borders. There are two major problems with globalisation. The first is disconnecting between the company and the state. Public companies have many owners (shareholders) from a number of countries whose focus is on the return on investment. The second major problem is that of the tipping point. In the past fourty years much of western manufacturing has been relocated to low-wage third world countries. One problem of globalisation is that it has increased the use of non renewable resources. Globalisation transfers consumption of limited oil supply from developed countries to developing countries. Globalisation lets countries move closer to each other. People, companies and organisations in different countries can live and work together.

References

1. Amar K J R Nayak, Kalyan Chakravarti and Prabina Rajib, *Globalisation Process in India: A Historical Perspective Since Independence, 1947, Retrieved from* http://www1.ximb.ac.in/users/fac/visiting/vfac.nsf23e5e3 9594c 064 ee 852564ae004fa010/9372a1cbc985527e652573340023a8e5/$FILE/S1-SAJM.pdf

2. *Costs and Benefits of Globalisation,* Retrieved from http://www.economicshelp.org/blog/81/trade/costs-and-benefits-of-globalisation/

3. *Development and Globalisation: Facts and Figures,* Retrieved from http://unctad.org/en/Docs/gdscsir20041_en.pdf

4. Dr. Meenu, Impact of globalisation and liberation on Indian economy, *International Journal of Marketing, Financial Services & Management Research, Vol.2, No. 9, September (2013),* http://indianresearchjournals.com/pdf/IJMFSMR/2013/September/13.pdf

5. Eddy Lee & Marco Vivarelli (2006), *The Social Impact of Globalisation in the Developing Countries,* Retrieved from http://ftp.iza.org/dp1925.pdf

6. *Education, globalisation and the knowledge economy: A Commentary by the Teaching and Learning Research Programme, Retrieved from* http://www.tlrp.org/pub/documents/globalisationcomm.pdf

7. *European Globalisation Adjustment Fund,* Retrieved from http://ec.europa.eu/social/main.jsp?catId=326

8. Gaurang R. Sahay, Globalisation, *Liberalisation and Agrarian Distress: A Study of Suicides among Farmers in India*, Retrieved from http://www.global-labour-university.org/fileadmin/GLU_conference_2010/papers/51._Globalisation_Liberalisation_and_Agrarian_Distress..pdf

9. *Globalisation (2014),* Retrieved from http://ec.europa.eu/economy_finance/international/globalisation/index_en.htm

10. *Globalisation (2014),* Retrieved from http://en.wikipedia.org/wiki/Globalisation

11. *Globalisation in India (2014),* Retrieved from http://en.wikipedia.org/wiki/Globalisation_in_India

12. *Globalisation,* Retrieved from http://www.english-online.at/economy/globalisation/advantages-and-disadvantages-of-globalisation.htm

13. *Globalisation and International Trade,* Retrieved from http://www.worldbank.org/depweb/beyond/beyondco/beg_12.pdf

14. Lalima Singh (2013), Globalisation and poverty in India, Voice of Research, Vol. 1 Issue 4, Retrieved from http://www.voiceofresearch.org/doc/mar-2013/Mar-2013_10.pdf

15. Marc Bacchetta & Marion Jansen (2011), *Making Globalisation Socially Sustainable,* Retrieved from http://www.wto.org/english/res_e/booksp_e/glob_soc_sus_e.pdf

16. Renuka Mahadevan, *Productivity growth in Indian agriculture: The role of globalisation and economic reforms.*

17. Rohini Hensman, *The Impact of Globalisation on Employment in India and Responses from the Formal and Informal Sectors,* Retrieved from http://socialhistory.org/sites/default/files/docs/publications/clara-wp15.pdf

18. Simon Reich (1998), what is globalisation? *Four Possible Answers,* Retrieved from https://kellogg.nd.edu/publications/workingpapers/WPS/261.pdf

19. SK Mishra & P Nayak (2006), Socio-economic Dimensions of Globalisation in India, Retrieved from http://freewebs.com/nehu_economics/secoglob_india.pdf

20. Stanley Fischer (2003), *Globalisation and Its Challenges,* Retrieved from http://www.iie.com/fischer/pdf/fischer011903.pdf

21. Tanveer Malik, *Impact of globalisation on Indian economy- An overview,* Retrieved from http://www.fibre2fashion.com/industry-article/8/738/impact-of-globalisation1.asp

22. *The impact of globalisation and increased trade liberalisation on European regions (2008),* Retrieved from http://ec.europa.eu/regional_policy/sources/docgener/studies/pdf/impact_liberalisation.pdf

23. *Twelve Reasons Why Globalisation is a Huge Problem (2013),* Retrieved from http://ourfiniteworld.com/2013/02/22/twelve-reasons-why-globalisation-is-a-huge-problem/

24. *Globalisation and Indian small scale industrial sector,* Retrieved from http://shodhganga.inflibnet.ac.in/bitstream/10603/5108/13/13_chapter%208.pdf

25. *Impact of Globalisation on Small Scale Industries in India,* Retrieved from http://theglobaljournals.com/gra/file.php?val=May_2014_1400151236_27704_08.pdf

26. Garima Chaudhary (2014), *Globalisation and its impact on SSI in India,* Retrieved from http://www.ermt.net/docs/papers/Volume_3/3_March2014/V3N3-178.pdf

27. *Globalisation and Small Scale Industry: Frequently Asked Questions (2006)*, Retrieved from http://www.cuts-citee.org/PDF/Mono-globalisation_small_scale_industry.pdf

28. Dr M H Bala Subrahmanya, *Small scale industry in India under globalisation: Does solace lie in technology,* Retrieved from http://www.econ.mpg.de/files/2006/workshops/india_workshop/papers/MHBala. pdf

29. Read more at http://www.brainyquote.com/quotes/keywords/globalisation.html#6xRFv5uOIqxpW3bD.99

2

Globalisation and Status of Women in India: A Study

Prof D. Pulla Rao

"Globalisation, as defined by rich people like us, is a very nice thing... you are talking about the Internet, you are talking about cell phones, you are talking about computers. This doesn't affect two-thirds of the people of the world."

– Jimmy Carter

Introduction

It was widely accepted that Indian women had enjoined equal and most dignified life in the society during the early Vedic period. They were highly educated. But after the introduction of the Manu Code, the status of women was converted into that of a 'servant'. Women in every Caste were placed below that of men folk of that Caste. They were stripped off all their rights, social, economic, and political and were treated as serfs with 'unquestionable' duties and responsibilities towards men folk.

However, during 1920s Mahatma Gandhi had given a clarion call to all the women of India to join the freedom struggle and trained them in the techniques to win freedom from the foreign rule. Lots of women had joined the freedom struggle and fought for independence on par with their men folk. And subsequently, the constitution of India had included special provisions to women to ensure gender equity in all walks of life including political 'empowerment'. But, the native government had accommodated only a few (prominent) women as members of Parliament, Ministers, Governors, etc. Many women freedom fighters were disappointed which signaled another 'struggle' against male chauvinism in a democratic country. They, along with several world women liberation organisations, continued their struggle for gender equity. In order to satisfy the agitating women, the government of India had introduced 33 percent reservation in Panchayati Raj's three tier institutions, village, block, and district Panchayats. The Indian women took it as a challenge, strived their every nerve, and made a history by wining more than the reserved seats. In some villages, blocks, and districts they had won 50 percent or more. This victory had blown out the 'myth' of the Law of Manu. The Indian women had proved that they are 'equal' to their men folk in all aspects. It is the Law of Manu, but not their inherent weakness as was propagated by Manu, that enslaved them to the men folk for centuries. It is due to the operation of the Law of Manu that their representation is only about 12 percent in the Parliament and about eight percent in the state legislatures. In spirit of the constitution, if the reservation is extended to the Parliament and the state legislatures they could have out witted their men folk in those bodies too. Hence the women of India are demanding extension of 'reservation' policy to the Parliament and the state legislatures also. Now the Indian men folk had no option except to extend the reservation policy to all levels basing on their proportion in the total population.

Independent India had raised greater hopes among the Indian women to obtain greater liberty and equality. They strongly believed that due to several types of sacrifices they had made during the freedom struggle their demands would be fulfilled. They ardently believed that they would be able to get rid of several undesirable religious, economic and social taboos that were imposed on them right from the Manu period. Mahatma Gandhi taught and trained the Indian women the technique of fighting for liberty and equality even at the cost of life. The Constitution of India had granted right to equality to every citizen, including women, in all walks of life. It is now for the women to fight for their constitutionally granted rights and thus elevate their status on par with their male counterparts in every field. This needs grabbing of political power through democratic process by which they can attain equal social and economic status. The Indian women had realised that only by winning in the elections they will get the decision making power into their hands, free themselves from dependency on men folk. Through political power they contemplated to influence the Parliament and State Legislatures to enact the 'gender equity' laws.

Gender Equity in the Constitution of India

The constitution of India had legally empowered women through clearly and candidly specified rights to equal status in all walks of life. It also prohibited discrimination on the grounds of religion, race, caste, sex etc. The following eight articles embodied in the Constitution of India stand as univocal testimony to the spirit and promise of 'equality' to Indian women:

1. Article 14 - Men and women to have equal rights and opportunities in the political, economic and social spheres.
2. Article 15(1) - Prohibits discrimination against any citizen on the grounds of religion, race, caste, sex etc.
3. Article 15(3) - Special provision enabling the State to make affirmative discriminations in favour of women.
4. Article 16 - Equality of opportunities in matter of public appointments for all citizens.
5. Article 39(a) - The State shall direct its policy towards securing all citizens men and women, equally, the right to means of livelihood.
6. Article 39(d) – Equal pay for equal work for both men and women.
7. Article 42 - The State to make provision for ensuring just and humane conditions of work and maternity relief.
8. Article 51 (A) (e) –To renounce the practices derogatory to the dignity of women.

Women at the National Level Politics

1. Sarojini Naidu, a poet and freedom fighter, was the first Indian woman to become President of the Indian National Congress and the first woman to become the governor of United Provinces of Agra and Oudh.
2. Vijayalakshmi Pandit, sister of Jawaharlal Nehru became the first women Ambassador to Soviet Union.
3. Amrit Kaur became the first woman and Christian Cabinet rank Minister of Health.
4. Aruna Asaf Ali was awarded International Lenin Peace Prize for the year 1964 and the Jawaharlal Nehru Award for International Understanding in 1991. She was awarded India's second highest civilian honour, the Padma Vibhushan in her lifetime in 1992, and finally the highest civilian award, the Bharat Ratna, posthumously in 1997. In 1998, a stamp commemorating her was issued.
5. Durugabai Deshmukh was a member of India's Lok Sabha. She was instrumental in the enactment of many social welfare laws. She was a member of the Planning Commission and Chairperson of Central Social Welfare Board in 1953, first Chairperson of the National Council on Women's Education, established by the Government of India in 1958.
6. Mrs. Indira Gandhi was the Fourth Prime Minister of India and served for two terms (1966 to 1977 and 1980 to 1984). She was the second-longest-serving Prime Minister of India and the only woman to hold this office so far.
7. Justice M. Fathima Beevi was the first female judge to be appointed to the Supreme Court of India and the first Muslim woman to be appointed to any higher judiciary. She is the first woman judge of a Supreme Court of a nation in India and Asia. Later she served as a member of the National Human Rights Commission and also as the Governor in Tamil Nadu (1997–2001).
8. Pratibha Devisingh Patil was the 12th President of the Republic of India and first woman hold this office.
9. Ms. Meira Kumar was the first woman Speaker of Lokh Sabha.

Women Chief Ministers of India

1. Sucheta Kriplani, Uttar Pradesh (1963 – 1967)
2. Nandini Satpathy, Orissa (1972 – 3 March 1976)
3. Shashikala Kakodkar, Goa (1973 – 1979)
4. Syeda Anwara Taimur, Assam (1980 – 1981)
5. Janaki Ramachandran, Tamil Nadu (7–30 January 1988)
6. J. Jayalalithaa, Tamil Nadu (1991 – 1996; 14 May 2001 – 21 Sept. 2001;2 March 2002 – 12 May 2006; 16 May 2011– present)
7. Mayawati, Uttar Pradesh (13 June 1995 – 18 October 1995; 21 March 1997 – 21, Sept. 1997; 2002 –2003; and 2007 –2012)
8. Rajinder Kaur Bhattal, Punjab (1996 – 1997)
9. Rabri Devi, Bihar (1997 –1999; 1999 –2000; & (2000 – 2005)
10. Sushma Swaraj, Delhi (13 October 1998 – 3 December 1998)
11. Sheila Dikshit, Delhi (1998 – 2013)
12. Uma Bharati, Madhya Pradesh (2003 – 2004)
13. Vasundhara Raje, (2003 – 2008; December 2013 – present)
14. Mamata Banerjee, West Bengal (20 May 2011 – present)
15. Anandiben Patel, Gujarat (21 May 2014 – present)

Gender Variations in Literacy Levels

The most important characteristic of population is literacy, which is a pre – requisite for the overall development of the country both socially and economically. Female literacy is considered to be a more sensitive index of social development compared to overall literacy rates. Female literacy is negatively related with fertility rates, population growth rates, infant and child mortality rates, and shows a positive association with female age at marriage, life expectancy and participation in modern sectors of the economy. In spite of all the special constitutional provisions and governmental efforts, in the field of education, the disparities between males and females are still large. According to the Census of 1951, the average general literacy rate was 18.33 with male 27.16 and female 8.86 per cent. The gap between male and female is 18.30. As per Census 2011 Report, general literacy rate is 74.04, with male 82.14 and female 65.46. This achievement in terms of general literacy growth is quite impressive, but when we compare the gap between male and female, it is contrary to the progress made in general literacy. It has increased from 18.30 to 16.68, which in ideal situation should have been reduced. Even through national average is relatively better, interstate variations are very large.

Table - 1: General Literacy Rate Since Independence with Gender Gap

Census year	Persons (%)	Males (%)	Females (%)	Male Female Gap in literacy rate (%)
1951	18.33	27.16	8.86	18.30
1961	28.30	40.40	15.35	25.05
1971	34.45	45.96	21.97	23.98
1981	43.57	56.38	29.76	26.62
1991	52.21	64.13	39.29	24.84
2001	65.38	75.85	54.16	21.70
2011	74.04	82.14	65.46	16.68

Source: Census of India, 2011.

In progressive states like Kerala, male and female literacy rates are 96.02 and 91.98 respectively with a gap of only 4.04 per cent. Similar situation exists in Mizoram and Lakshadweep. Compared to this, Bihar has male literacy of 73.39, female literacy of 53.33 with the gap of 20.06. State of Jharkhand has also similar situation. This variation depicts gap in social and overall human development among the states. If the country as a whole is to be considered, then these gaps are to be reduced.

Table - 2: State-wise Variation

Literacy Rate (States)	Males (%)	Females (%)	Gap (%)
Kerala	96.02	91.98	4.04
Mizoram	93.72	89.40	4.32
Lakshadweep	96.11	88.25	7.86
Bihar	73.39	53.33	20.06
Jharkhand	78.45	56.21	22.24

Source: Census of India, 2011.

Women in the Parliament of India

Indian Republic had adopted the unitary type of government wherein the political power is concentrated at the center with limited powers to the states. Parliament plays the supreme role in shaping the national policies and programmes. Indian Parliament got powers sufficient to guide the destiny of the country. If women get into the Parliament in sufficient numbers, they can influence the Central government to bring forth 'gender equity' legislation, policies, and programmes. Now let us have a glance at the number of women elected/nominated to the Indian Parliament. Of course, Lokh Sabha (Lower house) is directly elected while the Rajya Sabha (Upper house) is being filled with persons indirectly nominated from various walks of life. However, the legislation has to be approved by both the houses to get the assent/consent of the President of India.

Table -3: Women in Indian Parliament

	Lokh Sabha			Rajya Sabha		
Year	**Total Seats**	**Women**	**%**	**Total Seats**	**Women**	**%**
1952	499	22	4.4	219	16	7.3
1957	500	27	5.4	237	18	7.6
1962	503	34	6.8	238	18	7.6
1967	523	31	5.9	240	20	8.3
1971	521	22	4.2	243	17	7.0
1977	544	19	3.5	244	25	10.2
1980	544	28	5.1	244	24	9.8
1984	544	44	8.1	244	23	11.5
1989	517	27	5.2	245	24	9.8
1991	544	39	7.2	245	38	15.5
1996	543	39	7.2	223	24	9.0
1998	543	43	7.9	245	15	6.1
1999	543	49	9.0	245	19	7.8
2004	539	44	8.2	245	28	11.4
2009	544	59	10.8	232	21	9.1
2014	545	62	11.8	245	30	12.2

Sources: Lokh Sabh.gov.in. & Rajya Sabha Secretariat, New Delhi

It is obvious from Table-3 that Indian Parliament is still male dominated one. In the First Parliament only 22 women got elected to the Lokh Sabha that had a total strength of 499 members. Almost all of them were either freedom fighters themselves or spouses of the freedom fighters. Most of them or their female children repeatedly got elected in the subsequent elections on 'sympathy' mode. This tradition is being continued even till now restricting the entry of 'new' faces into the Parliament.

Women Representation in State Legislatures

State legislatures influence state governance. In some states there are two houses as in our Parliament while in some states there is a single house, lower house only. The Indian women thought it equally important to win majority seats in the state legislatures as well. But the ground realities are not in their favour as can be observed from the Table 4.

Table -4: Percentage of Women MLAs in State Legislatures: All India

Period	1952	1957	1960-65	1967-69	1970-75	1977-78	1979-83	1984-88	1989-92	1993-97	1998-99	2000-04	2005-09
India	2	6	4.7	2.5	4.5	2.6	3.2	4.2	4.3	3.7	5.4	5.1	6.3

Source: Centre for the Study of Developing Societies (CSDS), New Delhi.

Women Representation in Panchayati Raj Institutions

The Panchayti Raj system otherwise called the 'local self government' was introduced in India basing on the recommendations of Sri Balwant Rai Mehata Committee Report 1957. Basing on the Asoka Mehta Committee Report, 1977 the Panchayati Raj institutions were transformed from mere programme implementing agencies into effective decentralised political institutions at the grassroots level. In the beginning years, the Indian women did not dare to counter their men folk politically at the local level. But as the time passed, the aspirant women that failed to get into the national and state level political bodies wanted to settle down in the local bodies at least. But the men folk that are already entrenched in the local politics did not like women to be their rivals at the local level. Besides, the local politicians constitute the 'core cadre' for the national parties. This cadre shall be in power at the local level to have firm grip over the electorate at the grass root level. As the women brought pressure on the central government to allot special quota in the PRIs, it had taken initiatives to look into this demand.

The Committee on the Status of Women in India (CSWI) report suggested reservation of seats for women in political field at least in the local bodies to start with. In 1988, the National Perspective Plan for Women had suggested that a 30 per cent quota for women in all levels of local self-governance. Several women's groups had also brought pressure on the government of India demanding special quota in Indian polity. The net result of all those efforts was the adoption of the 73rd and 74th Amendments to the Indian Constitution in 1993 that guaranteed reservation of 33 per cent of seats for women in the Panchayati Raj Institutions. This reservation policy had brought a great change in the gender composition of women in the Panchayati Raj Institutions which can be seen clearly in the Table - 5.

Table -5: Women Representation in PRIs (All India)

Panchayat level	Total no. of PRI	Elected Represen-tatives	Women Represen-tatives	Women Percentage
District Panchayat	633	15581	5778	37.08
Intermediate Panchayats	6094	156557	58012	37.10
Village Panchayats	232855	2645880	974255	36.82
All India	239582	2818018	1038045	36.84

Source: GOI, Ministry of Panchayat Raj, Annual Report, 2007-08.

The New Initiatives

The overwhelming success of women in the Panchayati Raj elections had made the Indian women to agitate for their 'rightful' share of 50 percent in Parliament and state legislatures as well. The women liberation organisations from all over the world are encouraging the Indian women to fight for 'equal' status in all walks of life. Now the Indian women organisations are training their guns to achieve gender empowerment and equity.

The Failures of the Government of India

Though the government of India had introduced two bills, one for enhancement of women quota in PRIs and the other for sanction of special quota of 33.3 percent in Parliament and the state legislatures, the male chauvinism in the Parliament is sitting pretty on both of them as they against their vested interests. The present status of those two bills is as follows:

1. ***Enhance of Women Quota in PRIs:*** The government of India had contemplated to increase the present quota of 33 percent to 50 percent in all three tiers of Panchayati Raj Institutions (PRIs). A Bill to amend Article 243D was introduced in the Lok Sabha on 26th November, 2009 to that effect. But that is left to rest there. Once the Bill is passed the women representation will rise to more than 1.4 million.

2. ***Sanction of Quota in Parliament and State Legislatures:*** A Bill to reserve 33.3 percent seats in Parliament and state legislatures for women was introduced first by the H. D. Deve Gowda led United Front government in the Lok Sabha on 12th September, 1996, but it was not passed. Subsequently, the successive governments had tried to get it passed but failed due to lack of political consensus. However, Rajya Sabha, the Upper House had passed that Bill on 9th March, 2010. But that could not be sent to the President until the Lok Sabha also clears it.

Summary

Women of India had enjoyed high respect and dignity in the early Vedic period. They were treated on par with men respect and dignity and were allowed to write/recite Vedas, the most holy assignment of that era. But in the later Vedic period, the Law of Manu had place women as second category citizen with only duty to serve men folk without any rights of their own. From that time onwards male chauvinism was on the rise to the extent of making the life of women miserable and horrible until the entry of British Raj in India. The Indian renaissance was possible through English education, librated women from many social evils practice of 'sati', child marriage etc. Women were permitted to go to schools and colleges to pursue higher studies and Widows were permitted to remarry.

Gandhiji's call to women to join the freedom struggle had emboldened women to come out and mingle with the society freely and a large number of them had joined the rank and cadre of the freedom fighters. Some had even joined the women brigades of Nethaji to fight with the British soldiers in the battle field. And having fought for the liberty and freedom of the country, they had started their fight for their own rights and liberties on the native soil. Their aspirations were roused and clamour for equal status on social, economic, and political spears was intensified. Added to that, the news of fast growing women movements across the globe had encouraged them to fight for their rights and get liberated from the age old fretters of injustice.

The moment that the government of India had introduced 33 percent reservation in Panchayati Raj's three tier institutions, village, block, and district Panchayats, the women of India made a bee line to the electoral officers to enlist themselves as the contestants. The result was astounding to one and all. In all cases, the women representatives had exceeded the reserved quota of 33 percent. And in many cases, they had filled to the brim of their naturally rightful quota of 50 percent. Indian women had proved that given the chance they are second to none. Lack of special quota, women could not cross 12 percent mark in the Parliament and six percent mark in the state legislatures over the last six decades. Therefore, 'special quota' proved to be the panacea for their 'full' political empowerment. Thus the prescriptions of Dr. Baba Saheb Ambedkar in respect of scheduled castes and tribes, becomes the ultimate solution for empowerment of women too in India. Now it is for the women of India to fight for their quota, get it, and then finish their journey from serfdom to freedom.

Suggestions

1. ***Inter Gender Equity :*** Since Manu had divided and discriminated the Hindu society on caste and gender and excluded them, let the democratically elected government include them by giving 'special quota' on the basis of caste and gender.

2. ***Intra Gender Equity*:** Implement caste quota within the women quota lest the women from upper castes corner all political slots and exclude the women from lower castes from the political arena and thus defeat the very 'spirit' of special reservation for the 'excluded' categories.

3. ***Check Political Houses:*** Implement one family, one position, one time norm to expand political canvass to all the families of the country and practically make everybody 'equal' in the political arena.

4. ***Check Money and Muscle Power in Elections:*** As the money and muscle corrupt politics of the country is excluding the poor and women from entering into the fry take remedial measures to check their influence in the election process.

5. ***Intensify the Fight for Gender Parity:*** Men are not fools to give 'power' to women in a golden plate. The women should fight for it. 'Gone rights are not restored by begging but by relentless struggle only' said Dr. Baba Saheb Ambedkar.

References

1. Agnew and Vijay, (1979): *Elite Women in Indian Politics*, Vikas Publications, New Delhi.
2. Indrabhusan Singh and Ușha Kumari, (2007): Rural Development and Women Empowerment, *Kurukshetra,* March, 2007, pp. 3-8.
3. Kalpana Roy, (1999): *Women in Indian Politics*, Rajat Publications, New Delhi.
4. Kanna B.S. (1994): *Panchayati Raj in India (Rural Local Self Government),* Deep &Deep Publications, New Delhi.
5. Kaushik Susheela, (1993): *Women's Participation in Politics,* Vikas Publication, New Delhi.
6. Mira Seth, (2001): *Women and Development – The Indian Experience*, Sage Publications, New Delhi.
7. Pandey, A.K, (2002): *Emerging Issues in Empowerment of Women*, Anmol Publications, New Delhi.
8. Pande, G.S, (2001): *Political Participation of Women in India (Implementation of 73rd And 74th Amendments),* New Royal Book, Lucknow.
9. Shahana Das Gupta, (2005): *Indira Gandhi: The Story of Leaders Book Description*, Rupa Publications, New Delhi.

10. Sinha, Archana, (2004): Women in Local Self Governance, *Kurukshetra*, August, 2004, pp. 11-15.

11. Vidya, K.C, (1997): *Political Empowerment of Women at Grass root,* Kanishka Publishers, New Delhi.

12. Read more at http://www.brainyquote.com/quotes/keywords/globalisation.html#6xRFv5uOIqxpW3bD.99

3

Global Export Crisis and Chiken Impact on the Poor in India: A Synthesis of Sector Studies

Shikha Chantia

"Globalisation has produced a new of level of interdependence among us. The economy and multinational supply chains do not abide by political boundaries. A computer ordered in Brazil is designed in California and assembled in several other countries. Economic integration was the first strong evidence of a new era."

–Eduardo Paes

Introduction

Fashion is ever changing. India is a country with diversified customs and cultures. People following various traditions live here, their way of dressing also differ from each other. The traces of Indians being fashionable can be found out from the ancient remains of Harappa and Mohenjo-Daro civilisations. After the independence, globalisation is being witnessed in the Indian fashion industry, due to which changes have occurred in the style of Indian dressing. There are models called as theories of fashion which affects the change and dissemination of fashion in a population. The trickle across theory is the most popular theory especially in the 21st century because technology allows designer fashions to be copies quickly and easily, making them available to all consumers sooner. In the 1970s international fashion arrived in India much before the MTV culture with the bold colors, flower prints and bell-bottoms. Synthetics turned trendy and the disco culture affected the fashion scenario.

For the global fashion industry, India is a very big exporter of fabrics and accessories. India's strengths not only depend on its tradition, but also in its raw materials. World over, India is the third largest producer of cotton, the second largest producer of silk and the fifth largest producer of man-made fibers, apart from having cheaper skilled work force. India provides these fabrics to the international fashion houses at competitive prices with shorter lead time and an effective monopoly in designs which covers elaborated hand embroidery. Indian garments embellishment with bead work is another area which is in demand in the international market.

There is now considerable evidence (NCEUS 1009, Mahajan 1009, Kumar 1009) to show that the global economic crisis has had a significant impact on developing economies. The initial idea that developing countries are 'decoupled' from the global crisis is no longer accepted as valid, as it is clear that multiple channels have transferred the crisis to these countries. The International Labour Organisation (ILO) has described the impact of the crisis as 'a global catastrophe' (ILO 1009). It has estimated that about 19 million jobs have been lost already at the global level and that this figure may go up to 59 million, in the worst case scenario. This number is in addition to 90 million new entrants in the labour market, who are unlikely to find jobs in the prevailing recessionary situation. Estimates made by the Food and Agriculture Organisation (FAO) show that the number of hungry people has increased from 915 million people in 1008 to 1.01 billion people in 1009 (FAO 1009). Similarly, World Bank estimates say that there is an unforeseen increase in the number of poor, with about 10 million people being pushed into poverty by 1009 and 100 million likely to be pushed into poverty by 1010, in Asia alone (Chhibber et al. 1009).

The Indian economy has been quite adversely affected by the global crisis, through the channels. Indian exports crashed in the second half of 1008-09, showing a decline in the quantum of exports of about 14 percent. The decline was more than 50 percent in some sectors like gems and jewellery, textile and garment manufacturing and leather goods. On the financial side, the capital outflows as well as decline in revenue resulted in a severe liquidity crisis. The first survey of the Labour Bureau, Government of India, stated that the employment in the economy fell by 500,000 jobs during October-December 1008. The next survey, reported that one million jobs were lost, during January 1009. Though a slight improvement is observed in employment during January-March 1009, it is not clear whether this is sustainable (Labour Bureau 1009, Economic Survey 1009). In April 1009, UNDP India supported a quick survey in some of the major affected sectors, in selected states of India, to get a better understanding of the impact of the global crisis on small producers and informal workers. The sectors for the quick surveys were identified on basis of emerging reports that highlighted the impacts on specific sectors, viz., agriculture, auto parts, Chikan craft, engineering industry, home based garments and gems and jewellery.

All the sector studies have used a common approach, with some modifications to meet sector specific requirements. The common approach consists of the following basic core:

1. An analysis of the available literature and secondary data to understand the impact of the global crisis on the selected sector. This included in-depth discussions with concerned Government officials, sector (industry) leaders, office bearers of associations and labour leaders.
2. Selection of a centre or two, for an in-depth empirical study in the selected sectors; and to prepare a profile of the selected centre (s) to understand the impact of the crisis at the local level. This involved discussions with sector leaders, officials and labour leaders in the selected centres, as well as focus group discussions (FGDs), with men and women workers, small entrepreneurs and self employed / own account workers and household members (including women members) of workers.
3. Sample survey of a selected 100-150 workers and small producers. The sample was selected purposively, on the basis of the information of typologies of workers and location of workers.

Though the sample size is small, the sample survey does provide 304 a good understanding of the impact of the global crisis on workers.

4. Two questionnaires, were prepared, one for the selected workers and their households and the other for small producers, in each of the sectors.
5. Case studies were undertaken in order to understand the impact of the crisis, at the household level. The quick study covered 1,085 workers and producers, across six sectors, in five major states, in India. Even though some impact of the global crisis was evident as early as July 1008, when the exports started to decline, the larger decline in demand for export products (leading to the closure of units or a decline in production and employment) was observed after the festival of Diwali, in October 1008. Thus, in all the sector studies, October 1008 has been taken as the cutoff date; and the terms 'before the crisis' and 'after the crises refer to this date.

The specific objectives of the study are (i) to examine the impact of the crisis on the workers and small producers, working in the selected sectors, (ii) to draw inferences for interventions to address the adverse impacts on the workers and the sectors in the short and medium terms and (iii) to examine and recommend measures to mitigate the impact of similar crises.

Overview of the Chikan with Selected Sectors through Data

Chikken Craft

Handicrafts (Chikan) are a unique expression of the culture, tradition and heritage of India and the Handicrafts (Chikan) industry is an important sector of the Indian economy, providing employment to a large section of the population. Though exports of Chikan craft, like other handicraft export products, have been seeing a decline in their markets during the last 15 years or so, there has been a sudden and huge fall in the exports after the global financial crisis.

According to the figures released by the Export Promotion Council of Handicrafts (EPCH), exports of embroidered and crocheted goods, which amounted to Rs. 51,450 million in 1001-08, declined to

Rs. 19,110 million in 1008-09; a decline of more than 40 percent. Since majorities of the Chikan workers are informal workers, who work at home and are paid very low wages, and do not have access to any social protection, this crisis has meant the loss of livelihoods for a number of people. Lucknow is a major centre for Chikan craft and was therefore selected for this study.

The sectors vary in organisation of production, with Chikan craft and garments being significantly home based, agriculture carried out on family farms with participation of family members; while auto parts, engineering and diamond cutting and polishing have small production units outside the homes.

The home based garments and Chikan craft sectors employ a large number of women. Agriculture also has significant participation by women; while in the remaining sectors, women constitute less than five percent of the workforce (Hirway 1009, Shah 1009, Kumar 1009).

Wages and incomes of the workers differ considerably across the sectors. The average monthly income before the crisis was the highest in the engineering industry (Rs.1,888) followed by the gems and jewellery industry (Rs.5,841) and in third place by the auto parts industry (Rs.1,850).

The average monthly income in the other sectors was much less, Rs.1,111 in agriculture, Rs.1,811 in home based garments and Rs.918 in the Chikan craft sector.

It is important to note that that most workers in home based garments and Chikan craft industries were poor even before the crisis. However, their condition became much worse after the crisis.

The features that are common to all the sectors are (i) all these sectors have grown rapidly in the last few years, largely due to growing export markets. (ii) small producers or informal units are predominant in all these sectors and (iii) most workers engaged in these industries are informally employed.

Key Findings

Data Compiled from Sample Surveys in the Six Sectors

Table 1.1 Selected Sectors, Centres and Sample

Sector	State/s	Location Study	Sample		Total	Organization
			Worker	Small enterprise		
Gems and Jewellery Industry	Gujarat	Surat	127	35	162	CFD
		Bhavnagar (returned migrants)	34		34	
Auto parts Industry	Punjab	Ludhiana	125	31	156	EDII
Engineering	Gujarat	Rajkot	120	30	150	GIDR
Industry	Tamil Nadu	Coimbatore	123	40	163	
Home based	Gujarat	Ahmadabad	100		100	SEWA
garments industry	Madhya Pradesh	Indore	100		100	
Agriculture	Gujarat	Gujarat	78	22	100	SEWA
Chikan craft	Uttar Pradesh	Lucknow	100	20	120	SEWA
Total			907	156	1085	

Note: CFDA: Centre For Development Alternatives, EDII: Entrepreneurship Development Institute of India, GIDR: Gujarat Institute of Development Research, SEWA: Self-employed Women's Association

There are certain characteristics that are common to the workers, across the six sectors:

1. The workers in all these sectors are young. The average age varies from 10 to 11 years, in the six sectors. Only about 11 percent of workers are above 50 years old.
2. The level of literacy is quite low for these workers. The share of illiterate workers (without any formal education) is significant, varying from 10 percent in agriculture to less than 10 percent in 313 engineering, gems and jewellery and home based garments sectors. About 40 percent of the workers have studied up to Standard X and only about six percent workers have studied beyond Standard X. The percentage of graduates is less than one percent and they are employed mainly in the auto parts industry and engineering industry. Many workers are school drop-outs and have received on the job training in the specific sectors.

3. Almost all workers, with a few exceptions, are not permanent workers (they are regular workers3 or contract workers). They do not receive any social security benefits.

4. The share of women workers is less than five percent, in the auto parts, engineering and the gems and jewellery industries, these three industries happen to be primarily male dominated industries. In the other three sectors, women are predominant, 99 percent in home based garment industry, 84 percent in Chikan craft, 81 percent in agriculture.

5. The majority of workers in the gems and jewellery industry and auto parts industry live in pucca (permanent) houses, while the proportion of workers living in pucca houses is much less in the Chikan craft, agriculture and home based garment industries. About one fifth of the workers in these sectors live in kutcha (temporary) houses.

6. The majority of workers (more than 10 percent) live in joint families, 10 percent live in nuclear families and the rest live in single person families. Impact of the Crisis is on Employment, Wages and Incomes. The impact on the crisis on employment was observed in a number of ways: workers had lost jobs and were unemployed, workers got much less work than before in the same sector, some workers had shifted to other work, often less remunerative and with lower productivity, such as petty services (domestic service, helpers to drivers or masons, office peons, etc), petty trade (vegetable selling, street vending, etc), home based work (manufacturing incense sticks, spices, food items like papads and pickles, etc). There are some workers who did not experience any change.

A large number of skilled workers in the selected sectors have been forced to shift to unskilled work. The percentage of such workers is 18 percent in the Chikan craft sector, 11 percent in gems and jewellery industry and eight percent each in the auto parts and in the engineering industries. On an average, about 11 percent of skilled workers have shifted to unskilled work, implying waste of their skills acquired over the years. The higher percentage of such workers in Chikan craft is due to the huge loss of demand for these products in the global market. Such a shift can result in deskilling of the workers in the long run. There has been a significant deterioration in the employment status, even of these informal workers, from 'regular' to 'casual' or 'temporary' status, implying less regularity of work and increased employment insecurity. This deterioration from 'regular' to 'casual' status is significant in all the industries, though the percentage of casual workers varies from 15 percent in the engineering industry, to 11 percent in the gems and jewellery industry, to as much as 10 percent of workers in the auto parts industry. The average monthly income of workers has declined significantly in all the sectors. About 91 percent of the workers in the sample pertaining to the gems and jewellery industry experienced a decline in their incomes. This figure was much lower in the engineering industry (55 percent). In terms of percentage decline in income, the monthly incomes of the workers in the respective samples declined by about 11 percent in the home based garment industry, by 41 percent in the gems and jewellery industry, by 41 percent in the auto parts industry, by 11 percent in the Chikan craft industry and by 11 percent in engineering industry.

References

1. Report of Labor Bureau, *Economic survey*, Govt. of India.
2. Expert Promotion Council for Handicrafts, (EPCH)
3. *ICRIER (Indian Council for Research in International Economic Relations),* New Delhi.
4. Read more at http://www.brainyquote.com/quotes/keywords/globalisation.html#6xRFv5uOIqxpW3bD.99

4

Women Empowerment and Microfinance: Bridging the Gender Gap

Krupa D. Bhatt

"Outsourcing and globalisation of manufacturing allows companies to reduce costs, benefits consumers with lower cost goods and services, causes economic expansion that reduces unemployment, and increases productivity and job creation."

–Larry Elder

Introduction

Microfinance both credit and savings has potentials to improve the well-being of poor women in developing countries. Women-empowerment essentially means giving women the right towards a greater socio-economic and political participation, an effective decision-making capability, power and control. It plays a significant role in their participation in the process of development. While 'gender' is an assemblage of biological features and social interactions, 'gender inequality' is purely a social construct. Today, when economies are facing a serious challenge towards achieving a sustainable socio-economic development, women-empowerment and thereby bridging the gender-gap has become a critical issue. This paper seeks to address the crucial issue of women participation in the process of development. Paper try to put forward the issue of gender-disparity and the need for women-empowerment, the emergence of microfinance in the global perspective as an instrument for women empowerment, into the microfinance movement in India and tries to evaluate its effectiveness as a social instrument in achieving socio-economic development in general and women empowerment in particular with special reference to SEWA (Gujarat) in this regard.

Gender Inequality and the Need for Women Empowerment

The United Nations Commission on Status of Women states, *"Women who constitute half of the world's population by virtue of an accident of birth, perform two thirds of world's work, receive one tenth of its income and own less than one hundredth of its property."* Despite their significant contribution to the household sector and the national economy, women, particularly rural womenfolk have been largely disregarded and marginalised. They have been deprived of the basic economic opportunities and entitlements that men have access to. In the less-developed countries (LDC's) there is usually an under reporting of women in the workforce due to the traditional cultural norms and practices. In India, according to the National Family Health Survey-2 (NFHS-2) report, only about 25 percent of the Indian women reported themselves to be employed in the year preceding the report and only about six percent were reported to be self-employed. However, rural women in India and other LDC's are largely involved in agricultural production, in storage and marketing of agricultural produce, food processing, animal husbandry and poultry farming and in community development services.

In large plantations and paddy farming women are actively employed, yet they earn meagre wages or remain as unpaid workers. Discrimination against women results in their lack of proper education, which implies that they lack access to the skilled labor-market and in times of economic repression they are the first ones to face retrenchment. The United Nations International Children's Fund (UNICEF) approximated that in 2008, more than 100 million children of primary school age were out of school and 52 percent of them were girls. Women in rural areas are not provided with the basic necessary health care and sanitation facilities. They are deprived of access to information, skills, resources and credit facilities; therefore, leading to a lack of economic self-sufficiency. Strong patriarchal society, women have been largely subjugated and forced to bear the maximum burden of poverty. Empowerment has been essentially related to the concept of power. The concept of empowerment has been the subject of much intellectual discourse and analysis. Empowerment is defined as the processes by which women take control and ownership of their lives through expansion of their choices. Thus, it is the process of acquiring the ability to make strategic life choices in a context where this ability has previously been denied. The core elements of empowerment have been defined as agency (the ability to define one's goals and act upon them), awareness of gendered power structures, self-esteem and self-confidence (Kabeer 2001). Empowerment can take place at a hierarchy of different levels individual, household, community and societal-and is facilitated by providing encouraging factors (e.g., lack of resources and skills).

The decade of eighties witnessed a growing concern for empowering women and thereby, bridging the gender gap. According to Moser women empowerment is *"giving women the right to determine choices in life and to influence the direction of change through the ability to gain control over crucial material and non-material resources"*. Beteille opines that empowerment is both a means to an end and an end in itself. Empowerment is an ongoing and dynamic process, which enhances women's and any other marginalised and alienated group's abilities to change the structures and ideologies that keep them subordinate. It is a process of making present power structures more inclusive, including all women and men, senior citizens, dalits, indigenous people and people with disabilities. According to Sachidananda and Kumar, empowerment has been defined as a redistribution of power that challenges ideology and male dominance. It refers to the transformation of the structures or institutions that reinforces and perpetuates gender discrimination. The emphasis has been on the rearrangement of power relations in society, bringing about positive changes in the status and decision-making power of women, prioritising their needs and making them economically self-sufficient.

The questions surrounding the empowerment and emancipation of women have now become essentially crucial to the human rights based approaches to development. Empowering women was the central focus of The Cairo Conference organised by the United Nations on Population and Development in 1994. The United Nations Development Program has developed the Gender Empowerment Measure. It focuses on the three variables that reflect on women's participation in society. These are political power or decision-making, education and health. The 1995 UNDP report was devoted to women empowerment and it declared that if human development is not engendered it is endangered. Equality, sustainability and empowerment were emphasised and the stress was that women's emancipation does not depend on national income but is an engaged political process.

Micro finance and Women Empowerment: Global Perspective

In the South Asian region alone, microcredit covered at least 35 million of some 270 families and met around fifteen percent of the overall credit need of the low-income groups. The microfinance movement has been remarkably striking in Bangladesh, Sri Lanka and India. In Bangladesh and Sri Lanka microfinance services have stretched to more than 60 percent of the poor. The growth of microfinance has been indeed astonishing in this country. Since 1972, along with the government programs the Non-Government Organisations have played a remarkable role in forming microcredit institutions and reaching out to the rural women. It has been estimated that about 690 NGOs operate within the country and these cover around 80 percent of the villages. Also about 95 percent of the microfinance services are devoted to the rural areas and reports suggested that 88 percent of the recipients of benefits from the NGO programs were women. In a socially conservative region like Iran, a case study on Self Help Groups conducted in the Hamedan Country province by Homa Soroushmehr, Khalil Kalantari, Hossein Shabanali

Fami and Valiollah Sarani showed that formation of SHGs has led to an improvement in women's participation in family budget and their educational skills and awareness. Now they are able to fight for their rights which have led to a change in the inheritance laws of the land. They are now able to manage better their household cash transactions, start new business activities and additionally pay for the household purchase and sale of assets like jewels. This region was specifically chosen for the case study because the women population here constituted 8,46,430 persons, the highest in the province and a striking 93.5 per cent were classified under low socio economic status according to the Planning & Budgeting Organisation.

In a study on the Arua and Mukono Districts of Uganda, Florence Wakako has shown that participation in informal financial groups has been the most important micro financial resource that has played an active role in the empowerment of women in the Ugandan rural households. The study also confirms that the provision of microfinance has led to a greater increase in women's decision making capability in their traditional function, agriculture, and also in their non-traditional role, which is in the use of their household income. African countries like Uganda are trying to initiate NGOs and Micro Finance Institutions as, part of their national development plans and strategy.

India has witnessed a mini boom in the formation of the SHGs in the recent past. The Indian Constitution stands for the principle of gender equality since its very inception. Through the directive Principles of State Policy and Fundamental Rights, it upholds the guidelines for creating a just socio economic order. In order to eradicate rural poverty and to bring women on an equal footing with men, the emergence of SHGs, as microcredit institutions, has been an important step in our country.

Microfinance in India-Success and Flaws

The microcredit sector in India has been categorised into three major segments: The SHG Bank linkage program, The Co-operatives and MFIs linked to the NGOs and the Non-Banking Finance Companies (NBFCs). However, the earliest institutional form of microfinance that emerged in India is that of the SHGs and today the SHG Bank linkage program is the leading model of delivering microcredit in the country. Its growth has resulted into a massive movement to mobilise rural women, to help them access financial services like credit, savings and insurance that basically aim at their socio economic development. The formal credit institutions, typically the commercial banks, are not interested in providing credit to the rural poor for the simple reason that they usually demand small loans, they lack the necessary collaterals to support their borrowing and they may probably default; hence, they are categorised as bad borrowers. The introduction of the SHGs targeted at providing credit to these people by organising them into groups. Hence, SHGs have not only minimised the inadequate banking facilities among them, but have also helped to instill in them banking habits.

Its notion largely concentrates and centers on women and the movement has become the basis for upgrading the socio-economic condition and status of women through encouraging self-employment activities. Not only are the SHGs an important step towards poverty alleviation, but are also instruments initiating entrepreneurial capabilities among rural women. At the formal level the promotion of SHGs in India started in 1992 when the National Bank for Agricultural and Rural Development launched its SHG Bank Linkage Program with the policy-support of the Reserve Bank of India (RBI). The program has been planned, devised and developed by NABARD for more than 15 years. The Working Group on NGOs and to SHGs was set up by the RBI in 1994. It brought out a range of recommendations and the program was mainstreamed with the Commercial and Cooperative Banks in 1996.

A SHG is defined to be a small, economically homogeneous and affinity group of about 10-20 individuals. The group is formed to save small amounts regularly, mutually agree to contribute to a common fund, meet their emergency needs, have collective decision making, resolve conflicts through collective leadership and mutual discussions and provide collateral free loans on terms decided by the group at market driven rates. They are self-managed. The members themselves decide on how to mobilise the funds. The Self-Help

Promoting Institutions or the Self Help Promotion Agencies are usually responsible for grooming and promoting. Their three main types: NGOs, government agencies and banks. Majority of the SHGs are financed by the branches of the ordinary commercial banks that are also involved in their usual intermediation business. A large number of them have savings accounts in their banks. Initially SHGs were launched by the subsidised NGOs. However, today development program initiated by the government are setting up SHGs. In spite of SHGs being independent institutions, beyond their own individual savings their freedom is fairly constrained by the banks to which they are linked. NABARD has been playing an active role in their propagation.

It is keenly involved in providing favourable environment, capacity building support and encouraging the Regional Rural Banks and Cooperatives for their promotion. The NABARD has also formed the Micro Finance Development and Equity Fund for meeting the promotional costs. According to its estimates over 33 million women were linked to banks for financial services through 2.2 million SHGs. The National Council of Applied Economic Research has conducted a national level study Impact and Sustainability of SHG Bank Linkage Program in association with the German Collaboration. The study has shown that rural women have now gained much more political presence, voice and self-confidence as a result of the SHG movement. By generating access to savings and credit, it has helped women in rural India to take care of their family's financial requirements for production and consumption in a much improved manner. This has led to a much better gender relations within the family and also in the society.

SEWA

The role played by SEWA in Gujarat has been quite impressive. It is a Self Employed Women's Association that was founded by Ela Bhatt in 1972 with the aim of ensuring self-reliance, work and income security and an access to the social security needs for women working in the informal sector. It has been an active membership based organisation trying to generate awareness about the plight of the poor women workers in the informal sector in India and help them to reclaim their rights. The Work Security Fund, where members contribute a certain pre decided amount, helps to encounter adverse conditions in times of natural calamities or unemployment thereby reducing the dependency on external support and aids. With the formation of SHGs the members are able to access banking and insurance services. The Saving SHGs help the members to own land and secure their land rights. Its Village Resource Centers facilitate the access of better quality agricultural inputs like fertilizers, pesticides and implements, market information and technical advice. The formation of the 'Sabarkantha Women's Farm Cooperative has enabled women farmers in the reclamation of 3,000 hectares of ravine land in 73 villages. Also with the creation of this cooperative, the income of the women farmers' has increased from an average of 5000 rupees to as much as 15,000 rupees in a year.

However, the fact remains that the SHG movement has not been fully successful in its endeavor. Evidences from India suggest that while it has been able to achieve dramatic positive results in the Southern states, the situation has been somewhat discouraging in quite a large part of the country. The SHG movement has been characterised by a skewed growth pattern in India, where the growth has largely encountered in southern India. The table below show the ranking of states based on the Microfinance Penetration Index (MPI) and the Intensity of Penetration of Microfinance among Poor (MPPI).

Table 1: Top 5 States Based on MPI and MPPI

Name of State	MPI	Name of State	MPPI
Manipur	4.13	Manipur	7.06
Pondicherry	3.46	Andhra Pradesh	6.24
Andhra Pradesh	3.34	Pondicherry	4.67
Tamil Nadu	2.32	Sikkim	3.28
West Bengal	2.19	Tamil Nadu	2.76

Source: *Venugopalan Puhazhendhi, Microfinance India: State of the Sector Report 2012 (New Delhi: Sage Publications India Pvt. Ltd. Access Development Services: 2012.*

The table below show the ranking of states based on the Microfinance Penetration Index (MPI) and the Intensity of Penetration of Microfinance among Poor (MPPI).

Table 2: Last 5 States Based on MPI and MPPI

Name of State	MPI	Name of State	MPPI
Mizoram	0.32	Jammu & Kashmir	0.46
Punjab	0.27	New Delhi	0.45
New Delhi	0.24	Bihar	0.42
Meghalaya	0.21	Uttar Pradesh	0.38
Jammu and Kashmir	0.07	Mizoram	0.23

Source: *Venugopalan Puhazhendhi, Microfinance India: State of the Sector Report 2012 (New Delhi: Sage Publications India Pvt. Ltd. Access Development Services: 2012.*

Conclusion

To conclude, we say that women empowerment essentially refers to giving women the right towards a greater participation in the socio economic and political processes. It implies creating a much wider space for women in decision making so that women can increasingly participate in and contribute to the process of development. In today's globalised environment bridging the gender gap and bringing women into the mainstream will evidently lead to greater economic benefits and prosperity for nations. This incorporates giving women access to land, capital and other essential economic resources; i.e., making them economically self-sufficient. All these can be achieved only through strong collective social effort. The significance of women-empowerment has been recognised worldwide and it has become a crucial issue. In this regard the emergence of microfinance has been formidable. Not only has it been popular in the South Asian nations, where its origin lies, but also in the Latin American and Caribbean Countries.

It has seen a socio economic breakthrough with the advent of microfinance in the recent past. The SHGs form the principal mode or the prime institutions in this regard. There have been several lacunae in the spread of the microfinance movement in India. People have asserted that it has been over promising with very little efforts put towards achieving its aims and social objectives. Now the collective concern has been to overcome the growing constraints that this sector is facing. This implies an increased investment by the government towards capacity building and generating a favourable environment for the propagation of microfinance. The government has to play an active role towards proper implementation and orientation of its policies and programs. Simultaneously, the SHGs and the microfinance institutions have to be concerned with their social goals along with their commercial sustainability.

They have to see the continued specialised training of their staff and try to nurture and bring out exceptional leaders in the field because their performance to a large extent depends on their quality, management skills and leadership. The fact that the movement has not been able to reach the regions of extreme backwardness poses a major challenge. Sustainable socio economic development can only be achieved when we include those hands that rock the cradle, empower them and give them the dignity that they deserve.

References

1. A. Ramanathan, "Linkage between Self-help Groups (SHGs) and Banks in India" in *Micro Finance and Poverty Eradication: Indian and Global Experiences*, ed. Daniel Lazar and P. Palanichamy (New Delhi: New Century Publications, 2008), 124.

2. Denis Herbel, "SEWA's Model of Institution Building: Empowering Small-scale Women Farmers", *Gender, Equity and Rural Employment Division, economic and Social Development Department, Food and Agriculture Organisation*, (2010): 6.

3. Frances Sinha, Ajay Tankha, K. Raja Reddy and Malcolm Harper, *"Microfinance Self-help Groups in India: living up to their promise?"* (Warwickshire, UK: Practical Action Publishing Ltd, 2009), 4.

4. H.S. Shylendra, "Role of Self Help Groups", *Yojana* 52, January 2008.

5. Homa Soroushmehr, Khalil Kalantari & Hossein Shabanali Fami and Valiollah Sarani, "Investigation of Self-help Groups (SHGs) Effect on Rural Women Empowerment (Hamedan County, Iran)", *Journal of Agricultural Science* 4, no.1(2012): 1.

6. Isobel Coleman, "Defending Microfinance", *The Fletcher Forum of World Affairs* 29, no. 1 (2005):186.

7. Ann Marie Goetz and Rina Sen Gupta, "Who Takes the Credit? Gender, Power and Control Over Loan Use in Rural Credit Programs in Bangladesh," World Development 24, no. 1 (1996): 45-63;
8. Brooke A. Ackerly, "Testing the Tools of Development: Credit Programs, Loan Involvement and Women's Empowerment", *IDS Bulletin* 26, no. 3 (1995): 56-68.
9. Isobel Coleman, "Defending Microfinance", *The Fletcher Forum of World Affairs* 29, no. 1 (2005): 182. The Micro credit Summit Campaign defines "poorest" as those living on less than a one dollar per day or anyone in the bottom half of those living below their nation's poverty line.
10. Johnson W. Makoba, University of Nevada, Book Reviews, *Journal of Third World Countries*, Fall 2011.
11. Florence Wakoko, *Microfmance and Women's Empowerment in Uganda: From Rhetoric to Empowerment* (VDDM Verlag Publishers, 2010), 2.
12. K. Rajimwale, "Women Empowerment: Socio Cultural Constraints", *Man in India* 84, no. 3-4 (2004): 353-360.
13. John Harris, "Antinomies of Empowerment — Observation on Civil Society, Politics and Urban Governance in India", *Economic and Political Weekly* 42, no. 26 (2007): 2716-2724.
14. S. Batliwala, *"Women's Empowerment in South Asia: Concept and Practices" in Exchange Change* 1, no. 2 (1994).
15. Katherine Driscoll, "Microcredit: Not Yet A Panacea to End Trafficking in Women", University of *Pennsylvania Journal of Business Law* 13, no. 1 (2010): 280.
16. Kiran Prasad, "Critical issues in the economic development alternatives, ed. George O. Tsobanoglou (Delhi: The women Press 2010), 92.
17. International Institute of Population science (2000); *National Family Health Survey-2* (NFHS-2), India, 1998-99, Mumbai: IIPS
18. M.J.Osirim,"Making Good on Commitments to Grassroots Women: NGOs and empowerment for women in contemporary Zimbabwe", *Women Studies International Forum* 24, no. 2 (2001): 168.

19. C. Moser, "Gender Planning in the Third World: Meeting Practical and Strategic Needs", *World Development* 17, no. 11 (1989): 1799--1825.
20. Mahmuda Hogue and Yoshihito Itohara, "Women Empowerment through Participation in Micro-Credit Program: A Case Study from Bangladesh", *Journal of Social Sciences* 5, no. 3 (2009): 244.
21. Mahmuda Hogue and Yoshihito Itohara, "Women Empowerment through Participation in Micro-Credit Program: A Case Study from Bangladesh", *Journal of Social Sciences* 5, no.3 (2009): 244-245.
22. Meena Acharya and Puspa Ghimire, "Gender Indicators of Equality, Inclusion and-Poverty Reduction: Measuring Program/Project Effectiveness", *Economic and Political Weekly* 40, no. - 44/45 (2005): 4720.
23. Naila Kabeer, "Is Microfinance a 'Magic Bullet' for Women's Empowerment? Analysis of Findings from South Asia", *Economic and Political Weekly* 40, no. 44/45 (2005): 4709-4718.
24. "Microfinance Insight, World Bank Report: South Asia", *Yojana* 52, January, 2008.
25. Naila Kabeer, "Resources, Agency, Achievements: Reflections on the Measurement of Women's Empowerment", *Development and Change* 30, no. 3 (1999): 435-64.
26. Nathalie Holvoet, "The impact of Microfinance on Decision-making Agency: Evidence from South India", *Development & Change* 36, no 1 (2005): 76.
27. Heloise Weber, "The imposition of a global development architecture: the example of microcredit", *Review of International Studies* 28, no. 3 (2002): 540.
28. Pallavi Chavan, "Gender Inequality in Banking Services", *Economic and Political Weekly* 43, no. 47 (2008):18.
29. Rakesh Chandra, "*Women Empowerment in India — Milestones and Challenges*", National Conference on 'What it Takes to Eradicate Poverty' 2007, organized by PACS Program, New Delhi.
30. S. Chinnammai, "Micro Credit and Upliftment of Women through Education," in *Micro Finance and Poverty Eradication: Indian and Global Experiences,* ed. Daniel Lazar and P. Palanichamy (New Delhi: New Century Publications, 2008), 256.

31. Sachidananda and Kumar, "On Women's Empowerment", The Eastern Anthropologist 59, no. 1 (2006); A. Beteille, Empowerment", The *Economic and Political Weekly* 34, no.11 and 12 (1999): 589-97.
32. Tara S. Nair, "Commercial Microfinance and Social Responsibility: A Critique", *Economic and Political Weekly* XLV, no. 31 (2010): 32.
33. V. Sucharita, "Self-Help Groups, (SHGs) and Empowerment of Women: An Anthropological Study" in *Micro Finance and. Poverty Eradication: Indian and Global Experiences*, ed. Daniel Lazar and P. Palanichamy (New Delhi: New Century Publications, 2008), 133.
34. Read more at http://www.brainyquote.com/quotes/keywords/globalisation.html#6xRFv5uOIqxpW3bD.99

5

Acceptance of Birth Control Methods: The Prevailing Pattern among Yerava Tribe in Karnataka

P. Prabhuswamy

"Masterpieces of art possess immense potential to advance a worldview that could help assuage the societal terrors posed by globalisation, the most thoroughgoing socioeconomic upheaval since the Industrial Revolution, which has set off a pandemic of retrogressive nationalism, regional separatism, and religious extremism."

—Martin Filler

Introduction

India has the largest tribal concentrations in the world next to Africa. About 8.6 per cent of the India's population belongs to tribes in 2011. About 577 communities are notified as Scheduled Tribes spread all over India. However, some states like Haryana, Punjab, Delhi and Pondicherry do not have settlements notified as tribes. The union territory of Chandigarh also belongs to this category. In general, tribal groups differ in terms of their language, social organisation, culture and religious practices. One of the most conspicuous features of many tribal groups of India has been that they are economically poor and socially backward. This trend continues to prevail among them, even today. Their health and living conditions are dwindling because of their displacement from their native environment. The condition of the primitive tribes is worse when compared to other tribal groups.

Generally, majority of the tribal work as labourer and with continued dependency on minor forest produce for their livelihood. They evolve and maintain their own system to treat their illness and to upkeep their health condition. Traditionally, they use herbs/roots to treat illness and to maintain good health. This approach is used to avoid unwanted pregnancies or to delay births. This is in spite of the fact that most tribal settlements have been provided with modern system of medicine and cost free medical facilities at their door step. The changes initiated after independence have been able to bring about some changes in the life of tribal communities. The present paper is an attempt to analyse the nature of changes that have taken place with regard to '*Small Family Norm*' among the tribal communities with special reference to the Yeravas living in Karnataka.

In India, most tribal communities have their family size higher than the non-tribal population (Guntapalli and Nangia, 2009). While majority of the tribal people consider the birth of a child as '*gift of God*', many have begun to recognise and understand various aspects relating to child-birth. There are evidences to indicate that the tribal people have been using traditional methods to avoid unwanted pregnancies or to space births. Even today, this practice continues to prevail along with the use of modern methods of birth control. The majority of tribal people are aware of different methods of family planning. The use of birth control measures by the tribal womenfolk is more prominent than by the men folk. The use of family planning methods is female oriented among general population. This attitude is prevalent even among tribal groups as about 43 per cent of the currently married tribal women aged 15-49 years have been reported to be using any one of the modern family planning methods (IIPS and Macro International, 2007). It is found that a majority of them have been using female sterilisation while a negligible proportion has been using temporary methods of contraception.

The Context

The knowledge of modern family planning methods has reached each and every corner of the country. However, awareness about different temporary method is poor among tribal folk when compared to general population. Similarly, the use of temporary methods by the currently married women has been found to vary among different social groups in India (Table 1). The data reveals that the ratio of accepters among the scheduled tribes has been the least. This implies the fact that the tribal people may not consider temporary methods as effective measures for birth control. It is also likely that the tribal people would like to use any method of birth control which is convenient and most effective. As a matter of fact, there is higher ratio of scheduled caste and other caste groups who have accepted temporary methods of birth control. Thus, it could be concluded that temporary methods are not popular among tribal communities.

Table-1: Acceptance of Temporary Methods by the Currently Married and their Social Category in India

	Period		
Social Category	1992-93	1998-99	2005-06
SC	5.7	8.4	15.6
ST	4.2	7.3	10.0
Others	11.1	13.7	18.9
Total	9.8	12.2	17.5

Source: Micro data files: NFHS 1992-93, 1998-99 and 2005-06. Note: Temporary Methods include Pill, IUD, Condom and Traditional Methods.

Acceptance of permanent methods by the currently married has divergent pattern. The most commonly prevailing trend all over the nation has been that a few men accept permanent method of birth control. In the last two decades, the number of men accepting permanent method of birth control has not only declined but it is also low. This trend is not only restricted to tribes alone but it is also true among general population as well. The way the society is looking about the use of male sterilisation is not cheering. All this indicates that male methods of birth control do not have encouraging numbers of accepters.

Table-2: Acceptance of Male Sterilisation by the Currently Married and their Social Category in India

	Period		
Social Category	1992-93	1998-99	2005-06
SC	3.3	1.9	1.1
ST	5.7	3.1	2.5
Others	3.2	1.8	0.8
Total	3.4	1.9	1.0

Source: Micro data files: NFHS 1992-93, 1998-99 and 2005-06.

The ratio of accepters of permanent method is also on the decline from 1992-93 to 2005-06 among all categories of people. The trend prevailing among scheduled tribes also justifies a non-popular trend in accepting permanent methods of birth control. Further, it is seen that an increasing number of female accepters have been contributing towards the successful implementation of Family Planning Programme (Table 3).

The trend prevailing among women accepters has been the most promising at the all India level. It is seen that the ratio of accepters is more or less the same for all categories of women. Moreover, the acceptance of female sterilisation among tribal women folk is encouraging between 1998-99 and 2005-06 when compared to other communities.

There is consistency in the rate of increase over the last two decades. This trend could be justified in many ways. First, women accept permanent method of birth control as it entitles them with permanent solution to limit family size. Secondly, the use of temporary methods involves either periodical or time bound assistance or help from doctors or paramedical staff.

Such assistance is not only difficult to get but also unavailable at their door step. Lastly, women accepters prefer permanent method as it conveniently reduces the risk and problems associated with another pregnancy.

Table-3: Acceptance of Female Sterilisation by the Currently Married and their Social Category in India

	Period		
Social Category	1992-93	1998-99	2005-06
SC	25.7	34.4	38.3
ST	23.2	28.7	35.4
Others	28.0	34.9	37.7
Total	27.3	34.3	37.6

Source: Micro data files: NFHS 1992-93, 1998-99 and 2005-06.

Karnataka Scenario

The pattern of acceptance of family planning methods differs from the all India situation. While the broad trend remains similar, the actual ratio varies significantly. It is observed that the rate of acceptance of temporary methods is lower than the all India ratio. This is true for all social categories (Table 4). The lowest ratio prevails among the scheduled tribes. Simultaneously, it is also observed that the ratio has remained relatively constant from 1992-93 to 2005-06.

Table-4: Acceptance of Temporary Method among Currently Married Women by Social Group in Karnataka

	Period		
Social Category	1992-93	1998-99	2005-06
SC	3.9	2.8	2.6
ST	2.7	2.2	2.5
Others	7.3	7.2	7.0
Total	6.6	6.2	6.0

Source: Micro data files: NFHS 1992-93, 1998-99 and 2005-06. Temporary Methods include Pill, IUD, Condom and Traditional Methods.

In contrast, the ratio of men accepting permanent method has declined from 1992-93 to 2005-06. Another important thing to be noted is that the ratio of accepters is lowest for all social categories. As a matter of fact, the male sterilisation is the least popular method of birth control. This has been primarily due to an attitude of non-acceptance among both men and women towards male sterilisation. Even health workers at the gross-root level are not making much effort in promoting male sterilisation as birth control methods. Besides, there is a popular opinion among the tribal people that male sterilisation would affect physical strength of men and they may not able to do hard work. Such attitudinal disposition is not restricted to tribal people alone but also among other non-tribal communities.

Table-5: Acceptance of Male Sterilisation by the Currently Married and their Social Category in Karnataka

	Period		
Social Category	1992-93	1998-99	2005-06
SC	1.7	0.8	0.2
ST	2.7	0.4	0.4
Others	1.4	0.6	0.2
Total	1.5	0.7	0.2

Source: Micro data files: NFHS 1992-93, 1998-99 and 2005-06.

Further analysis indicates that the ratio of women accepting permanent methods has not only been consistent but also increasing over the last two decades. There has been significant increase during the last 6-7 years. The ratio of increase has been highest among scheduled tribes when compared to other social groups (Table-6). One of the main reasons for this kind of a trend is due to an attitude among women that they would not hesitate to accept permanent measure of birth control as it would enable them to permanently avoid pregnancies and associated problems. Thus, a detailed analysis of acceptance of permanent method of birth control by the tribal communities gains significance.

Table-6: Acceptance of Female Sterilisation by the Currently Married and their Social Category in Karnataka

	Periods		
Social Category	1992-93	1998-99	2005-06
SC	40.0	53.8	62.6
ST	40.9	42.1	58.5
Others	41.1	51.8	55.5
Total	41.0	51.6	56.8

Source: *Micro data files: NFHS 1992-93, 1998-99 and 2005-06.*

Awareness and Acceptance of Birth Control Methods among Tribes

Many studies have been made to understand the awareness and use of birth control measures by the tribes. Sharma and Sharma (1993) have analysed the status of women, fertility and acceptance of family planning methods among the tribes of Rajasthan. The study found that those who had exposure on different family planning methods manifested a little higher positive attitude towards the use of family planning methods. It was observed that the use of certain indigenous methods to avoid or space the birth was also the reason for lower level acceptance. It was also found that acceptance of family planning method is associated with the status of women in the family.

The family planning behaviour among scheduled caste and scheduled tribe women has been analysed by Roy and Paswan (1995) in rural Uttar Pradesh. The study has drawn data from NFHS for analysis. It reveals that acceptance of contraception among both the communities is by and large similar. Similarly, an attempt has also made to understand reasons for lower level acceptance of family planning methods among scheduled tribes in Rajasthan by Singh and Srinivasan (2000). The tribes selected for the study were Bhils, Garassias and Meenas. The study employed an in-depth interviews and focus group discussion methods to collect data. The study found that socio-cultural and socio-economic factors have been playing a crucial role in acceptance of family planning methods. Another finding of the study was the non-existence of client and provider relationship. The knowledge, attitude and practice of family planning were studied by Basu et.al. (2004). The Santal and Lodha tribes from Madinapore district of West Bengal were included in the study. It was found that lack of awareness; backwardness and absence of monitory incentives were influencing family planning acceptance level.

Bhasin and Nag (2007) have analysed women's knowledge and use of family planning methods among sahariyas, Minas, Bhils, Kathodis, Damors and Garasias tribes in Rajasthan. The study has found that knowledge of family planning methods is widespread and most commonly used method was tubectomy in the study area. However, the use of family planning methods is not up to the mark. An analysis provided by Kumar and Joshi (2008) has explored knowledge and practices about family planning methods among the tribes of Gujarat. The study examined the reasons for non-use and discontinuation of modern contraceptive methods by tribal people.

Guntapalli and Nangia (2009) have tried to understand the differences between the tribes and non-tribal population in terms of their education, standard of living, child mortality, women's autonomy, exposure to media, use of contraception and reproductive behaviour. The study found that the use of family planning method is low among tribal women though most of the women know at least one method of contraception or the other. The knowledge about temporary methods is much lower than the knowledge about sterilisation. It is found that the mean number of children ever-born is significantly higher among scheduled tribe women when compared to non-scheduled tribe women. Another study by Sharma and Rani (2009) has made an analysis on the use of contraceptive methods and its status among scheduled tribes of Central India. It also emphasises on how it differ from non-scheduled tribes. The study found that the knowledge of different family planning methods has reached all and most of the tribal women. The study also found that users of temporary method constituted only three per cent of the total accepters indicating low level attitude towards use of modern temporary method.

The socio-cultural factors and fertility behaviour among the Kanuri tribe was analysed by Mairiga et.al (2010). The study employed an in-depth interviews and focus-group discussion to collect data. The study found that children among Kanuri tribe were highly valued and desired, irrespective of their sex. Couples with many children were respected and given importance. Among them, prolonged breast-feeding, religious ceremonies, and herbs were used to avoid or delay births. However, a few Kanuari women have been found to practice modern family planning methods. Most of the studies mentioned above have made a broad analysis of awareness and acceptance of birth control measures among various tribal communities in different parts of India. It is evident that the tribal people manifest a common pattern. The use of temporary methods has not encouraging. It is also true that tribal communities have been showing a positive attitude towards permanent methods of birth control. This has been particularly true in case of women. It is in this context, the present study intends to analyse the prevailing pattern of birth control method among tribes in general and Yerava tribal in particular.

The Pattern among Yeravas

In Karnataka, there are 49 communities notified as scheduled tribes which constitute about seven per cent of the state's total population. The Gond, Koli Dhor, Marati, Meda, Soliga, Jenu Kuruba and Yerava are considered as the major tribes in Karnataka. The Yerava is one of the largest among the 10 major tribal groups in the state. They are socially backward and economically poor when compared to other tribes. According to 2001 census, the Yerava population was 22, 000 persons. They predominantly live in Coorg district. There are a few of them living in adjoining districts, namely Mysore and Chamarajnagar. Thus, a study of Yerava tribe and acceptance of birth control method is gains importance.

In general, Yerava do not accept bareness as it is seen as a curse of the God. They expect every married woman to give birth to a child within a year or two. If a woman fails to conceive within a specified time, elderly members of the family consult their priest or traditional healer. Sometimes, the traditional healer suggests specified pooja or offerings to the tribal deity. If all these attempts fail, a man may seek second partner with or without separation from the first wife. Generally, Yerava prefer small family. It is difficult for them to rare more number of children as most of them work as labourer in the plantation. There are many measures like using herbal method of contraception, prolonged breast-feeding and abstinence helping them to limit family size. All the tribal communities have been provided with basic facilities of health and family planning. These services are provided through Sub-centres, Primary Health Centres and District Hospitals. Although the tribal communities have been given health and family planning facilities with free of cost, the availability of such facilities are far from satisfactory. There are also private clinics providing these facilities. Yeravas have not been able to be benefitted to a desirable extent. With regard to health and family planning services, the most crucial role is being played by the ANM working in the sub-centre or the health worker living in the community.

Objectives

The present study is an attempt to analyse the acceptance of birth control methods by the Yerava tribe. It also proposes to examine various aspects associated with the prevailing pattern with special reference to the use of permanent measures of birth control by women.

Methodology

The present paper mainly relies on primary sources for data. The data for this paper has been obtained from household survey. All Yerava tribes living in Virajpet taluk of Coorg district constituted the universe for the study. The taluk, is considered as it is most dominant tribal habitat particularly of the Yeravas.

The sampling design was based on the tribal household list collected from the District Social Welfare Department of the state government. The method of stratified- random sampling procedure was adopted for the selection of tribal colonies. The tribal colonies were grouped in to two categories i.e., inclusive colonies (where Yerava tribes live with other tribal groups) and exclusive colonies (where only Yeravas live). A total of 10 tribal colonies were selected for the study with both inclusive and exclusive colonies. The fieldwork was carried out in 10 selected tribal settlements during January-May 2009.

The individual households were selected on a random basis. A total of 124 households from 10 tribal colonies constituted the sample for the study. There were only 77 currently married women have been included for the present study. These currently married women constituted the respondents for the study. A pre-tested schedule has used to collect data. The data relating contraception, prevailing pattern, health problems due to use of contraception and so on has obtained from the households schedule. The simple computation of data has carried out to understand the prevailing pattern among Yerava tribe. The SPSS package has been used to group the data for analysis and interpretation.

Analysis and Findings

The use of modern contraceptive methods by the currently married women or by their spouses would be one of the significant determining factors of fertility behaviour among currently married women. It directly influences the size of the family.

It has been found that nearly 60 per cent currently married women are reported to be using modern methods of birth control. However, it doesn't mean that those women who are not using any method have not been making effort to limit family size. It is also found that a few couples are using traditional methods like contraceptive herbs/roots to avoid unwanted pregnancies or to space the births.

The local traditional medicinal man has been found to play a crucial role in the use of traditional methods of contraception like contraceptive herbs. The traditional medicinal man advises couple and encourages them to use roots/herbs as contraceptive methods. It is found that the use of contraceptive herbs is culturally accepted by majority of the tribal people. However, field notes suggested that very negligible proportion of women have been found to be users of contraceptive herbs.

It is also found that most tribal women do not use any contraceptive method in the initial stage of their married life. The Yeravas of Kodagu believe that "*child is a gift of God*".

They do not tolerate bareness and they want to get a child immediately after marriage (Census of India, 1981). After having 2-3 children, they either use traditional method or adopt modern birth control method. This is a usual practice that exists among majority of the Yerava households in the study area. Since Yeravas mainly work as labourers or depend on minor forest produce for the livelihood, their limited income prompts them to be inclined towards small family norm.

An analysis of the data collected from the currently married women has been examined by taking into account of variables like age-group, literacy, household size and type of family. The grouped data reveals the number of currently married women in each category with number of acceptors.

1. **Household Size:** The size of the household is one of the variables which seem to be correlated with the level of acceptance of birth control methods by the currently married women. It is found that there are almost equal numbers of currently married women with less than five and more than five members in the sampled household. There are 53.8 per cent of those with less than five members and 63.2 per cent of those with more than five members accepting contraceptive methods of birth control. This implies the fact that an increasing number of Yeravas would like to use birth control methods as the size of the family increases. This could be possible as most of them work as labourer in the estate. These estate owners play a vital role on them in limiting the family size. Besides, the exposure to urban areas and interaction with wider society has also been considered as an important factor.

2. **Type of Family:** Another important observation is that there is an increasing ratio of currently married women accepting birth control measures (75 per cent) with extended families than those living in nuclear families (54.1 per cent). This could be seen as contrary to the popular notion that joint family and extended families tend to be resistant towards birth control methods.

3. **Literacy:** One of the most significant factors influencing acceptance of birth control methods is the literacy. It is an established fact that higher the literacy level, higher would be the level of acceptance of birth control methods. Simultaneously, it is also found that educational level is inversely proportional to the size of the family or number of children. This aspect has been examined in the context of the data collected. It is found that as many as 43.3 per cent literate and 68.1 per cent illiterate Yerava women have been found to be using different methods of contraception. Thus, literacy has not been an

influential factor /promoting factor among Yerava currently married women in accepting birth control measures.

Table 7: Variation in the Use of Modern Contraception by Currently Married Yerava Women

Characteristics	Number of Currently Married Women	Number of Acceptors	Per cent of Acceptors
Household Size			
Up to 4 Members	39	21	53.8
5 + members	38	24	63.2
Type of Family			
Nuclear	61	33	54.1
Extended	16	12	75.0
Literacy Level			
Illiterates	47	32	68.1
Literates	30	13	43.3
Age-group			
Up to 20 Years	04	00	0.0
21-30	39	19	48.7
31-40	19	15	78.9
Above 41Years	15	11	73.3
Total	77	45	58.4

Source; Field Survey

4. **Age-group:** It is evident from the data that nearly 50 per cent of the currently married women are in the age-group of 21-30 years and only half of them have been found to be acceptors of any one method of birth control. There has been a significant increase in the ratio of the currently married women using birth control measures. Nearly 75 per cent of them have been found to be the acceptors in the age-group of 31 years and above. This could be seen as the most prominent trend among the currently married women. Thus, it could be concluded that the currently married among Yeravas prefer to use different measures of birth control after a few years of married life.

Further analysis on the use of different methods of birth control has indicated that about 58 per cent of the currently married women in the sample have accepted permanent method namely sterilisation

(Table-8). Among these acceptors, most of them (50.6 per cent) have accepted laparoscopic sterilisation. The popular acceptance of this method by women has been mainly due to the merits of the method. There are a few advantages identified by the currently married women. First, laparoscopy does not demand stay in the hospital. Second, laparoscopy is considered to involve simple surgical procedure when compared to the traditional procedures of tubectomy. It is true that the post-operative recouping time and care required is minimum. Another interesting data from the study is that none of the currently married women in the sample are using other modern temporary methods like IUD, Pill or any other. However, some of the respondents have indicated that they are using herbal methods of contraception to space births or to avoid pregnancies. In-depth interview and discussion held with traditional healer has brought out this established fact during the fieldwork.

Table 8: Type of Contraceptive Methods Opted by the Yerava Women

Sl. No.	Type of Contraceptive Methods	Number of Currently Married Women	Per cent
1	Laparoscopic	39	50.6
2	Tubectomy	06	7.8
3	Not using any method	32	41.6
	Total	77	100.0

A follow-up analysis of sterilisation acceptors among currently married women has been another significant aspect. It is found that only 15.6 per cent of acceptors of laparoscopy had indicated side effects and complications. Some of these complications are also generally associated with women with advancing age and longer tenure of married life. Most of these problems are resolved by women either by taking help from local ANM or health centres. These happenings have not made any significant impact on women either in their attitudes towards birth control or in their attempts to establish small family.

Conclusion

The tribal and the non-tribal communities have been found manifest different patterns in their level of awareness, attitude and practice of birth control measures. There is a definite trend among tribal communities with regional and cultural variations between and among them. Although these variations have been examined by scholars, such attempts have been successful in identifying significant factors associated with either the success or failure of the programme. One of the most prominent and popular methods of birth control among tribes is the permanent method of sterilisation. This is justified by the fact that they could permanently replace the risks of recurring pregnancies with possible risks of sterilisation.

Yerava tribe has been found to be favourable in limiting family size and in accepting different methods of birth control. They have been found to use traditional and herbal methods of birth control. The use of temporary methods has not been popular both among men as well as women. As a matter of fact, laparoscopy has been found to be most popular and acceptable permanent method among Yeravas. All this implies that efforts are needed to promote and popularise all methods of birth control with due consideration to the traditionally prevailing tribal methods. Health personnel working at the gross-root level have to promote modern temporary methods in the tribal area to space or avoid the birth. Thus, it could be concluded that Yerava tribe has been promoting small family norm with its own choices for modern methods of birth control.

Acknowledgement

Author is grateful to his Ph. D guide, Dr. B. Vijaya Raghava Rao, former Head, Department of Sociology, St. Joseph's College, Bangalore for his constant support, encouragement, valuable comments and suggestions on earlier draft of this paper. This paper has presented in the National Seminar "Population, Health and Environment" held in Bhopal organised by the IIPS, Mumbai in collaboration with Indian Institute of Forest Management (IIFM) Bhopal during 21-23rd March 2013.

References

1. Basu, S., Kapoor, A.K. and Basu, S.K (2004). Knowledge, Attitude and Practice of Family Planning among Tribals. *Journal of Family Welfare*. 50 (1): 24-30.

2. Bhasin, M.K., and Nag. S (2007). Demography of the Tribal Groups of Rajastan: Dynamics of Family Planning Methods Usage, *Anthropologist*. 9 (2): 99-106.

3. Guntapalli, A.M., and Nangia, P (2009). Women's Autonomy, Contraceptive use and Fertility: A Comparative Study of Tribal and Non-tribal Women in India, *Man in India.* 89 (3): 323-340.

4. IIPS and Macro International (2007). National Family Health Survey (NFHS- 3), 2005-06: India: Volume 1, Mumbai: IIPS.

5. IIPS and Macro International (2008). National Family Health Survey (NFHS- 3), India, 2005-06: Karnataka, Mumbai: IIPS.

6. IIPS (2010). District Level Household and Facility Survey (DLHS - 3), 2007-08: India. Mumbai: IIPS.

7. Kumar, A and Joshi, K.M. (2008) Family Planning Methods among the Tribal population in South Gujarat: A case Study of Access and Usage. *Journal of Development in Practice*, 18 (2): 258-266.

8. Mairiga,A. G, Kullima, A.A, Bako, B, and Kolo, M. A. (2010). Socio-cultural Factors Influencing Decision-making Related to Fertility among the Kanuri Tribe of North-eastern Nigeria. *Afr J Prm Health Care Fam Med.* 2 (1), Article no. 94, 4 pages. DOI: 10.4102/phcfm.v2i1.94.

9. Mutharayappa, R. (2001). Is Culture Influences Family Planning Acceptance? *Man in India.* 3 & 4:277-289.

10. Office of the Registrar General and Census Commissioner (1981). The Yeravas of Kodagu, Ethnographic notes and Special Studies on Scheduled Castes & Scheduled Tribes, Series-9, Karnataka, Part xi, New Delhi.

11. Roy, T.K and Paswan, B. (1995). Demand for Family Planning Among Scheduled Castes and Scheduled Tribes In Hari Mohan Mathur (Eds.), *The Family Welfare Programme in India*(pp.157-175. New Delhi, Vikash Publishing.

12. Sharma, R and Rani, M. (2009). Contraceptive use among Tribal Women of Central India: Experiences among DLHS-RCH-II Survey, *Research and Practice in Social Sciences.* 5 (1): 44-66.

13. Sharma, V and Sharma, A (1993). The Status of Women, Fertility and Family Planning among Tribals of South Rajasthan: *Journal of Family Welfare*. 39 (4): 20-25.

14. Family Planning Practices among Tribals of South Rajasthan, India, *The Journal of Research and Education in Indian Medicine.* 10 (4):5-9.

15. Singh, L.P. and Srinivasan, K (2000). Family Planning and the Scheduled Tribes of Rajastan: Taking Stock and Moving Forward. *The Journal of Health Management.* 2 (1):55-80.

16. Read more at http://www.brainyquote.com/quotes/keywords/globalisation.html#6xRFv5uOIqxpW3bD.99

6

Economic Development in India: Progress and Challenges

R.Prasad & Sukanta Sarkar

"Globalisation and the neoliberal economic model have already been rejected in Latin America; it simply hasn't been a solution for our people. At the same time, Latin countries like Venezuela and Argentina are anti-imperialist and anti-globalisation, and yet their economies are growing again."

– Evo Morales

Introduction

The post independence-era Indian economy (from 1947 to 1991) was a mixed economy with an inward-looking, centrally planned, interventionist policies and import-substituting economic model that failed to take advantage of the post-war expansion of trade and that nationalised many sectors of its economy. India's share of global trade fell from 1.3 percent in 1953 to 0.5 percent in 1983. This contributed to widespread inefficiencies and corruption, and it was poorly implemented. Until the liberalisation of 1991, India was largely and intentionally isolated from the world markets, to protect its economy and to achieve self-reliance. Foreign trade was subject to import tariffs, export taxes and quantitative restrictions, while foreign direct investment was restricted by upper-limit equity participation, restrictions on technology transfer, export obligations and government approvals; these approvals were needed for nearly 60 per cent of new FDI in the industrial sector. Local economic development (LED) offers local government, the private and not-for-profit sectors, and local communities the opportunity to work together to improve the local economy. It focuses on enhancing competitiveness, increasing sustainable growth and ensuring that growth is inclusive. LED encompasses a range of disciplines including physical planning, economics and marketing. It incorporates many local government and private sector functions including environmental planning, business development, infrastructure provision, real estate development and finance.

What is Economic Development?

Economic development is the sustained, concerted actions of policy makers and communities that promote the standard of living and economic health of a specific area. It is a wealth spends on country's population. It can be referred to as the quantitative and qualitative changes in the economy. The scope of economic development includes the process and policies by which a nation improves the economic, political, and social well-being of its people. In economics, the study of economic development was borne out of an extension to traditional economics that focused entirely on national product, or the aggregate output of goods and services. It is the development of economic wealth of countries, regions or communities for the well-being of their inhabitants. From a policy perspective, economic development can be defined as efforts that seek to improve the economic well-being and quality of life for a community by creating and/or retaining jobs and supporting or growing incomes and the tax base.

Development economics considers how to promote economic growth in countries by improving factors like health, education, working conditions, domestic and international policies and market conditions. It examines both macroeconomic and microeconomic factors relating to the structure of a developing economy and how that economy can create effective domestic and international growth. The definition of economic development given by Michael Todaro is an increase in living standards, improvement in self-esteem needs and freedom from oppression as well as a greater choice. The most accurate method of measuring development is the Human Development Index which takes into account the literacy rates & life expectancy which affects productivity and could lead to Economic Growth. It also leads to the creation of more opportunities in the sectors of education, healthcare, employment and the conservation of the environment. It implies an increase in the per capita income of every citizen.

Indicators for Economic Development

The International Economic Development Council defines economic development as an *"activity that seeks to improve the economic well-being and quality of life for a community, by creating and/or retaining jobs..."* The World Bank is the primary international organisation that measures economic development on a national and global scale. Of the more than 2,000 indicators it uses to assess development, five measure it the most directly.

1. *Public Sector:* Every year the World Bank assigns low income nations a set of ratings called Country Policy and Institutional Assessment.
2. *Private Sector and Trade:* Under the heading "Private Sector and Trade" will find many indicators of the business environment, including imports and exports measured both in dollar value and by time-study indexes.
3. *Poverty:* This subcategory covers income distribution and poverty. Poverty is measured nationally and separately as a percentage of rural population and urban populations.
4. *Financial Sector:* There are five subcategories under this heading. Asset and Capital Markets are the two most general, and they include bank capital and market capitalisation.
5. *Economic Policy and Debt:* There are three main subcategories in this class: Balance of Payments, External Debt and National Accounts. Indicators measure capital and financial accounts, as well as the current account and reserves.

The gross domestic product (GDP) is the godfather of the indicator world. As an aggregate measure of total economic production for a country, GDP represents the market value of all goods and services produced by the economy during the period measured, including personal consumption, government purchases, private inventories, paid-in construction costs and the foreign trade balance. Real GDP is the one indicator that says the most about the health of the economy and the advance release will almost always move markets. It is by far the most followed, discussed and digested indicator out there useful for economists, analysts, investors and policy makers.

Economic Development in India since Independence

India's economic development strategy immediately after Independence was based primarily on the Mahalanobis model, which gave preference to the investment goods industries sector, with secondary importance accorded to the services and household goods sector. The model downplayed the role of the factory goods sector because it was more capital intensive and therefore would not address the problem of high unemployment in India. Any increase in planned investments in India required a higher level of savings than existed in the country. Investments were carried out both by the government and the private sector, with the government investing in strategic sectors (such as national defense) and also those sectors in which private capital would not be forthcoming because of lags or the size of investment required (such as infrastructure). The private sector was required to contribute to India's economic growth in ways envisaged by the government planners. India's environment of regulated economic development led to the formulation of policies that were concerned with both macroeconomic and microeconomic aspects.

Economic development in India still depends on the various sectors that constitute the Indian economy – agriculture, services and manufacturing industries. Production volume has gone up in Indian agriculture at a consistent rate since the 1950s. Much of this improvement can be attributed to the five-year plans that were established for the development of Indian agriculture. Developments in irrigation processes, as well as various modern technologies used have contributed to the overall advancement of agricultural processes. India is rated as one of the top economies in the world in terms of purchasing power parity (PPP) of the gross domestic product (GDP) by leading financial entities of the world, such as the International Monetary Fund, the World Bank, and the CIA. Financial sector reforms have led to a booming stock market that has helped large firms finance their expansion easily. However, small and medium enterprises, which are an important engine of growth and productivity, have not been able to access finance as they are too small to be of interest to equity markets or FDI. Growth in lending to this sector has been slow due to the closely regulated publicly owned banking sector which has few incentives for innovation, and a large deficit with the attendant fears of making new loans.

The economic development in India followed socialist-inspired policies for most of its independent history, including state-ownership of many sectors. Favourable macroeconomic performance has been a necessary but not sufficient condition for the significant reduction of poverty amongst the Indian population. India is fifteenth in services output. Service industry employ English-speaking Indian workers on the supply side and on the demand side, has increased demand from foreign consumers interested in India's service exports or those looking to outsource their operations. During the Internet bubble, heavy investments in undersea fibre-optic cables linked Asia with the rest of the world. The fall that followed the economic boom resulted in the auction of cheap fiber optic cables at one-tenth of their original price.

Industrialisation has a major role to play in the economic development of the under developed countries. Rapid industrial growth has resulted in the expansion of infrastructural facilities. The development of modern industries has stimulated the growth of banking, insurance, commerce, shipping, air services etc. India started her quest for industrial development after independence. The industrial policy resolution of 1948 marked the beginning of the evolution of Industrial policy. In 1977 the Congress Party was thrown out and Janata Party assumed power, new Industrial Policy was introduced to make radical changes in the existing policy. The Industrial policy stated that industrial units found guilty of mismanagement leading to sickness would be dealt firmly. All the industrial policies recognised the need for securing participation of foreign capital and enterprise. The role of foreign direct investment are support domestic investment for achieving a higher level of economic development. FDI benefits domestic industry as well as the Indian consumer by providing opportunities for technological upgradation access to global managerial skills and practices etc.

India and China signed a five-year trade and economic cooperation agreement to improve the trade balance that is loaded heavily in favour of the latter, a sore point in economic relations between the neighbours. The agreement also envisages $20-billion Chinese investment in India. The Five-Year Trade and Economic Development Plan were signed by Commerce Minister Nirmala Sitharaman and her Chinese counterpart Gao Hucheng in the presence of Prime Minister Narendra Modi and visiting President Xi Jinping. Sitharaman and Gao also signed the minutes of the 10th session of the India-China Joint Economic Group held in Beijing. India had a $36.2 billion goods trade deficit in fiscal 2014 with China. This wide trade imbalance is often blamed for hurting many of the manufacturing sectors in India. The total trade between the two countries was nearly $66 billion. India sought greater access for bovine meat, rapeseed meal and oil meals and also flagged the issue of the country's basmati exports facing restrictions in China. China provided market access for basmati rice in 2012 but shipments have been stuck because authorities in Shanghai were not aware of the quarantine clearance given by the Chinese government for import of the aromatic grain, New Delhi has pointed out. India exported $4.1 billion worth of bovine meat in fiscal 2014. Basmati rice accounted for $4.8 billion of the total rice exports of $7.8 billion. India has also sought market access for five fruit and vegetables on an urgent basis. China had provided market access for mangoes in 2004 and for grapes and bitter gourd in 2005. India also suggested lower tariffs on textiles and handmade carpets, casein and caseinates, diamonds and oil seeds. China has suggested this could be taken up under the framework of the Asia-Pacific Trade Agreement. Chinese investments in India are abysmally low. Increasing investments in key sectors like infrastructure will not only bring in capital inflows but would also provide impetus to the manufacturing sector. This would help India increase its exports and lower trade deficit.

Five Year Plans

Though the planned economic development in India began in 1951 with the inception of First Five Year Plan, theoretical efforts had begun much earlier, even prior to the independence. Setting up of National Planning Committee by Indian National Congress in 1938, The Bombay Plan & Gandhian Plan in 1944, Peoples Plan in 1945 (by post war reconstruction Committee of Indian Trade Union), Sarvodaya Plan in 1950 by Jaiprakash Narayan were steps in this direction. Five-Year Plans (FYPs) are centralised and integrated national economic programs. Joseph Stalin implemented the first FYP in the Soviet Union in the late 1920s.

Since 1947, the Indian economy has been premised on the concept of planning. This has been carried through the Five-Year Plans, developed, executed, and monitored by the Planning Commission. With the Prime Minister as the ex-officio Chairman, the commission has a nominated Deputy Chairman, who holds the rank of a Cabinet Minister. Montek Singh Ahluwalia is the last Deputy Chairman of the Commission (resigned on 26 May 2014). The Eleventh Plan completed its term in March 2012 and the Twelfth Plan is currently underway. The First Five-Year Plan was one of the most important because it had a great role in the launching of Indian development after the Independence. It strongly supported agriculture production and it also launched the industrialisation of the country. The first Indian Prime Minister, Pandit Jawaharlal Nehru presented the First Five-Year Plan to the Parliament of India and needed urgent attention. The First Five-year Plan was launched in 1951 which mainly focused in development of the primary sector. The First Five-Year Plan was based on the Harrod–Domar model. At the end of the plan period in 1956, five Indian Institutes of Technology (IITs) were started as major technical institutions. The University Grant Commission (UGC) was set up to take care of funding and take measures to strengthen the higher education in the country. The Second Plan, particularly in the development of the public sector. The plan followed the Mahalanobis model, an economic development model developed by the Indian statistician Prasanta Chandra Mahalanobis in 1953. The plan attempted to determine the optimal allocation of investment between productive sectors in order to maximise long-run economic growth.

The Third Five-year Plan stressed agriculture and improvement in the production of wheat, but the brief Sino-Indian War of 1962 exposed weaknesses in the economy and shifted the focus towards the defence industry and the Indian Army. Many primary schools were started in rural areas. In an effort to bring democracy to the grass-root level, Panchayat elections were started and the states were given more development responsibilities. Due to miserable failure of the Third Plan the government was forced to declare *"plan holidays"* (from 1966–67, 1967–68, and 1968–69). Three annual plans were drawn during this intervening period. During 1966-67 there was again the problem of drought. At this time Indira Gandhi was the Prime Minister. The Indira Gandhi government nationalised 14 major Indian banks and the Green Revolution in India advanced agriculture. In addition, the situation in East Pakistan was becoming dire as the Indo-Pakistan War of 1971 and Bangladesh Liberation War took funds earmarked for industrial development. The Fifth Five-Year Plan laid stress on employment, poverty alleviation (Garibi Hatao) and justice. The plan also focused on self-reliance in agricultural production and defence. In 1978 the newly elected Morarji Desai government rejected the plan.

The Sixth Five-Year Plan marked the beginning of economic liberalisation. Price controls were eliminated and ration shops were closed. This led to an increase in food prices and an increase in the cost of living. This was the end of Nehruvian socialism. Family planning was also expanded in order to prevent overpopulation. The Sixth Five-Year Plan was a great success to the Indian economy. The target growth rate was 5.2 per cent and the actual growth rate was 5.4 per cent. The Seventh Five-Year Plan marked the comeback of the Congress Party to power. The plan laid stress on improving the productivity level of industries by upgrading of technology. The main objectives of the Seventh Five-Year Plan were to establish growth in areas of increasing economic productivity, production of food grains, and generating employment. The Seventh Plan had strived towards socialism and energy production at large. The thrust areas of the Seventh Five-Year Plan were: social justice, removal of oppression of the weak, using modern technology, agricultural development, anti-poverty programmes, full supply of food, clothing, and shelter, increasing productivity of small- and large-scale farmers, and making India an independent economy.

The Eighth Plan could not take off in 1990 due to the fast changing political situation at the centre and the years 1990-91 and 1991-92 were treated as Annual Plans. The Eighth Plan was finally launched in 1992 after the initiation of structural adjustment policies. Under pressure, the country took the risk of reforming the socialist economy. P.V. Narasimha Rao was the ninth Prime Minister of the Republic of India and head of Congress Party, and led one of the most important administrations in India's modern history, overseeing a major economic transformation and several incidents affecting national security. The Ninth Five-Year Plan came after 50 years of Indian Independence. Atal Bihari Vajpayee was the Prime Minister of India during the Ninth Five-Year Plan. The Ninth Five-Year Plan tried primarily to use the latent and unexplored economic potential of the country to promote economic and social growth. The Ninth Five-Year Plan also saw joint efforts from the public and the private sectors in ensuring economic development of the country. The main objective of the Ninth Five-Year Plan was to correct historical inequalities and increase the economic growth in the country.

There have been several important developments during the Eleventh Plan that have implications for financing of the Twelfth Plan. The Indian Economy resiliently faced the global financial crisis of 2008. However, slower growth adversely impacts growth in Centre's resources, particularly taxes. The Sixth Central Pay Commission award has been implemented. The 13th FC award for 2011–15 is under implementation with some changes in the fiscal responsibility and budget management framework targets. Service tax has emerged as a very promising source of revenue. Efforts are being made to introduce unified Goods and Service Tax (GST) in consultation with States.

The Twelfth Five-Year Plan of the Government of India has decided for the growth rate at 8.2 percent but the National Development Council (NDC) on 27 Dec 2012 approved eight percent growth rate for 12th five-year plan. The government intends to reduce poverty by 10 percent during the 12th Five-Year Plan. Mr Ahluwalia said, *"We aim to reduce poverty estimates by nine percent annually on a sustainable basis during the Plan period. 12th Five Year Plan of the Government of India (2012–17) is under drafting which aims at one direction will help in doing so the growth rate at eight percent."* The broad vision and aspirations which the Twelfth Plan seeks to fulfill are reflected in the subtitle: *'Faster, Sustainable, and More Inclusive Growth'*. Inclusiveness is to be achieved through poverty reduction, promoting group equality and regional balance, reducing inequality, empowering people etc whereas sustainability includes ensuring environmental sustainability, development of human capital through improved health, education, skill development, nutrition, information technology etc and development of institutional capabilities, infrastructure like power telecommunication, roads, transport etc. The policy challenge in the Twelfth Plan is two-fold. The immediate challenge is to reverse the observed deceleration in growth by reviving investment as quickly as possible. This calls for urgent action to tackle implementation constraints in infrastructure which are holding up large projects, combined with action to deal with tax related issues which have created uncertainty in the investment climate. From a longer term perspective, the Plan must put in place policies that can leverage the many strengths of the economy to bring it back to its real Growth potential.

Finance Commissions

The Finance Commission of India came into existence in 1951. It was established under *Article 280* of the Indian Constitution by the President of India. It was formed to define the financial relations between the centre and the state. The Finance Commission Act of

1951 states the terms of qualification, appointment and disqualification, the term, eligibility and powers of the Finance Commission. As per the Constitution, the commission is appointed every five years and consists of a chairman and four other members. With the objective of giving a structured format to the Finance Commission of India and to bring it at par with world standards, The Finance Commission (Miscellaneous Provisions) Act, 1951 was passed. It lays down rules regarding qualification and disqualification of members of the Commission, their appointment, term, eligibility and powers.

A finance commission is a body of five experts including a chairman constituted under Article 280 of the Constitution of India by the President. The primary mandate of the Commission is to recommend a formula for sharing net proceeds of tax revenues of the Centre with the states, principles which should govern the transfer of grants-in-aid of the revenues of the states out of the Consolidated Fund of India and measures required to augment the Consolidated Fund of individual states during a five year period.

The first finance commission was constituted on November 1951. The Constitution requires the President to constitute a fresh panel every fifth year or earlier. The Twelfth Finance Commission (TFC) recently handed over its recommendation for the five-year period starting April 1, '05. While the states have a preponderant share of spending responsibilities to improve the lot of the people, the Centre has been vested with a preponderant share of the powers of taxation. To remedy this imbalance, from the collections by the Centre, funds must devolve to the states and must be distributed among the states in a fair manner.

The finance commission undertakes this task, as well as additional ones referred to it by the President in its terms of reference. Stamp duty and local sales tax are major source of income for states. The Centre retains power to impose and collect taxes on very large number of items. For instance, customs and excise, income and corporation tax are levied and collected by the Centre even though the service or activity that generates these duties and taxes takes place at the state level.

The Finance Commission takes into account various parameters for deciding its awards. The TFC, for instance, assigned specific weights to population, income distance, poverty, geographic area and tax efforts of the states to decide the quantum of taxes that should be transferred to the states. The Constitution only requires the Centre to report to Parliament what action it has taken on the recommendations of the Finance Commission. However, normally the Centre accepts and implements all the recommendation of such panels. The Constitution requires the Centre to lay an action taken report in Parliament detailing implementation of the recommendations. A significant change is in the quantum of resources sought to be transferred as grants-in-aid of revenues. The main function of finance commission is to recommend how the Union government should share taxes levied by it with the states. These recommendations are meant for the period of five years. The commission also lays down rules by which the centre should provide grants-in-aid to states out of the Consolidated Fund of India and also in case of special provision of states. Finance Commission is also assigned the duty of suggesting measures to augment the resources of states and ways to supplement the resources of Panchayati Raj institutes and municipalities.

It is the duty of the Commission to make recommendations to the President as to: (a) the distribution between the Union and the States of the net proceeds of taxes which are to be, or may be, divided between them and the allocation between the States of the respective shares of such proceeds; (b) the principles which should govern the grants-in-aid of the revenues of the States out of the Consolidated Fund of India; (c) the measures needed to augment the Consolidated Fund of a State to supplement the resources of the Panchayats in the State on the basis of the recommendations made by the Finance Commission of the State; (d) the measures needed to augment the Consolidated Fund of a State to supplement the resources of the Municipalities in the State on the basis of the recommendations made by the Finance Commission of the State; and (e) any other matter referred to the Commission by the President in the interests of sound finance.

Centre-State Financial Reforms

The Constitution assigned taxes with a nation-wide base to the Union to make the country one common economic space unhindered by internal barriers to the extent possible. States being closer to people and more sensitive to the local needs have been assigned functional responsibilities involving expenditure disproportionate to their assigned sources of revenue resulting in vertical imbalances. In addition to provisions enabling transfer of resources from the Centre to the States, a distinguishing feature of the Indian Constitution is that it provides for an institutional mechanism to facilitate such transfers. The institution assigned with such a task under Article 280 of the Constitution is the Finance Commission, which is to be appointed at the expiration of every five years or earlier. Under the Constitution, the main responsibilities of a Finance Commission are the following. (a) The distribution between the Union and the States of the net proceeds of taxes which are to be divided between them and the allocation between the States of the respective shares of such proceeds; (b) Determination of principles and quantum of grants-in-aid to States which are in need of such assistance; (c) Measures needed to augment the Consolidated Fund of a State to supplement the resources of the Panchayats and Municipalities in the State on the basis of the recommendations made by the Finance Commission of the State.

Initially, the Constitution provided for the sharing of only two Central taxes with States. Article 270 permitted mandatory sharing of the net proceeds of income tax levied and collected by the Union with the States. Such proceeds assigned to States did not form part of the Consolidated Fund of India. Article 272 provided for sharing of Union excise duties, if Parliament by law so provided. The shares of the States in Union excise duties were to be paid from the Consolidated Fund of India. This position continued till the 80th amendment of the Constitution in 2000 which provided for sharing of the proceeds of all Union taxes and duties with the States, except the Central sales tax, consignment taxes, surcharges on Central taxes and earmarked cesses. As far as the distribution of the proceeds of Union excise duties was concerned, initially the share of States was restricted to certain specified commodities. From the Fourth Commission onwards, States were being given a share in the proceeds of the tax on all the commodities. The Eleventh Finance Commission, for the first time, introduced the concept of overall ceiling on total Central transfers to States from all channels on the revenue account. The indicative ceiling recommended by the Commission was 37.5 per cent of the gross revenue receipts of the Centre. Under Article 275 of the Constitution, Finance Commissions are mandated to recommend the principles as well as the quantum of grants to those States which are in need of assistance and that different sums may be fixed for different States. It has become customary for the Presidential Order to mention certain considerations that a Commission shall have regard, among others, while making its recommendations. These considerations by and large reflected the emerging developments in Centre-State finances.

Over the period covered by twelve Finance Commissions, the key constitutional change was brought about by the 80th Constitutional amendment, which provided for a mandatory sharing of the net proceeds of all central taxes except earmarked cesses and surcharges and Article 268/269 taxes (including the service tax). Historically, the distinction between Article 270 and 272 had led the earlier Finance Commissions to use the sharing of income taxes far more as an instrument of vertical transfers and the sharing of Union excise duties as a tool to achieve more horizontal equity. The main criteria for determining shares of the states used by the different Finance Commissions have related to: population criterion, distance criterion, inverse income criterion, criterion based on area, index of infrastructure, index of fiscal discipline, and index of tax effort. The two core criteria in the scheme of sharing of central taxes are: population and distance. States get grants from the Finance Commission, Planning Commission and other Central Ministries. The Finance Commission grants are for meeting the assessed revenue gap of the states as also for various other purposes including for special needs and upgradation of standards. The Finance Commissions particularly from Ninth Finance Commission onwards have attempted to apply, to some extent normative principles for making an assessment of state's own tax and non-tax revenues as well as revenue expenditures.

For the Ninth and Tenth Finance Commissions, the relative share of vertical transfers was 59 and 57 per cent, respectively. This share came down to 39 per cent for the Eleventh Finance Commission and 48 percent for the Twelfth Finance Commission. Correspondingly the Eleventh Finance Commission devoted 61 per cent of total transfers for meeting the horizontal objectives. In relation to grants, there are two duties cast upon the Finance Commission conjointly by Articles 280(3) (b) and 275. Article 280(3) (b) requires the Commission, to make recommendations as to the principles which should govern such grants-in-aid. Following from Article 275(1), specific sums are to be recommended to be paid to the States which are assessed to be in need of assistance. It is significant to note that while Article 270 (for division of taxes) speaks of percentage share, Article 275 refers to specific sums. The Constitution prescribes that these grants are to be charged on the Consolidated Fund of India and have to be recommended by a Finance Commission. The First Finance Commission had considered the principles of determining grants at length and had opined that both unconditional and specific purpose grants can and should be considered by the Finance Commission under the Article 275 read with Article 280(3) (b).

The Seventh Finance Commission (1978), while recommending grants-in-aid for up-gradation of standards of administration, felt that grants should be made for meeting capital expenditure as well. In principle, Article 275(1) makes no restriction as to whether needs should be considered only on revenue account, and further only on the non-plan revenue account. There has been a running debate for some time as to whether the whole revenue account or only the non-plan revenue account should be considered by the Finance Commission. The distinction between non-plans versus plan revenue expenditure became material with a minute of dissent given by the Member-Secretary of the Third Finance Commission (1961). The Third Finance Commission took into account the needs of the States for the 3rd Five Year Plan and recommended by a majority that the quantum of grants-in-aid should be fixed in such a way as to enable the States, along with any surplus out of devolution, to cover 75 per cent of the revenue component of their plans. The revenue gap grants are the main grants given under Article 275.

The government announced the constitution of the 14th Finance Commission under the chairmanship of former RBI Governor Y. V. Reddy. The five-member panel is to submit its report by October 31, 2014. Apart from its recommendations on the sharing of tax proceeds between the Centre and the States which will apply for a five-year period beginning April 1, 2015, the Commission has been asked to suggest steps for pricing of public utilities such as electricity and water in an independent manner and also look into issues like disinvestment, GST compensation, sale of non-priority PSUs and subsidies. Among other things, the Commission would look into the need for insulating the pricing of public utility services like drinking water, irrigation, power and public transport from policy fluctuations through statutory provisions. The 14 Finance Commission would suggest measures for maintaining a stable and sustainable fiscal environment consistent with equitable growth.

14th finance commission has been constituted by the Government of India consisting of Dr. Y.V. Reddy, former Governor Reserve Bank of India, as the Chairman and the following four members: Prof Abhijit Sen, Ms. Sushma Nath, Dr. M.Govinda Rao, and Dr. Sudipto Mundle. The new commission shall make its report available by the 31st October, 2014, covering a period of five years commencing on the 1st April, 2015. Apart from its recommendations on the sharing of tax proceeds between the Centre and the States which will apply for a five-year period beginning April 1, 2015, the Commission has been asked to suggest on:

1. Pricing of public utilities such as electricity and water in an independent manner and also look into issues like disinvestment, GST compensation, sale of non-priority PSUs and subsidies.
2. Measures for maintaining a stable and sustainable fiscal environment consistent with equitable growth including suggestions to amend the Fiscal Responsibility Budget Management Acts.
3. With regard to debt-stressed states, the Commission has been asked to suggest steps for augmenting revenues of states which are lagging.

4. Review the present arrangements as regards financing of Disaster Management with reference to the funds constituted under the Disaster Management Act, 2005(53 of 2005), and make appropriate recommendations thereon.

Conclusion

Economic development is the sustained, concerted actions of policy makers and communities that promote the standard of living and economic health of a specific area. It is a wealth spends on country's population. Economic development in India still depends on the various sectors that constitute the Indian economy – agriculture, services and manufacturing industries. Industrialisation has a major role to play in the development of the under developed countries. Rapid industrial growth has resulted in the expansion of infrastructural facilities. The development of modern industries has stimulated the growth of banking, insurance, commerce, shipping, air services etc. India and China signed a five-year trade and economic cooperation agreement to improve the trade balance that is loaded heavily in favour of the latter, a sore point in economic relations between the neighbours. The agreement also envisages $20-billion Chinese investment in India. Indian planning commission and financial commissions are playing vital role for its development. Five year plan and finance commission plays vital role for economic development of the nation.

References

1. *Economic development (2014),* Retrieved from http://en.wikipedia.org/wiki/Economic_development
2. *Definition of development economics (2014),* Retrieved from http://www.investopedia.com/terms/d/development-economics.asp
3. *What is economic development? (2014),* See http://www.svbic.com/node/24
4. *What is local economic development?* Retrieved from http://web.worldbank.org/WBSITE/EXTERNAL TOPIC SEXTURBAN DEVELOPMENT/EXTLED0,,content MDK: 20185186~menu PK:399161~page PK: 148956~pi PK:216618~the Site PK: 341139,00.html

5. *Economic development Vs. Economic growth (2014),* Retrieved fromhttp://www.diffen.com/differenceEconomic_ Development_ vs_ Economic_Growth

6. Steve Greechie, *What Are Indicators of Economic Development? (2014),* Retrieved from http://smallbusiness.chron.com/indicators-economic-development-3883.html

7. *Economic Indicators: Gross Domestic Product (GDP), (2014)),* Retrieved from http://www.investopedia.com/university/releases/gdp.asp

8. Anil K. Lal and Ronald W. Clement, Economic development in India: The role of individual enterprise, *Asia-Pacific Development Journal,* Vol. 12, No. 2, December 2005, Retrieved from http://www.unescap.org/sites/default/files/apdj12-2-5-lal.pdf

9. *India economic development (2014),* Retrieved from http://www.economywatch.com/indianeconomy/india-development.html

10. *Growth in India (2014),* Retrieved from http://web.worldbank.org/WBSITE/EXTERNAL/COUNTRIES/SOUTHASIAEXT/EXTSARREGTOP MACECOGRO 0,, conten tMDK: 20592481~menu PK: 5 79404~page PK: 34004173~pi PK: 34003707~the Site PK: 579398, 00.html

11. *Economy of India (2014),* Retrieved from http://en.wikipedia.org/wiki/Economy_of_India

12. *Economic development in India (2014),* Retrieved from http://en.wikipedia.org/wiki/Economic_development_in_India

13. Puja Mondal *(2014)*, *Role of Industrialisation in the Economic Development of India*, Retrieved from http://www.yourarticlelibrary.com/economics/role-of-industrialization-in-the-economic-development-of-india/4664/

14. *The Economic Times (Sep 19, 2014),* China President Xi's India visit: Five-Year Trade and Economic Development Plan signed, Retrieved from http://articles. economictimes.indiatimes.com/2014-09-19/news/54108754_1_market-access-trade-deficit-gao-hucheng

15. *Finance Commission of India (2014*), Retrieved from http://en.wikipedia.org/wiki/Finance_Commission_of_India

16. *Finance commission India, (2014),* Retrieved from http://fincomindia.nic.in/ShowContentOne.aspx?id=8&Section=1

17. *Finance commission of India (2014),* Retrieved from http://fincomindia.nic.inShowContent. aspx? uid1= 2&uid 2= 1& uid 3=0&uid4=0

18. *Review of Trends in Fiscal Transfers in India, (2014),* Retrieved fromhttp://fincomindia.nic.in Show Content. aspx?uid1=11&uid2=6&uid3=0&uid4=0&uid5=0&uid6=0&uid7=0

19. The Economic Reforms (Feb, 2005), *what is finance commission?* Retrieved from http://articles.economictimes.indiatimes.com/2005-02-07/news/27499485_1_the-tfc-twelfth-finance-commission-states

20. *The Hindu (Jan 2, 2013),* Y.V. Reddy to head 14th Finance Commission, Retrieved from http://www.thehindu.com/business/Economy/yv-reddy-to-head-14th-finance-commission/article4264593.ece

21. Parveen Kaswan (2013), *14th Finance Commission and its Role*, Retrieved from http://www.simplydecoded.com/2013/01/10/14th-finance-commission-and-its-role/

22. *Five-Year Plans of India (2014),* Retrieved from http://en.wikipedia.org/wiki/Five-Year_Plans_of_India

23. *Five years plans*, chapter 7, Retrieved from http://mospi.nic.in/Mospi_New/upload/SYB2014/CH-7-FIVE% 20YEAR%20PLANFive%20Year%20Plan%20 writeup.pdf

24. See http://www.brainyquote.com/quotes/keywords/globalisation_2.html

7

Globalisation and Poverty Eradication: An Assertive Approach in 21st Century

Deepali Singh

"We cannot wait for governments to do it all. Globalisation operates on Internet time. Governments tend to be slow moving by nature, because they have to build political support for every step."

– Kofi Annan

Introduction

The problem of poverty is considered as the biggest challenge to development planning in India. High poverty levels are synonymous with poor quality of life, deprivation, malnutrition, illiteracy and low human resource development. Poverty can be defined as a social phenomenon in which a section of the society is unable to fulfill even its basic necessities of life. It is one of the perennial and intractable problems facing governments and populations throughout the world. India is home to 22 per cent of the worlds poor. Reducing and eventually eliminating poverty is vital if the country is to attain national and international goals of development and good governance. Various studies have drawn attention to the fact that some segments of the population find it especially hard to escape poverty. The government has initiated, sustained, and refined many programs since independence to help the poor attain self sufficiency in food production. All those whose income or expenditure is below to minimum per capita consumer expenditure are considered to be below the poverty. Two types of standards may be used to define poverty the absolute and the relative:

(a) Absolute poverty: Minimum physical quantities of cereals, pulses, milk, vanaspati, cloth are determined for a subsistence level and are converted into monetary terms on the basis of price quotations.

(b) Relative poverty: It is used to explain the extent of deprivation of resources in an economy to one section of the population against other. In many parts of the world the poor are the overwhelming number of the population. In my country, India, they make up approximately 30 per cent, who are living below poverty line, i.e. Rs. 12000/- (US$400) income per annum. About 80 percent of them live in rural areas that are usually illiterate or semiliterate and the majority is women. The poor are also economically very active. They contribute to the national economy each year, and they grow, produce, transport, and sell most of the commodities.

Probably the most important initiative has been the supply of basic commodities, particularly food at controlled prices, available throughout the country.

The poor spend about 80 percent of their income on food while the rest of the population spends more than 60 per cent. The price of food is a major determinant of wage scales. Often when food prices rise sharply, rioting and looting follow. Until the late 1970s, the government frequently had difficulty obtaining adequate grain supplies in years of poor harvests.

During those times, states with surpluses of grain were cordoned off to force partial sales to public agencies and to keep private traders from shipping grain to deficit areas to secure very high prices; state governments in surplus-grain areas were often less than cooperative. After the late 1970s, the central government, by holding reserve stocks and importing grain adequately and early, maintained sufficient supplies to meet the increased demand during drought years. It also provided more remunerative prices to farmers.

Causes of Poverty

There are many reasons for poverty, few of them are:

- Geographic factors for example access to fertile land, fresh water, minerals , energy , and other natural resources .
- Inadequate nutrition in childhood in poor nations may lead to physical and mental stunting that may lead to economic problems.
- Disease, specifically diseases of poverty; AIDS, malaria and tuberculosis and others overwhelmingly afflict developing nations, which perpetuate poverty by diverting individual community from investment and productivity liability to find a well – paying job.

Poverty in India

In India, more than 65 per cent of the country's population lives in rural areas and about 193 million rural people are poor and every three of the four people in India survive on less than US $1 a day live in rural areas. For more than 15 per cent of rural poor people, poverty is a chronic condition. India adopted a development strategy which was based on the trickle down concept. Then the government realised the need for direct intervention in favour of the poor, since that development strategy failed to meet the basic needs of million of the rural poor. Consequently, the implementation of comprehensive and coherent anti poverty programmes. However, the Planning Commission has cautioned that the poverty ratios over the two time period (1993-94 and 1999-2000) are not strictly comparable. The survey methodology has undergone changes over the two surveys in 1993-94 and 1999-2000. There are two basic pre-requisites of a poverty eradication programmes: (a) reorientation of the agricultural relations so that the ownership of land is shared by a larger section of the people, and (b), no programme of removal of poverty can succeed in an economy plagued by inflation and spiralling rise of price.

Government Policies

The government of India has taken various steps from time to time to reduce poverty in rural areas which are follows:

(1) Small farmers development programme

(2) Draught area development programme

(3) Food for work programme

(4) Minimum needs programme

(5) Integrated rural development programme

(6) National rural development programme

(7) Rural labour employment guaranty programme

The largest of the other programmes is the Indira Awaas Yojana, which provides houses free of costs to below the poverty line scheduled casts and scheduled tribe families living in rural areas. Recently, several other poverty alleviation programmes have been launched including: Pradhan Mantri Gramodaya Yojana, Pradhan Mantri Gram Sadak Yojana, Antyodya Anna Yojana, The Annapurna Scheme, Valmiki Ambedkar Awas Yojana. In the 1980s and early 1990s, Indian government programms attempted to provide basic needs at stable, low prices; to increase income through pricing and regulations, such as supplying water from irrigation works, fertilizer, and other inputs; to foster location of industry in backward areas; to increase access to basic social services, such as education, health, and potable water supply; and to help needy groups and deprived areas. The total money spent on such programs for the poor was not discernible from the budget data, but probably exceeded 10 percent of planned budget outlays. Government's implementation of Policies:

(1) Government around the world have recently made moves towards increased liberalisation of trade, but these policies have benefited only the private sector , while the people sector has experienced increased regulation.

(2) Government economic policies tend to favour those business people who are rich in assets, and the people's sector trends to be asset – poor. The private sector can enjoy the benefits of the free – market economy since it had the assets to go to where profits can be made.

(3) The people's sector is often tied to middlemen and operates in a much more restricted market structure. They are unable to travel

to sell goods in wholesale markets and therefore only realise a fraction of the profits on the final price of their goods.

(4) Similarly in the case of capital markets, the private sector can obtain capital at competitive rates, whereas the people's sector is forced to borrow from money lenders at exorbitant interest rates.

In order to meet the problem of poverty various measures are to be taken. They are discussed below:

(1) Poverty and unemployment are interred related. Adequate employment opportunities should be created in rural areas particularly in agricultural sector. In order to eliminate agricultural unemployment it is necessary to improve agriculture in the country.

(2) There is the need to strengthen all the poverty alleviation programmes, particularly IRDP. All the organisation deficiencies in an execution of the programme such as the shortage of technical and expert staff, delays in release of funds and inadequacies in funds, lack of proper co ordination should be removed. It is essential to see that the target groups are not wrongly selected to ensure leakage of benefits to the non poor. Other drawbacks in the programme implementation such as right and non-co-operative attitudes of the officials, corrupt practices in sanctioning of loans should also be taken into consideration.

(3) Efforts are to be made to remove the deficiencies in the implementation ofTRYSEM programme such as poor infrastructural support to enable the trainees to follow the pursuits, lack of co-ordination among DIC, banks and Training Institute and lack of follow up to the trained. Govt. instead of sticking to only few traditional crafts, new vocations conducive for income generating activities should be selected in order to make TRYSEM and DWCRA programmes more effective.

(4) Adequate care is to be taken that while implementing JRY. The ingredient are not missed in it on the whole, for smooth implementation of various programmes the entire administrative set up should be properly co ordinate.

(5) The recent increase in population and pressure exercised on the limited resources of the country has brought to the forefront the urgency of the problem of family planning and population control.

Thus, family planning or family welfare programmes should be effectively implemented.

(6) There is lack of political and social awakening among the rural people. The programme of poverty alleviation is not so simple as to be successfully solved by the Government, thus there is a great need for political and social awakening. People should be made aware of various programme and benefits of these programmes.

(7) Eradication of poverty needs a multiplied strategy. But as things stand the most important, indeed the central one, has to be the creation of massive wage employment opportunities both on private and public accounts in rural areas.

There are several participants in the developmental arena such as national and international agencies, private companies and non-governmental organisations which have taken up projects to improve the quality of education and healthcare, focusing on specific critical areas such as HIV/AIDS, illiteracy and women's empowerment. State governments are important participants in antipoverty programs. The constitution assigns responsibility to the states in a number of matters, including ownership; redistribution, improvement, and taxation of land. State governments implement most central government programs concerned with land reform and the situation of small landless farmers. The central government tries to establish programs and norms among the states and union territories, but implementation has often remained at the lower bureaucratic levels. In some matters concerning subsoil rights and irrigation projects, the central government exerts political and financial leverage to obtain its objectives, but the states sometimes modify or retard the impact of central government policies and programs.

By Swaminathan S Anklesaria Aiyar, the world has learnt to live with terrorism, treating it like any other accident. As evil cannot be completely eradicated, terrorism too may not be completely eliminated. But it could be contained and many preventive and protective actions could be taken. Having mere power is not enough. We should be able to use it to attack poverty and destroy it. It is incorrect to say that all the poverty eradication programmes have failed because the growth of the middle class people indicates that economic prosperity has indeed been very impressive in India, but at the same time, the distribution of wealth is not at all even across the country. Poverty eradication is expected to make better progress in the coming years than in the past due to the increasing stress on education, reservation of seats in government jobs and the increasing empowerment of women have contributed much to the eradication of poverty in India.

BJP's prime ministerial candidate Narendra Modi, Education is the route to eradicate poverty and every child in India must be educated. Speaking at the 9th convocation of the SRM University, Modi said, *"This is an era of knowledge. This is the only potent route to fight poverty. We have to review our commitment to education."* He also said that the private sector should be given a free hand to promote education. Education will help eradicate poverty. The Indian government spends significant funds on subsidies for electricity; fertilizer fuels etc. food rations, price supports, land allocation / distribution, job training and financial assistance for initiatives in agriculture and small business. The beneficiaries are usually corrupt officials who manage and distribute funds and landlords and powerbrokers, who directly from any government programmes due to bribery, political influence in the allocation of fund, diffused focus and priorities, poor execution, shortage of rural infrastructure and social inequality. Similarly corruption and misallocation of development funds are ultimately the result of failed governance. Eradication of poverty in India is a long term goal.

Below Poverty Line

There has been a sharp decline in poverty with the percentage of population Below Poverty Line (BPL) declining to 26.1 percent in 1999-2000 from 35.97 percent in 1993-94. According to the estimates of the Planning Commission, while the percentage of rural BPL population has dropped to 27.09 percent from 37.27 percent, in urban India, it fell to 23.62 percent from 32.36 percent during the five year period. In absolute term too, the BPL population has dropped by over 19 percent to 26.03 crore in 1999-2000, from 32.04 crore in 1993-94. The rural poor stands at 19.32 crore while the urban poor stands at 6.71 crore. At the state level, the percentage of

BPL population in Orissa is declined to 47.15 percent from 48.56 percent. It has overtaken Bihar to reach the top slot with the highest incidence of poverty. The other big states with highest incidence of poverty were Madhya Pradesh at 37.43 percent (as against 43.52 per cent), Assam 40.86 percent (36.09), U.P. 31.15 percent (40.85), and West Bengal 27.02 percent (35.66).

The Planning Commission's press report claiming that the overall number of poor households declined from 37 per cent in 2004-05 to around 22 per cent in 2011-12 has invited criticism from several quarters. Civil society is not happy with the low poverty cut-off line of Rs. 27 per day per capita for rural areas and Rs. 33 for urban areas at 2011-12 prices, as it is difficult to meet one's basic expenses and survive on such an inadequate income. Economists are questioning the need for subsidised food for 67 per cent of the population if poverty levels are really so low. Opposition parties are accusing the Planning Commission of fudging the figures so as to help the Congress in its electoral propaganda. The present methodology for determining poverty based on consumption expenditure is certainly flawed, and leads to under-reporting of the actual number facing acute deprivation. For instance, in Mumbai and Delhi the number of poor is only six and ten percent of the total city population respectively, whereas the slum population alone in these districts is 53 and 30 per cent respectively. Therefore, the estimates for the number of poor should be reworked by taking into account their deprivations and living conditions, such as access to basic services, shelter, public health, and education.

Estimating the scale of poverty with respect to a fixed poverty line which was Rs. 1.63/1.90 per capita per day for rural/urban populations in 1973-74, and since then has remained unchanged after adjusting it for inflation is still relevant for many purposes, including judging whether the development process is helping the poor and how fast poverty is declining over time. It also helps to assess which states are doing better in poverty eradication. Any line that we choose would be arbitrary and the number below that line would certainly go up if the threshold is increased. For instance, if in place of Rs. 27 per day per capita as the rural cut-off line we choose Rs. 40, the rural poverty figure would jump from 26 to 50 per cent. The present cut-off is surely too low, it could be called the destitute or starvation line; still, 270 million people are surviving on such a meager amount. One should worry more about them rather than attack the line itself. The government has undertaken programms to mitigate the worst effects of adverse monsoon rainfall, which affects not only farmers but village artisans and traders when the price of grain rises. The government has supplied water by financing well digging and, since the early 1980s, by power-assisted well drilling; rescinded land taxes for drought areas; tried to maintain stable food prices; and provided food through a food-for-work program. The actual work accomplished through food-for-work programs is often a secondary consideration, but useful projects sometimes result. Employment is offered at a low daily wage, usually paid in grain, the rationale being that only the truly needy will take jobs at such low pay.

The popular outrage over the official definition of poverty at abysmally low levels of daily income, of Rs. 26 in rural areas and Rs. 32 in urban areas, assumes the state will deny basic services to a household whose income is above the figure. This is totally erroneous. There is no mechanism in the hands of the government to ascertain income or expenditure to identify the 'poor' on the ground. Economist Suresh Tendulkar has estimated that 37 percent of Indians are poor, not 27 percent as we have been led to believe by the Planning Commission, say reports. Apart from warming the cockles of leftist hearts, which have been skipping quite a few beats at the steady decline in the official poverty count over the past decade and a half of 'neo-liberal, anti-people' growth, this revelation means little.

Conclusion

High poverty levels are synonymous with poor quality of life, deprivation, malnutrition, illiteracy and low human resource development. Poverty can be defined as a social phenomenon in which a section of the society is unable to fulfill even its basic necessities of life. In India, more than 65 percent of the country's population lives in rural areas and about 193 million rural people are poor and every three of the four people in India survive on less than

US $1 a day live in rural areas. For more than 15 percent of rural poor people, poverty is a chronic condition. India adopted a development strategy which was based on the trickle down concept. Government have been implemented various poverty ersdication programme for welfare of poor people.

References

1. Aasha Kapur Mehta, Chronic Poverty and Development Policy in India, Andrew Shepherd SAGE, 09-Mar-2006 - Business & Economics
2. Amitabh Kundu, Understanding the poverty line, Oct 15, 2011, The Economic Times.
3. Bibhuti Bhushan Malik, Poverty in India: Fundamental Issues: a Social Science Perspective, (Google eBook),Mittal Publications, 2009.
4. Jose Murickan, Poverty in India: Challenges and Responses, Xavier Board of Higher Education in India, 1988.
5. K. Nageswara Rao, Poverty in India: Global and Regional Dimensions, Deep and Deep Publications, 01-Jan-2005.
6. K. Nageswara Rao, Poverty in India: Global and Regional Dimensions, Deep and Deep Publications, 01-Jan-2005.
7. Krishna A. Jalihal, Murudaiah Shivamurthy, Pragmatic Rural Development for Poverty Alleviation: A Pioneering Paradigm, Concept Publishing Company, 2003.
8. Kulwant Rai Gupta, Poverty in India, Atlantic Publishers & Dist, 01-Jan-2008.
9. Mahadeo Dandekar, with Nilakantha Rath, Poverty in India, Vishnu Year, 2009. K.S. Mohindra, Women's Health and Poverty Alleviation in India, 2009.
10. Meeta Krishna, Poverty Alleviation and Rural Poor, Mittal Publications, 2003.
11. Narendra Modi, Education will help eradicate poverty: Modi, February 9, 2014 | IANS the Times of India.
12. Naresh Chandra Saxena, A poor debate on poverty in India, July 25.

13. Neepa Saha, Independent Commission on Development and Health in India, Independent Commission on Development and Health in India, 2005.
14. Poverty in India: Fundamental Issues: a Social Science Perspective (Google eBook) Mittal Publications, 2009.
15. Poverty: (scenario in Indian Subcontinent),Indian Economic Association. Conference, Deep and Deep Publications, 2010.
16. Prof Tendulkar's, Poverty estimates rise, December 12, 2009, ET Bureau.
17. Raka Ray, Mary Fainsod Katzenstein, Social Movements in India: Poverty, Power, and Politics, Rowman & Littlefield, 01-Jan-2005.
18. S. G. Bhanushali, Poverty alleviation programmes in India, Book well Publications, 2000.
19. S.N. Misra, Poverty and Sustainable Development: Concepts and Measures, Deep and Deep Publications, 01-Jan-2005.
20. Sanjivi Guhan, Poverty in India: research and policy, Oxford University Press, 1992.
21. Swaminathan S Anklesaria Aiyar, Poverty, the evil, September 16, 2006 | TNN the Economic Times, .
22. T. L. Jain, Poverty in India: An Economic Analysis, Ess Publications, 1987.
23. The Poverty and Justice Bible: Contemporary English Version American Bible Society Bible Society, 2008.
24. V M Dandekar, Nilakantha Rath, Poverty in India, eBook Description UPDF.
25. Vishnu Mahadeo Dandekar, Nilakanth Rath, Poverty in India, Ford Foundation, 1970.

8

Changes of Economic Sectors in India: Progress and Challenges

Rakesh Joshi & Sukanta Sarkar

"The current global landscape is quite different from the not-too-distant past. The process of globalisation has intensified, and the world is moving towards new forms of governance."

— Michelle Bachelet

Introduction

The financial sector of the economy is an important contributor to economic growth. Disruptions that interfere with the ability of the financial sector to intermediate financial work might be expected to restrain economic activity. It helps by facilitating funds from investors to borrowers.[1] Cultural industries are increasingly becoming important components of the modern economy and knowledge-based society due to their impact on the enrichment of development. The culture sector generates two types of impacts: non-economic and economic. The first decade of the 21st century was marked by changes in the participation of the culture sector in economic development. The cultural industries have gained importance.[2] The postal sector has been undergoing a paradigm shift over the last 30 years, from a relic of the industrial era to a facilitator of exchanges of goods and messages in the era of global Internet connectivity. The transformation has taken place from a perspective of both supply and demand. Since the beginning of the 1980s, a key driver of change in the postal sector has been the introduction of new means of communication, which have entered into direct competition with the traditional postal communication business.[3]

Economic statistics describe the activities of economic transactors and the transactions that take place between them. In the real world, economic entities engaged in the production of goods and services vary in their legal, accounting, organisational and operating structures.[4] Economic growth is necessary for poverty reduction, but the magnitude and speed by which growth can reduce poverty are strengthened and accelerated when income distribution is equitable, and when the poor can participate in the economic activities that experience expansion. For rapid poverty reduction in developing countries, it is not enough simply to focus on rapid aggregate economic growth; attention must also be given to removing the types of inequalities that limit the poor's access to, and capacity to exploit, the opportunities for economic advancement. In low-income agrarian economies, livestock form an integral part of predominantly smallholder diversified crop-livestock farming systems. Superseded only by larger-scale staple crops, the livestock sector is the second most important contributor to the agricultural economy.[5] Public sector information, like much other information, has the important feature that there are many heterogeneous ways in which it can be used and reused.[6] The financial sector and its role in the process of economic development have attracted notable attention since the early 1990s. In particular, the crucial need for a stable banking system was highlighted in the wake of the Asian financial crisis of the late 1990s. The rapid influx of short-term, speculative capital flows to Asian economies was a major contributing factor to the crisis.[7]

Government interventions to redistribute income and to improve living standards are part of a policy package, the components of which will be interdependent but not necessarily consistently integrated. Efforts to alleviate poverty in rural areas, to redistribute income, to promote agricultural development or to create jobs will be constrained by other macroeconomic and sectoral policies, and will, in turn, affect the outcomes of those policies. Furthermore, the outcomes of policies will be modified by exogenous shocks, which may themselves require action by the government to reduce their impact.[8] The informal economy plays an important role for employment creation, income generation and poverty reduction in many countries, especially developing and transition countries. Statistics on the informal economy are needed as an evidence-based tool for research and policy-making. They enhance the visibility of the many workers in the informal economy and of their economic contribution.[9]

Types of Economic Sector

The three-sector theory is an economic theory which divides economies into three sectors of activity: extraction of raw materials (primary), manufacturing (secondary), and services (tertiary). It was developed by Alan Fisher, Colin Clark and Jean Fourastie. According to the theory, the main focus of an economy's activity shifts from the primary, through the secondary and finally to the tertiary sector.[10]

1. *Primary sector:* It is the sector of an economy making direct use of natural resources. This includes agriculture, forestry, fishing and mining. This is contrasted with the secondary sector, producing manufactured goods, and the tertiary sector, producing services. The primary sector is usually most important in less developed countries, and typically less important in industrial countries. In developed countries primary industry is becoming more technologically advanced, for instance the mechanisation of farming as opposed to hand picking and planting. In more developed economies additional capital is invested in primary means of production.[11]

2. *Secondary sector:* It includes those economic sectors that create a finished, usable product: production and construction. This sector generally takes the output of the primary sector and manufactures finished goods or where they are suitable for use by other businesses, for export, or sale to domestic consumers. This sector is often divided into light industry and heavy industry. Many of

these industries consume large quantities of energy and require factories and machinery to convert the raw materials into goods and products.[12]

3. *Tertiary sector*: It is one of the three economic sectors, the others being the secondary sector and the primary sector (agriculture, fishing, and extraction such as mining). The tertiary sector of industry involves the provision of services to other businesses as well as final consumers. Services may involve the transport, distribution and sale of goods from producer to a consumer, as may happen in wholesaling and retailing, or may involve the provision of a service, such as in pest control or entertainment. The goods may be transformed in the process of providing the service, as happens in the restaurant industry.[13]

Importance of Economic Sectors

Everything that grows also changes its structure. Just as a growing tree constantly changes the shape, size, and configuration of its branches, a growing economy changes the proportions and interrelations among its basic sectors i.e. agriculture, industry, and services and between other sectors i.e. rural and urban, public and private, domestic and export-oriented. One way to look at the structure of an economy is to compare the shares of its three main sectors i.e. agriculture, industry, and services, in the country's total output. Conserving natural capital and building up human capital may help global development become more environmentally and socially sustainable. Growth of the service sector will not be a miracle solution to the problem of sustainability, because agricultural and industrial growth is also necessary to meet the needs of the growing world population.

Agricultural productivity gains and/or diversification into high-value agricultural products leading to increased income through increased value of output per area of land and, more important, per unit of labour input are an essential means of raising rural incomes and improving food security. Because a large share of the rural poor keep livestock, because livestock can make important contributions to sustainable rural development, and because the demand for livestock products is growing rapidly in developing countries, diversification into livestock, and increasing livestock productivity should form part of a strategy for poverty reduction and agricultural productivity growth. Livestock contribute to human food and nutrition security directly, by transforming vegetation from non-arable land, crop residues, by-products from food processing, and organic waste into human food of high nutrient density and nutritional quality. Livestock are an important means of conferring income and status to women. Although women seldom hold property or usage rights to land they often independently own livestock.

A strong manufacturing base creates a broad foundation on which the rest of the country's economic sector grows. Manufacturing production and the workers they employ generate demand for other manufactured goods. Manufacturing also drives supply chain growth by generating innovation and creating new technologies throughout the country. Industrial development has had an important role in the economicgrowth of countries like China, the Republic of Korea (Korea), TaiwanProvince of China (Taiwan), and Indonesia. Along with accelerated growth, poverty rates have declined in many countries. Industrialisation has an important role to play in the economic development of the under-developed countries like India with huge man power and large and varied resources. It plays a vital role in the economic development of an underdeveloped country. The historical facts reveal that all the developed countries of the world broke the vicious circle of underdevelopment by industrialisation. It makes possible the optimum utilisation of the scarce resources of the country. It helps in increasing the quantity and quality of various kinds of manufactured goods and thereby makes a larger contribution to gross national product. Industrialisation brings structural changes in the pattern of foreign trade of the country. It helps in increasing the export of manufactured goods and thus earns foreign exchange.

The services sector plays an increasingly important role in the global economy and the growth and development of countries. Services are becoming crucial in a country's development, including for the achievement of the Millennium Development Goals, such as poverty reduction and access to basic services, including education, water and health services. For developing countries and least developed countries (LDCs), service trade is the new frontier for enhancing their participation in international trade and, in turn, realising development gains.

Economic Sectors of India: Changing

Tertiary sector has becoming important sector in India by replacing the primary sector. In modern welfare state such as India, the government is supposed to provide basic services such as hospitals, educational institutions, defense, posts and telegraphs for welfare of the people. These functions have led to the importance of the tertiary sector. With the introduction of new agricultural tools, the production increased. As the income of the people rose, there was more need for services such as, public schools, shops, private hospitals etc, for better facilities. Service sector in India employs two different kinds of people. There are highly skilled & educated workers such as teachers and doctors. On the other hand, a large number of workers are engaged in services such as small shopkeepers, repair persons etc. who barely manage to earn a living. They perform these services because they do not have any other work to do. As a result of this only a portion of service sector is growing in importance.

There was change in the share of GDP of the three sectors but the primary sector continues to be the largest employer in 1973 as well as in 2000 because enough jobs were not created in the secondary and tertiary sectors. Industrial output or production of goods increased by eight time i.e., from 6000 crore to 50,000 crore approximately but the employment increased 2.5 times only, similarly in tertiary sector, the production increased 11 times i.e., from 10,000 crore to 110,000 crore but employment increased only less than three times.[14] The service industry forms a backbone of social and economic development of a region. It has emerged as the largest and fastest-growing sectors in the world economy, making higher contributions to the global output and employment. Its growth rate has been higher than that of agriculture and manufacturing sectors. The most important services in the Indian economy have been health and education. They are one of the largest and most challenging sectors and hold a key to the country's overall progress. Accordingly, it is carrying out measures like National health policy, implementing National Rural Health Mission (NRHM) in different States, conducting surveys and studies, etc. The era of economic liberalisation has ushered in a rapid change in the service industry. As a result, over the years, India is witnessing a transition from agriculture-based economy to a knowledge-based economy. Another major and upcoming service industry has been media and entertainment. It is basically an intellectual property-driven sector with small to large players spread throughout the country.[15]

Private and public organisations have traditionally defined the boundaries of their operations firmly, thus restricting the extent to which they are prepared to act and report on the economic, social and environmental impacts associated with their activities. More recently, the introduction of Integrated Product Policy and Life-cycle thinking has provided organisations with the conceptual framework to transcend operational boundaries and track products throughout the entire supply chain. Though simple enough in principle, supply chain management requires the coordination of networks rather than isolated organisational initiatives. Businesses are increasingly expected to report on their supply chains, and proactive sustainability reporting can enhance the image of organisations and thus, returns.[16]

Among fast growing developing countries, India is distinctive for the role of the service sector. Where earlier developers grew on the basis of exports of labor-intensive manufactures, India has concentrated on services. Although there are other emerging markets where the share of services in GDP exceeds the share of manufacturing, India stands out for the size and dynamism of its service sector. Service-sector growth is widespread across activities. However, the fastest growing are business services, communication and banking. Business services, which include computer-related services, machinery rental, accounting, legal services, technical services, and research, of which computer services is the single fastest-growing segment. Financial services include banking and insurance, with banking being the largest and fastest growing. Other rapidly growing sectors include hotels, restaurants, education, and health.[17]

The Indian food processing industry is a high priority sector and is poised for excellent growth in the coming years because it holds the vital link between agriculture and industry. India is the world's largest producer of food after China. India is the world's largest producer of tea, sugarcane and milk. Processing industry is nascent but is growing rapidly. In India, the industry is largely dominated by ready to eat segment, which contributed nearly 90 percent of total sales of packaged foods in India in FY-13. Indian food industry is primarily export oriented. In this context, there are massive opportunities for export oriented food processing industries for medium scale entrepreneurs.

India's healthcare sector has been growing rapidly driven by a number of factors such as increasing the average life expectancy and average income level and rising awareness for health insurance. India's travel and tourism industry is one of the most profitable industries in the country, and also credited with contributing a substantial amount of foreign exchange. Foreign tourists spend more in India than almost any other country worldwide. Several reasons are cited for the growth and prosperity of India's travel and tourism industry.

The Indian Retail Industry is the largest among all the industries, accounting for over 10 per cent of the country's GDP and around eight per cent of the employment.[18] There is broad consensus that the global center of economic growth is moving to Asia, and as a large emerging nation with a growing middle class, India has captured the attention of developed economies looking for new investment and trade opportunities. By some estimates, India's economy will grow from its current $1.8 trillion GDP to be the world's third largest in 2030, with a GDP of close to $30 trillion. A recent report by the National Intelligence Council states that by 2030, India could be the rising economic powerhouse that China is seen to be today."[19]

India is primarily an agrarian country with 60 per cent of its population being dependent directly or indirectly on agriculture. The Indian agriculture sector has made considerable progress in the last few decades with its large resources of land, water and sunshine.

India produces all major crops to meet the requirement of food, fodder, fibre, fuel and inputs for its agricultural industry. Agriculture is expected to grow at 4.6 per cent in 2014. Agriculture production of food grains is expected to break the 2011-12 record of 259 million tonnes (MT). More importantly, agricultural profitability has increased over the last decade with record increases in MSPs (minimum support prices for agricultural produce) for all covered crops. Spice exports from India are expected to reach US$ 3 billion by 2016-17, on the back of creative marketing strategies, innovative packaging, strength in quality and a strong distribution network.

The Indian spices market is pegged at Rs. 40,000 crore (US$ 6.61 billion) annually, of which the branded segment accounts for 15 per cent. Indian basmati rice processing and marketing companies such as KRBL Ltd and LT Foods Ltd have seen their profits grow. Basmati exports to countries such as South Africa, Egypt, Azerbaijan, Tanzania, Poland and Ukraine, among others, have more than tripled in the past three years. The foreign direct investment inflows in agricultural services and machinery sector during April 2000 - April 2014 stood at US$ 1,699.96 million and US$ 359.68 million respectively, as per data released by Department of Industrial Policy and Promotion (DIPP).[20]

The cropping pattern in India has undergone significant changes over time. As the cultivated area remains more or less constant, the increased demand for food because of increase in population and urbanisation puts agricultural land under stress resulting in crop intensification and substitution of food crops with commercial crops. Increase in area under total oilseeds is not reflective of general rise in area across all oilseed crops, but seemed to be limited only to rapeseed and mustard, sunflower and soybean.

Favourable market conditions for refined oil and protein-rich soya food might have been responsible for inducing farmers to allocate larger areas for these crops.[21] The pattern of growth that the Indian economy is currently experiencing has received particular attention. This growth process has witnessed the slowing of agriculture at a time when the rest of the economy is growing at unprecedented rates. Growth of the services economy has been less spectacular but more steady over a longer period. The slow growth of agriculture has been explicitly noted as a matter of concern in the Approach Paper to the Eleventh Plan.[22]

The share of agriculture and allied sectors in India's GDP has declined to 13.7 per cent in 2012-13 due to shift from traditional agrarian economy to industry and service sectors. As per latest estimates released by Central Statistics Office (CSO) the share of agricultural products/Agriculture and Allied Sectors in Gross Domestic Product of the country was 51.9 per cent in 1950-51, which has now come down to 13.7 per cent in 2012-13 at 2004-05 prices. The decrease in the share of Agricultural and Allied Sectors in GDP of the country in comparison to other sectors is on account of structural changes due to a shift from a traditional agrarian economy to industry and service dominated on.

In a separate query, the minister said despite a decline in the sector's contribution to GDP, food grain production and productivity has risen. Despite this, the production of food grains has increased from 230.8 million tonnes in 2007-08 to 255.4 million tonnes in 2013-14. Similarly, productivity of food grains has increased from 1,860 kg per hectare in 2007-08 to 2,125 kg a hectare in 2012-13.[23]

The contribution of manufacturing sector in the country's Gross Domestic Product may fall below 15 per cent in 2013-14 owing to demand slowdown, leading to unutilised excess capacity. During 2012-13, the share of manufacturing sector in the GDP declined to 15.2 per cent, compared to 15.7 per cent in the previous financial year. The decline is witnessed in the backdrop of government aiming to bring manufacturing contribution to 25 per cent of the total economic activity within a decade, but the trend is certainly moving in the reverse direction. The government has introduced the National Manufacturing Policy in October 2011, which seeks to raise the share of manufacturing to GDP from 16-25 per cent within a decade and create 100 million jobs. Although the industrial production during March improved to 2.5 per cent, the factory output during 2012-13 worked out to be only one per cent, down from 2.9 per cent in the previous fiscal. The government has projected economic growth at above six per cent in the current fiscal.[24]

The service sector is contributing more than half of the Indian GDP. It takes India one step closer to the developed economies of the world. Earlier it was agriculture which mainly contributed to the Indian GDP. The Indian government is still looking up to improve the GDP of the country and so several steps have been taken to boost the economy. Policies of FDI, SEZs and NRI investment have been framed to give a push to the economy and hence the GDP.[25] Country estimates for 2012 show a deceleration in services growth in some major countries. For example, in 2012 it decelerated to 0.5 per cent from 0.9 per cent (in 2011) in the USA; 8.1 per cent in 2012 from 9.4 per cent (in 2011) in China; and 6.6 per cent in FY 2012-13 from 8.2 per cent (in FY 2011-12) in India. While the share of services in employment for many developed countries is very high and in many cases higher than the share of services in incomes, the gap between these shares is relatively less. Except China and India, all the other BRIC Countries also have a similar pattern. In the Indian and Chinese cases, there is a wide gap between the two; within order to be comparable with the healthcare parameters of other developing countries, India's healthcare sector faces many challenges. For example, to reach a ratio of two beds per 1000 population by 2025, an additional 177 billion beds will be required which will need a total investment of US$86 billion gap being wider for India. The growth of the services sector is closely linked to the FDI inflows and the role of transnational firms. While the ambiguity in classifying the different activities under the services sector continues, the combined FDI share of financial.[26]

The Union Cabinet gave its approval to the long-awaited ambitious National Manufacturing Policy (NMP), which seeks to set up mega industrial zones, create 100 million jobs by 2022 and put India at par with manufacturing powers like China and Japan. The NMP seeks to enhance the share of manufacturing in the GDP to 25 per cent within a decade and create 100 million jobs in manufacturing as part of the inclusive growth agenda of the UPA. The major objectives of the NMP are to increase the sectoral share of manufacturing in GDP to at least 25 per cent, create 100 million jobs by 2022 and enhance global competitiveness of the sector. Besides, it focuses on domestic value addition, technological depth and environmental sustainability of growth. Besides, it focuses on domestic value addition, technological depth and environmental sustainability of growth. The policy envisages specific interventions broadly in the areas of industrial infrastructure development and improvement of the business environment through rationalisation and simplification of business regulations. Besides, development of appropriate technologies, especially green technologies for sustainable development, and skill development of the younger population are envisaged. The contribution of the manufacturing sector is just over 16 per cent of India's GDP, currently. With a view to accelerating the growth of the manufacturing sector, the manufacturing policy proposes to create an enabling environment suitable for the sector to flourish in India.[27] In order to be comparable with the healthcare parameters of other developing countries; India's healthcare sector faces many challenges. For example, to reach a ratio of two beds per 1000 population by 2025, an additional 177 billion beds will be required which will need a total investment of US$86 billion.[28]

India's services sector has emerged as a prominent sector in terms of its contribution to national and state incomes, trade flows, FDI inflows and employment. For more than a decade the sector has been pulling up the growth of Indian economy with great stability. The share of services in India's GDP at factor cost (at current prices) increased from 33.3 per cent (1950-1951) to 56.5 per cent in 2012-13, as per advance estimates. Including construction, this would increase to 64.8 per cent. With 18 percent, trade, hotels and restaurants are the largest contributors to GDP among the various sub sectors. This is followed by financing, insurance, real estate and business services with 16.6 per cent share. Community, social, and personal services with 14 per cent share stand in the third place.

This is followed by construction at fourth place with 8.2 per cent share.[29] The growth of India's services sector, its contribution to GDP, and its increasing share in trade and investment has drawn global attention.

Unlike other countries, where economic growth has led to a shift from agriculture to industries, in India, there has been a shift from agriculture to the services sector. In this respect, some economists consider India as an outlier among South Asian countries and other emerging markets. After India's independence, for more than a decade share of services in the GDP was less than 30 per cent. In the last decade, the share of services has surpassed the combined share of agriculture and industry, making it the most important contributor to the country's output. In 2009-10, services, industries and agriculture respectively accounted for 57.3 per cent, 25.7 per cent and 16.9 percent of India's GDP. Nevertheless, the share of services is lower than that of developed countries (the United Kingdom (UK, 78.4 per cent) and the United States (US, 78.2 per cent)), but higher than that of China (41.8 per cent). In terms of size of total employment (both organised and unorganised), in 1993-94, close to 63 per cent of the population was engaged in agriculture sector and around 21 per cent in services. Over the years, the percentage of people employed in agriculture has declined and employment in services has increased, though the broad pattern of employment has remained the same with agriculture having the highest share. There has been a change in the pattern of employment within the services sector.[30]

India has the second fastest growing services sector with its compound annual growth rate at nine per cent, just below China's 10.9 per cent, during the last 11-year period from 2001 to 2012, the Economic Survey for 2013-14 said. Russia at 5.4 per cent is a distant third. Among the world's top 15 countries in terms of GDP, India ranked 10th in terms of overall GDP and 12th in terms of services GDP in 2012, services share in world GDP was 65.9 per cent but its share in employment was only 44 per cent in 2012. As per the survey, in India, the growth of services-sector GDP has been higher than that of overall GDP between the period FY2001- FY2014. Services constitute a major portion of India's GDP with a 57 per cent share in GDP at factor cost (at current prices) in 2013-14, an increase of six per cent points over. India's share in world services exports, which increased from 0.6 per cent in 1990 to 1.1 per cent in 2000 and further to 3.3 per cent in 2013, has been increasing faster than its share in world merchandise exports. While exports of software services, accounting for 46 per cent of India's total services exports, decelerated to 5.4 per cent in 2013-14 from 5.9 per cent in 2012-13, travel, accounting for a nearly 12 per cent share, witnessed negative growth of 0.4 per cent.[31]

Conclusion

Economic statistics describe the activities of economic transactors and the transactions that take place between them. In the real world, economic entities engaged in the production of goods and services vary in their legal, accounting, organisational and operating structures. Government interventions to redistribute income and to improve living standards are part of a policy package, the components of which will be interdependent but not necessarily consistently integrated. Efforts to alleviate poverty in rural areas, to redistribute income, to promote agricultural development or to create jobs will be constrained by other macroeconomic and sectoral policies, and will, in turn, affect the outcomes of those policies. Tertiary sector has becoming important sector in India by replacing the primary sector. In modern welfare state such as India, the government is supposed to provide basic services such as hospitals, educational institutions, defense, posts and telegraphs for welfare of the people. These functions have led to the importance of the tertiary sector.

References

1. Mark Carlson, Thomas King, Kurt Lewis (2008), *Distress in the Financial Sector and Economic Activity,* Retrieved from http://www.federalreserve.gov/pubs/feds/2008/200843/200843pap.pdf
2. *Measuring the economic contribution of cultural industries: A review and assessment of current methodological approaches*, Retrieved from http://www.uis.unesco.org/culture/Documents/FCS-handbook-1-economic-contribution-culture-en-web.pdf
3. *Development strategies for the postal sector: an economic perspective (2014),* Retrieved from http://www.upu.int/uploads/tx_sbdownloader/publicationTrendsDevelopmentStrategiesFor The Postal Sector En.pdf
4. *International Standard Industrial Classification of All Economic Activities,* Retrieved from http://unstats.un.org/unsd/publication/seriesM/seriesm_4rev4e.pdf

5. J. Otte, A. Costales, J. Dijkman, U. Pica-Ciamarra, T. Robinson, V. Ahuja, C. Ly and D. Roland-Holst (2012), *Livestock sector development for poverty reduction: an economic and policy perspective Livestock's many virtues,* Retrieved from http://www.fao.org/docrep/015/i2744e/i2744e00.pdf
6. Rufus Pollock, *The economics of public sector information,* Retrieved from http://rufuspollock.org/papers/economics_of_psi.pdf
7. Manuela W. Armenta, *The Financial Sector and Economic Development: Banking on the Role of Human Capital,* Retrieved from https://www.princeton.edu/jpia/past-issues-1/2007/9.pdf
8. Carolyn Jenkins (1997), *Economic Objectives, Public-Sector Deficits and Macroeconomic Stability in Zimbabwe,* Retrieved from http://www.csae.ox.ac.uk/workingpapers/pdfs/9714text.pdf
9. Ralf Hussmanns (2004), *Measuring the informal economy: From employment in the informal sector to informal employment,* Retrieved from http://natlex.ilo.ch/public/english/bureau/stat/download/papers/wp53.pdf
10. *Three-sector theory,* Retrieved from http://en.wikipedia.org/wiki/Three-sector_theory
11. *Primary sector of the economy (2014),* Retrieved from http://en.wikipedia.org/wiki/Primary_sector_of_the_economy
12. *Secondary sector of the economy (2014),* Retrieved from http://en.wikipedia.org/wiki Secondary_ sector_ of_ the_economy
13. *Tertiary sector (2014),* Retrieved from http://en.wikipedia.org/wiki/Tertiary_sector_of_the_economy
14. *Sectors of the Indian Economy,* Retrieved from http://www.educomponline.com/Uploads/InboxAttachment/80887f62-a66b-4568-965b-aedd31baf727.pdf
15. *Services Sector,* Retrieved from http://business.gov.in/Industry_services/services_sector.php
16. Dr. Sibylle Frey and Dr. Thomas Wiedmann (2008), *Identifying resource productivity for five key economic sectors in the South West region,* Retrieved from http://www.censa.org.uk/docs/SEI_SW-Sectors_BL3-CF.pdf

17. Barry Eichengreen & Poonam Gupta (2010), *The Service Sector as India's Road to Economic Growth?,* http://icrier.org/pdf/Working per cent20Paper per cent20249.pdf

18. Asha, Emerging Sectors of Indian Economy, *Global Journal of Management and Business Studies,* Volume 3, Number 5 (2013), pp. 491-196.

19. Persis Khambatta and Amb. Karl F. Inderfurth (2012), *India's Emerging Economy: Sector by Sector,* Retrieved from http://csis. org/ files/ publication/121 221 Wadhwani Chair_ USIndiaInsight. pdf

20. *Agriculture sector in India,* Retrieved from http://www.ibef.org/ industry/agriculture-india.aspx

21. Elumalai Kannan & Sujata Sundaram (2011), *Analysis of Trends in India's Agricultural Growth,* Retrieved from http://www.isec.ac.in/ WP per cent20276 per cent20- per cent20Elumalai per cent20Kannan_1.pdf

22. See http://rbidocs.rbi.org.in/rdocs/content/pdfs/85240.pdf

23. *The Economic Times (Aug 30, 2014),* Agriculture's share in GDP declines to 13.7 per cent in 2012-13, Retrieved from http:// articles.economictimes.indiatimes.com/2013-08-30/news/ 41618996_1_gdp-foodgrains-allied-sectors

24. *The Economic Times (May 12, 2013),* Manufacturing sector's contribution to GDP may fall below 15 per cent in FY14, Retrieved from http://articles.economictimes.indiatimes.com/2013-05-12/ news/39203854_1_assocham-survey-100-million-jobs-manufacturing-sector

25. *GDP of India,* Retrieved from http://www.tradechakra.com/indian-economy/gdp.html

26. Services Sector, Retrieved from http://indiabudget.nic.in/es2012-13/echap-10.pdf

27. *The Hindu (oct 25, 201),* Retrieced from http://www.ficci.com/ sector-overview.asp?secid=18

28. See http://www.ficci.com/sector-overview.asp?secid=18

29. See http : // www.brainyquote.com/ quotes/ keywords/ globalisation_3.html

30. Growth of the Service Sector, Retrieved from http://www.worldbank.org/depweb/beyond/beyondco/beg_09.pdf
31. Steve Krar, Importance of industry on community, Retrieved from http://www.automationmag.com/images/stories/LWTech-files/87 per cent20 per cent20Community.pdf
32. Matleena Kniivilä, Industrial development and economic growth: Implications for poverty reduction and income inequality, Retrieved fromhttp://www.un.org/esa/sustdev/publications/industrial_development/3_1.pdf
33. See http: // saif 113 sb .hubpages. com / hub / ROLE - OF-INDUSTRIALIZATION-IN-ECONOMIC-DEVELOPMENT-OF-THE-COUNTRY
34. Global importance of services (2014), Retrieved from http://unctad.org/en/conferences/gsf/2013/pages/importance-of-services.aspx

9

Effects of Globalisation on Language Lecturer's of International Postgraduates Language and Academic Culture in National University of Malaysia

Md. Momtazur Rahman

"In this age of globalisation, instant real time media and television, everyone all over the world realizes that high energy usage equates with a high standard of living and wealth."

— John Olver

Introduction

The national university of Malaysia with an international reach is one of the leading research-intensive universities in the country. Like other public universities in Malaysia, there are a large number of international postgraduate students in the fields of science and technology at the university. According to the university statistics (2006-2007 Session), 1229 international postgraduate students were pursuing masters and doctorate levels in various fields of the university. They are from the regions such as Southeast Asia, East Asia, South Asia, Africa and Middle-East. The international postgraduate students whose previous undergraduate and postgraduate degree programmes were not conducted in English or who cannot demonstrate acceptable English proficiency level (e.g., by providing acceptable TOEFL or IELTS scores) are required to sit for the English Proficiency Placement Test (EPPT).

Table 1 shows band scores of EPPT results of international postgraduate students from various faculties of the university (e.g., Faculty of Science, Technology, Faculty of Engineering, Faculty of Information Science and Technology, Faculty of Humanities and Social Sciences, Faculty of Law, Faculty of Economics and Management and Faculty of Education). It is apparent that many of these international students found it difficult to obtain bands 3, 4 and 5 (the passing grades) for the EPPT test and are required to take the ESP course offered by the School of Language Studies and Linguistics. Therefore, there is a need for an investigation into the ESP needs of these international postgraduate students. The study will suggest possible findings for incorporation in an ESP course framework. This study will focus on identifying international students' difficulty in the four language skills: reading, writing, listening and speaking skills.

Table- 1 : Band Scores of EPPT Results of International Postgraduate Students

Semesters	Numbers of Students	Percentages of Students	Obtaining Bands
Semester-II	90	36%	1 and 2 (failing scores)
(2008/2009)	150	61%	3, 4 and 5 (passing scores)
Semester I	135	53%	1 and 2 (failing scores)
(2009/2010)	119	46%	3, 4 and 5 (passing scores)
Semester II	114	60%	1 and 2 (failing scores)
(2009/2010)	75	39%	3, 4 and 5 (passing scores)

Source: *EPPT results by School of Language Studies and Linguistics of National University of Malaysia*

In addition to coping with the language demand, these international postgraduates may find difficulties in coping with the new academic norms, ethos and educational systems of the university as they are from the different academic cultures and educational backgrounds. Jordan (1997) notes that international students in an English educational environment have been face difficulties in learning the target language. He reasons, *"there may be easily a conflict between their customary learning style and that presumed in the target situation"* (Jordan, 1997, p.95). Jordan (1997) elucidates that if a student enters a new educational system as an outsider from a different academic culture, there will be some mismatches and misunderstandings. International students also frequently face difficulties in adjusting to their new social and academic environment (Al-Sharideh & Goe, 1998 and Chen, 1997). According to them, these problems can form frightening barriers to their success in academic performances and social adaptation. Therefore, based on these views, it is necessary to investigate whether there are such differences and whether the international postgraduate students have difficulties in adjusting to these differences. Hence, the study will suggest important findings about academic culture for incorporation in an ESP course framework.

Notions of Language Needs Analysis

Language Needs Analysis

Language Needs analysis is the corner stone of an English language course. Needs analysis leads to a focused course (Brown, 1995; Chambers, 1980; Dudley-Evans & St. John, 1998; Ellis & Johnson, 1994; Jordan, 1997). According to Robinson (1991), *needs analysis is generally regarded as critical to ESP, although ESP is by no means the only educational enterprise which makes use of it* (p.7). Hutchinson and Waters (1997) argue, *"Any language course should be based on needs analysis"* (p. 53). Dudley-Evans & St John (1998) state as, *"needs analysis is the process of establishing the what and how of a course"* (p.121). Dudley-Evans & St John (1998) stress three aspects of needs analysis: First, needs analysis aims to know learners as people, as language users and as language learners. Second, needs analysis study also aims to know how language learning and skills learning can be maximized for a given learner group. Third, needs analysis study aims to know the target situations and learning environment so that data can appropriately be interpreted (p.126).

Language needs analysis is considered as a very crucial first step prior to designing and developing a language course, producing materials for teaching and learning, and developing language test. West (1994) states that language needs analysis is a pragmatic activity, which focuses on specific situations and the nature of language and curriculum. In the ESP/EAP context or general English course, needs analysis is vital in determining the aspects of language that are crucial for a particular area of teaching (West, 1994). Robinson (1991) suggests, needs analysis is not only just for determining the "*what and how of a language of teaching*". Rather, she also suggests that needs analysis study should be repeated so that it can be built into the formative process (Robinson, 1991). The main sources of needs analysis include the learners, people working or studying in the field, ex-students, documents relevant to the field, clients, employers, colleagues and ESP research in the field (Dudley-Evans and St John, 1998). The main instruments for executing language needs analysis study are questionnaire, analysis of authentic spoken and written texts, discussions, structured interviews, observations and assessments (Dudley-Evans & St John, 1998; Hutchinson & Waters, 1987; Robinson, 1991).

Components of Language Needs Analysis

Target Situation Analysis (TSA)

Target Situation Analysis (TSA) is a form of needs analysis focuses on identifying the learners' language requirements in the occupational or academic situation they are being prepared for (Ewer and Hughes-Davies, 1971, p.6, cited in West, 1994). The earliest TSA procedures were designed to determine 'how much English' was used (Ewer and Hughes-Davies, 1971, p.6, cited in West, 1994). Robinson (1991) argues, *"A needs analysis, which focuses on students' needs at the end of a language course, can be called a TSA (Target Situation Analysis)"* (p.8). Chambers (1980) introduced and discussed this term. Munby (1978) formulates the best-known framework of TSA type of needs analysis. He presents a communicative needs processor, comprising a set of parameters within which information on the students' target situation can be plotted. Dudley-Evans & St. John (1998) define as, "*TSA refers to task and activities learners are/will be using English for target situation*" (p. 124). According to them, TSA generally uses questionnaire as the instrument. Dudley-Evans and St. John (1998) explain as: TSA includes objective, perceived and product-oriented needs. The objective and perceived needs are derived by outsiders from facts, from what is known and can be verified. Therefore, 'to be able to spell English words correctly' is an objective/perceived need. Product-oriented needs are derived from the goal or target situation (p.124).

Present Situation Analysis (PSA)

According to Robinson (1991) "PSA (Present Situation Analysis) seeks to establish what the students are like at the start of their language course, investigating their strengths and weaknesses" Dudley-Evans & St. John (1998) state that PSA refers to the strengths and weaknesses in language, skills and learning experiences. Richterich and Chancerel (1980) construct the most extensive aspects for establishing the PSA. They suggest that there are three basic sources of information: the students themselves, the language-teaching establishment, and the 'user-institution', for example the students' place of work. They also suggest that course designers/ ESP practitioners might also study the surrounding society and culture: the attitude held towards English language and towards the learning and use of a foreign language (Richterich and Chancerel, 1980).

Academic Culture and Some Studies on Academic Culture

There is a little scope of literature on the definition of academic culture. Jordan (1997) defines as "*academic culture consists of a shared experience and outlook with regard to the educational system, the subject or discipline, and the conventions associated with it*" (p. 98). Jordan (1997) argues that if a student gets touch with an academic culture as an outsider from a different academic culture, there will certainly be some mismatches of his/her experiences, or misunderstandings. According to Jordan (1997), *"these conventions may, for example, take the form of the respective roles of students and lecturers/tutors/supervisors, etc. and their customary behaviour; or the conventions attached to the academic writing, with its structuring and referencing system"* (p. 98).

Based upon literature, various studies have examined the difficulties international students experience as a result of differences in academic culture. Ballard and Clanchy (1984) also focused on different learning styles and academic cultures from a case of Asian students, studying abroad in an English education environment. They found that with prior knowledge, students could be prepared to adapt to an alien system. But, they will need to change habits of thinking, studying and learning to suit the demands of the foreign education system. Due to the differences in academic culture, they found students' difficulty in the following study activities: (1) working independently, (2) relations with supervisors, and (3) participating in discussions (Ballard and Clanchy, 1984). Some writers stated that international students frequently encounter difficulties in adjusting to their new social and academic environment (Al-Sharideh & Goe, 1998; Chen, 1997). According to them, these problems can form alarming barriers to their success in academic performance and social adaptation. Zimmermann (1995) regarded communication as the center of adaptation process, but he also noticed that international students often lack the opportunities to communicate with local students, academicians, or even other international students from different countries and cultures.

Furneaux et al. (1988, cited in Jordan, 1997) found major differences in expectations between international students and British university academics at Reading University, UK. Students were asked to rank the personal qualities they thought. He found that the students gave a low ranking to such qualities as curiosity, the ability to be critical and honest, but all of which the academics considered essential. According to Jordan (Jordan, 1997), difficulties can also arise due to difference in academic culture. As he pointed out, students might be from a culture based on close family groups. For example, students from Nepal, Hong Kong and other Southeast Asian countries frequently work together, solve problems as a group. They are also accustomed to studying in relatively crowded conditions (Jordan, 1997). Chen's study (1999) also indicated that Chinese students at North American university experienced considerable challenges in their academic learning: their unfamiliarity with the North American educational culture and their lack of North American academic background. Finally, a study by Rajapaksa and Dundes (2003) addressed the need for information helpful in retaining international students studying in the United States. The study explored whether students had greater difficulty in adjusting to study life. The study revealed that international students had difficulty in adapting to new study life in the US and they were more likely to feel lonely, homesick, and as if they had left part of themselves at home.

The problem of plagiarism is now a very important aspect of academic culture. According to Jordan (1997), students from many countries in Asia, have considerable respect for printed words and those in authority resulting in many of them quoting extensively from authorities/books without acknowledging the sources. These students may feel that criticisms of published works is disrespectful and do not realize what they are doing amounted to plagiarism. Students often present extracts from books or articles in an uncritical way (Jordan, 1997). He also asserted that a number of institutions are aware of the different attitudes towards plagiarism. For example, according to a Handbook by Hong Kong Polytechnic University for 1995, it contains an appendix, namely, Guidance notes on avoiding plagiarism, on bibliographic referencing and on photocopying of copyright materials. The university views plagiarism as a serious disciplinary and academic offence.

Niall and Lucas (2005) undertook a study on the overseas students studying in the United Kingdom. Their study considered differing cultural values among overseas students toward plagiarism and the implications for postgraduate education in a Western context. Their study showed that plagiarist practices were often the outcome of many complex and culturally situated influences (Niall and Lucas,

2005). A study by Dawn (2010) made a review on some studies from various disciplines on plagiarism and examined some factors (cultural, educational, and linguistic factors) that may affect the textual borrowing practices of international students. According to the study, the reasons, international students may employ inappropriate source use, are complex. Measures to address and combat plagiarism in higher education must be taken into consideration as his study suggested

Research Methodology

Sample involved in the Study

The samples for the semi-structured interview in the qualitative research involved the English language lecturers of the School of Language Studies and Linguistics of the National University of Malaysia. The language lecturers taught the international postgraduate students English courses in the university. They were chosen because they were able to provide detailed information on their perceptions concerning the international students' difficulties with regard to four language areas and some aspects of academic culture. They also helped to provide the information on their opinions and suggestions for overcoming students' difficulties in the target language and other aspects. Five English language lecturers of the school of the university were selected for the interview session. Purposive sampling strategy was also applied for the selection of the samples in the language lecturers' interview. The reason was that these lecturers were English language experts and had the experiences of teaching English courses designed for the international postgraduate students for some years in the university. Therefore, they were aware of international students' difficulties in the target language (English) and some aspects of academic culture.

Semi-structured Interview for the English Language Lecturers

Semi-structured interview for the English language lecturers of the School of Language Studies and Linguistics of the university was formulated on the basis of PSA (Present Situation Analysis), as a component of the language needs analysis of the study. The interview questions were open-ended items. The interview questions sought the information concerning the following themes/aspects: (1) language lecturers' perceptions concerning the international students' difficulties in reading, writing, listening and speaking areas in English for academic purposes, (2) their perceptions of students' difficulties in relation to the differences in academic culture, (3) their perceptions of students' most difficulties in skill/skills in the four language areas, and (4) their suggestions and comments on students' difficulties in the target language. In the interview, the questions of English language lecturers' perceptions concerning students' difficulty in reading, writing, listening and speaking areas were based on PSA (Present Situation Analysis) of the theoretical framework of the needs analysis. The questions of language lecturers' perceptions of students' difficulties related to the differences in academic culture were formulated on the aspects of academic culture of the theoretical framework of the needs analysis of the study.

Administration of the Interview

The semi-structured interview was conducted for the five English language lecturers from the School of Language Studies and Linguistics of the university during their free time. The interview sessions were also the type of individual interview. The interview sessions, which were also set up in the informal situation, were conducted in the lecturers' offices of the school of the university. Actually, prior permission of interviewing the five language lecturers was sought. The lecturers were informed the objective of conducting the interview. A tape recorder was used to record interviewees' responses to all questions. The time duration of the individual interview session was 40-50 minutes.

Analysis of the Qualitative Data

The qualitative data from the three interviews (students' interview, subject lecturers' interview and language lecturers' interview) were transcribed. For each of the questions in the interviews, all the responses were summarised and analysed in the qualitative way according to the different themes. The important points from the data of all interviews were highlighted. Any interesting insights provided in the interviews were also noted.

Analysis and Discussion of Language Lecturers' Interviews

This section delineates the analysis and discussion of the language lecturers' interviews. I will analyse the responses from the English language lecturers' interviews according to themes.

The Profiles of the Interviewees: General Information

The interviewees were five English language lecturers, who were selected from the School of Language Studies and Linguistics of the university based on their involvement in teaching international postgraduate students. They were lecturers with many years of teaching experience and were English language specialists. Table 2 depicts the profiles of these five lecturers of the school of the university.

Table -2 : Profiles of the Language Lecturers of School of Language Studies and Linguistics of National University of Malaysia.

Lecturers	Genders	Positions	Areas of expertise	Years of teaching	Years of teaching international Students
A	Male	Lecturer	Sociolinguistics	23 years	4 years
B	Male	Lecturer	ESP	20 years	3 years
C	Female	Lecturer	Reading in ESL	20 years	5 years
D	Female	Lecturer	Academic Writing	25 years	3 years
E	Male	Lecturer	Syntax Theory	20 years	5 years

Reading Skills in English

Theme One: Perceptions of Students' Difficulties in Reading Skills in English: A Focus on Present Situation Analysis

In general, a majority of the language lecturers (four out of five) stated that the international students faced difficulties in reading (Lecturers B, C, D and E). Lecturers C and D said that the students had difficulty particularly in vocabulary. On top of that, they did not have reading strategies to compensate for the lack of vocabulary. Lecturer C explained: *"You know....sometimes, there are strategies. If you do not have dictionary. You look at the contexts of the words if you do not understand. You can guess the meaning of the words. That is the something that they can not do."* (Lecturer C).

Lecturer B added that they are not able to think critically: *"They are not supposed to read and translate texts literally as they are in postgraduate levels. When they answer to phrases and single words in tests.....not based on critical thinking. They are supposed to read to infer the texts. They are not good in critical thinking."* (Lecturer B). Lecturer D supported this view: *"When they are asked to read journals, because they have to respond to some journal articles. They have to give critical views on the journals. They just cannot do it."* (Lecturer D)

Discussion of Findings

From the findings, it is apparent that lack of vocabulary knowledge was one of the weaknesses of these international students. Jinyan (2006) found this in her/his study too. She reported that Asian students at a Canadian university lacked vocabulary skills. In addition, they did not have the required reading strategies and were not able to read critically.

This finding is also similar to the findings of Margaret (2000). In her study, she revealed that international students at an Australian university had poor critical thinking skills. The English lecturers were experts in the target language and had taught English to international students for many years in this university. Therefore, they were able to identify students' difficulties in these two important areas, even though the students themselves and their subjects' lecturers were not aware of them. Evidently, emphasis should be placed on these reading skills in an ESP course framework. Table 3 depicts a summary of these findings.

Table -3 : Findings of Language Lecturers' Interviews

Difficulties in reading skills identified by language lecturers' interviews
Vocabulary skills
Strategies for guessing meaning of words
Critical thinking skills

Writing Skills in English

Theme Two: Perceptions of Students' Difficulties in Writing Skills in English: A Focus on Present Situation Analysis

Generally, most of the language lecturers (four out of five lecturers) stated that the international postgraduate students faced difficulties in punctuation in terms of writing skills (Lecturers A, B, C and D). Most of the lecturers (four lecturers) stated that the international students had also difficulties in grammar skills (Lecturers A, B, D and E).

Lecturer A specifically indicated: *"Another problem is that they do not have grammar skills. They mix up the tenses."* (Lecturer A). Lecturer B also explicitly indicated students' difficulties in grammar skills.

He explained: *"They can not write proper sentences. The concept of subject and verb agreement is not in their sentences. They have problems in spelling."* (Lecturer B). Many of the lecturers admitted that the students also faced difficulties in paraphrasing (Lecturers A, C and D). Lecturer A also pointed out:

"They have very minimal summary skills." (Lecturer A). Lecturer D supported this view: *"I think, they don't really appreciate how to do summarizing."* (Lecturer D). Lecturer D further added students' difficulty as: *"They have problems in capitalization in writing."* (Lecturer D). Lecturer A further explained students' difficulties in terms of paragraph/essay writing skills: "*They cannot give you the coherent and unified paragraphs or essay. Because most of the time, they do not understand what is a topic sentence. They do not understand what a thesis statement is. They do not know how to support the topic sentence."* (Lecturer A).

Discussion of Findings

From the findings, it is evident that the students had difficulties in punctuation in writing. They had difficulties in grammar skills (such as, knowledge of tenses and subject-verb agreement). In addition, they lacked paraphrasing, summarizing, spelling and capitalisation in their writing. Finally, they were not able to write proper paragraphs/ essays. The findings of Gina's study (2009) are partly similar to these findings. Gina's study (2009) reported that international students at a Canadian university encountered difficulties in spelling. It was possible for the English language lecturers to identify students' difficulties in some of these new writing skills because they were susceptible to students' writing capability through teaching. In fact, these findings contribute to reveal some new writing skills, necessary for the international students. Hence, these writing skills should be considered as focused components in an ESP course framework. Here is a summary of these findings as shown in Table 4.

Table- 4 : Findings of Language Lecturers' Interviews

Difficulties in writing skills identified by language lecturers
Punctuation
Grammar skills (such as, knowledge of tenses and subject-verb agreement)
Paragraph/essay writing skills
Paraphrasing
Summarizing
Spelling
Capitalisation

Listening Skills in English

Theme Three: Perceptions of Students' Difficulties in Listening Skills in English: A Focus on Present Situation Analysis

In general, two language lecturers stated that the international students had difficulties in listening (Lecturers D and E). Lecturer D, in particular, explained students' listening difficulties as: "*Most probably, during lecture, I use formal or standard English. So, they are not used to it. Basically, as a teacher when you see your students give you a signal that they don't understand. Then you can always simplify the language. So, from that situation, I know that they have problems in listening. The other reason is that they are not used to Malaysian accents."* (Lecturer D)

Lecturer E argued that listening is related with culture. He argued: "*For me, listening has a lot to do with culture. Students from some cultures tend to listen to you better than others.*

They are bound to cultures, because they are from different cultures." (Lecturer E). On the contrary, two lecturers stated that the international students were able to listen in classes or whatever situations. Lecturer B explained: *"I don't think, they have many problems in listening."* (Lecturer B). Lecturer C supported this view: "*I don't think that they have any problems in listening. They understand what I say."* (Lecturer C)

Discussion of Findings

From the findings, it is reported by some lecturers that the international students encountered difficulties particularly in following lectures in formal English and Malaysian accents in terms of listening. The reason was that they were not used to formal English language and Malaysian accent.

The findings also suggest that people from some cultures are more interested in listening than others. Ferris's findings (1998) are also partly similar to the findings derived from the language lecturers' interviews. Ferris (1998) conducted a comparative study on international students at three universities in the US.

Ferris found that international students lacked their listening abilities. For example, they were unable to understand/follow lecturers by their instructors (who were native speakers) in classes (Ferris, 1998).

Therefore, consideration should be given to this listening skill (e.g., ability to follow lectures in formal English and Malaysian accent) for inclusion in an ESP course framework. Table 5 shows the finding of the study.

Table- 5 : Findings of Language Lecturers' Interviews

Difficulties in listening skill Identified by Language Lecturers
Ability to understand/follow lectures in different accents (Malaysian accents) and formal English'

Speaking Skills in English

Theme Four: Perceptions of Students' Difficulties in Speaking Skills in English: A Focus on Present Situation Analysis

The majority of the language lecturers (four out of five lecturers) stated that the international postgraduate students in the university encountered difficulties in pronunciation in terms of speaking skills (Lecturers A, B, C and E). Lecturer A identified their different pronunciations. He explained: *"My interaction with them in classes is sometimes very hilarious.....very funny. Because the way they pronounce certain words...you can mean different words. They pronounce words differently."* (Lecturer A).

Three lecturers supported this view: *"The Arabs are the most difficult students to teach because their accents are very strong. 'R' is very strong oral sound for them. It is intonation problem. There are also simple vowel sound problems."* (Lecturer B). *"I don't understand the words that they have pronounced, although, they are actually talking to me. But it is very difficult for me to understand what they are saying. Maybe, their pronunciation is influenced by their mother tongues."* (Lecturer C). *"They are coming from different cultures. I have to listen to them carefully to make sense or what they say." (Lecturer E)*

Discussion of Findings

Apparently, the international students had faced difficulties in pronunciation. A study by Jinyan (2006) supports this finding. Jinyan's study (2006) revealed that Asian students at a Canadian university faced difficulty in pronunciation. The findings of the language lecturers' interviews also report that their pronunciation was different. The 'r' sound of the students from the Middle Eastern countries was so strong sound. It could be due to their Arabic language. The sound, 'r' in Arabic language is also strong. Therefore, this speaking skill should be one of the main speaking components in an ESP course framework

Differences in Academic Culture

Theme Five: Perceptions of Students' Difficulties in relation to Differences in Academic Culture

Lecturer A commented that the international students (especially students from Middle East countries) did not follow the manners and courtesy in terms of talking. He stated: *"Culturally.... I think....the students, who are especially from Middle Eastern countries, become very aggressive in talking. They believe, what they say, is always right."* (Lecturer A).

Lecturer E also supported this view: *"The students from Middle East countries tend to be more aggressive in and out side the class rooms."* (Lecturer E). Lecturer A tried to find the reason for their aggressiveness: *"It could be based on the centuries of histories where different groups of Arab people in the Middle East countries were territorial."* (Lecturer A). Lecturer B stated that the students (especially students from the Middle Eastern countries) did not tend to mingle with the local students in the university. He explained: *"I think, there is a lack of interactions between the international students and local students. Especially, Arab students like to keep to themselves."* (Lecturer B)

Lecturer D supported this view: *"But, I think, they don't interact much with local students."* (Lecturer D). Lecturer A explained his view about Arab students: *"They also don't work with students from certain countries. This could be due to their superstition."* (Lecturer A). Lecturer B also supported this view: *"Especially, Arab students like to keep themselves. I don't see much interaction between them and students from other countries."* (Lecturer B). Lecturer D elucidated the international students' learning habits: *"They are in very passive learning environment in their academic culture. I think, especially in the countries like Yemen and Jordan and Iraq, there is a one way interaction. They don't ask questions in classes. They just listen to lectures. They expect us to give everything, because they were so used to it in their home countries."* (Lecturer D)

Lecturer C implied pushy behaviour of the international students: *"Sometimes, we have a test in the evening, the next morning/day when we see them. They want their results. That is the kind of the majority of the students I get. They are from different norms."* (Lecturer C).

Lecturer E also supported this view: *"The students from the Middle East countries once pay their fees; they expect to get passing grades. Some of students follow me after my car to get me to pass them in their courses. That is the kind of thing in difference in academic culture."* (Lecturer E). All of the language lecturers stated that the international students in the university were so accustomed to plagiarism (Lecturers A, B, C, D and E). Lecturer A added: *"Plagiarism is a crime in academic setting. But to them, it is no big deal. In terms of those academic cultures, international students have very limited knowledge." (Lecturer A). Lecturer C commented: "In some countries, maybe, it is accepted."* (Lecturer C)

Table- 6 : Summary of Issues due to the Differences in Academic Culture: A Basis of the Findings of the Language Lecturers' Interviews

Issues Identified in Relation to Differences in Academic Culture	Who Indicated	Numbers of Respondents
1. The international students (especially students from Middle East countries) were very aggressive in terms of talking or inside and outside the classrooms.	Lecturers A and E	Two
2. The international students did not tend to mingle/interact much with local students in this university.	Lecturers B and D	Two
3. The international students (especially students from Middle East countries) were very passive learners and expected everything from lecturers	Lecturer D	One

4. They were pushy in the sense that once they finished their tests, the next days/morning, they wanted to know their results. Or they expected passing grades once they paid fees.	Lecturers C and E	Two
5. The international students were so accustomed to plagiarism.	Lecturers A, B, C, D and E	Five

Discussion of Findings

From the findings, it is evident that the international students (especially students from Middle East countries) did not follow the manners and etiquettes and were very aggressive in terms of talking in classrooms or out of the classrooms. It could be due to their different cultures and norms. They were not also interested in mingling with local students. It was also revealed that students from the Middle East countries were pushy, very passive learners and expected everything from teachers. They had difficulties in adapting to the new norms and convention of the academic system of the university.

The findings also report that the international students were in the habit of plagiarism. This is not surprising as the students, themselves, did not realise their own weaknesses. Therefore, ways to overcome this problem should be seriously considered in an ESP course. Dawn (2010) in his review of studies from various disciplines on plagiarism as a cross-cultural issue examined cultural, educational, and linguistic factors that influenced the textual borrowing practices of international students.

His recommended ways by which academic libraries could assist international students with understanding plagiarism through orientations and instruction, reference service, and web-based guides and tutorials. Jordan (1997) described: *Students from many countries in Asia had considerable respects for printed words and those in authority. As a result, it was quite normal for students to quote from authorities/books without acknowledging the source. Criticism of published works was unacceptable as students felt. Thus, students often presented extracts from books or articles in an uncritical way (p. 100).*

From the findings, it is evident that the international postgraduate students faced difficulties in adapting to the norms and conventions in the academic setting in National University of Malaysia. Ballard and Clanchy (1984) proposed that with prior knowledge, students could learn to adapt to an alien system. But, they will need to change habits of thinking, studying and learning to suit the demands of the foreign education system. Due to the differences in academic culture, they found that students had difficulties in the following aspects: (a) working independently, (b) relations with supervisors, and (c) participating in discussions (Ballard & Clanchy, 1984). Zhou (2009) on his study on Chinese postgraduate students in the United Kingdom found that many Chinese students faced difficulty in adapting to academic cultural differences as well as general cultural differences in the UK.

Conclusion

The paper aims at investigating language needs of the international postgraduate students of the National University of Malaysia. The paper reveals that international postgraduate students face difficulty in some skills in the four language areas (reading, writing, speaking and listening). The paper also suggests the skills in these four language areas for incorporation in an ESP course. In addition, the paper reveals some aspects of academic culture. For example, plagiarism is rife among the international students. In addition, the international students find difficulty in adjusting to new academic culture in the university. It is true that they are from different academic norms and conventions. The language lecturers of the university, as the experts, are able to identify strengths and weakness of these students. The course designers can benefit from the paper that they can design a language course based on the findings.

References

1. Al-Sharideh, K. A, & Goe, W. R. (1998). Ethnic communities within the university: An examination of factors influencing the personal adjustment of international students. *Research in Higher Education, 39*, 699-725.

2. Ballard, B, & Clanchy, J. (1984). *Study abroad: A manual for Asian students*. Kuala Lumpur: Longman Malaysia Sdn. Berhad.

3. Brown, J. D. (1995). *The elements of language curriculum: A systematic approach to program development*. Boston: Heinle and Heinle..

4. Chambers, F. (1980). Are-evaluation of needs analysis. *ESP Journal, 1*, 25-33.

5. Chen, C.P. (1999). *Common stressors among international college students: Research and counseling implications. Journal of College Counseling, 2, 49-65.*

6. Dudley-Evans, T., & ST John, M. J. (1998). *Developments in English for specific purposes*. Cambridge: Cambridge University Press.

7. Dawn, A. (2010). Deconstructing plagiarism: International students and textual borrowing practices. *Reference Librarian, 51*, 31-44.

8. Ellis, M. & Johnson, C. (1994). *Teaching business English.* Oxford: Oxford University Press.

9. Ferris, D. (1998). Students' view of academic aural/oral skills: A comparative needs analysis. *TESOL Quarterly, 32*, 298-318.

10. Gina, L. H. (2009). The component reading and writing *skills* of at-risk undergraduates with *writing difficulties. Journal of Language Disabilities*, 7, 59-72.

11. Hutchinson, T., & Waters, A. (1987). *English for specific purposes*. New York: Cambridge University Press.

12. Jordan, R. R. (1997). *English for academic purposes: A guide and resources book for teachers*. London (UK): Cambridge University Press.

13. Jinyan, H. (2006, June). English ability for academic listening: How confident are Chinese students? *College Student Journal, 40*. Retrieved from 2010, June 20 2010, from http:// www. gamilang. ukm. my.

14. Margaret, R. (2000). *International students*, learning environments and perceptions: A case study using the Delphi technique. *Journal of Higher Education Research & Development, 19*, 89 102.

15. Munby, J. (1978). *Communicative syllabus design: A sociolinguistic model for defining the content of purpose-specific language programmes*. London: Cambridge University Press.

16. Niall, H., & Lucas, D. I. (2005). Cultural values, plagiarism, and fairness: When plagiarism gets in the way of learning. *Journal of Ethics & Behavior, 15*, 213-231.

17. \Richterich, R., & Chancerel, J. (1980). *Identifying the needs of adults learning a foreign language*. Oxford: Pergamon Press.

18. Rajapaksa, S., & Dundes, L. (2003). It's a long way home: International student adjustment to living in the United States. *Journal of College Student Retention: Research, Theory and Practice, 4*, 15-28.

19. Robinson, P. (1991). *ESP today: A practitioner's guide*. New York: Prentice Hall.

20. West, R. (1994) Needs analysis in language teaching. *Language Teaching*, 27, 1-19.

21. Zimmerman, S. (1995). Perceptions of intercultural communication competence and international student adaptation to an American campus. *Communication Education, 44*, 321-335.

22. Zhou, Y. (2009). Patterns of adaptation of Chinese postgraduate students in the United Kingdom. *Journal of Studies in International Education, 13*, 467-486.

23. Seehttp://www.brainyquote.com/quotes/keywords/globalisation_3.html

PART-II

ECONOMIC DEVELOPMENT

10

Sustainable Development and Society: an Overview

P.K.Pandey & Sukanta Sarkar

"Whatever it is that leads human beings to hate, to destroy, and to kill has taken on a collective force like never before, as technology and globalisation now give it the capacity to not just strike, but to strike us all, together, as one."

— Marianne Williamson

Introduction

Different countries have different priorities in their development policies. But to compare their development levels, you would first have to make up your mind about what development really means to you, what it is supposed to achieve. Indicators measuring this achievement could then be used to judge countries' relative progress in development. Recent United Nations documents emphasise human development, measured by life expectancy, adult literacy, access to all three levels of education, as well as people's average income, which is a necessary condition of their freedom of choice. Population dynamics are one of the key factors to consider when thinking about development. GDP growth rates in developing countries are on average higher than those in developed countries. Capital is a stock of wealth used to produce goods and services. Most often, by capital people mean physical capital: buildings, machines, technical equipment, stocks of raw materials and goods.[1]

In order to meet the challenges of environment and development, States have decided to establish a new global partnership. This partnership commits all States to engage in a continuous and constructive dialogue, inspired by the need to achieve a more efficient and equitable world economy. It is keeping in view the increasing interdependence of the community of nations and that sustainable development should become a priority item on the agenda of the international community. It is recognised that, for the success of this new partnership, it is important to overcome confrontation and to foster a climate of genuine cooperation and solidarity. It is equally important to strengthen national and international policies and multinational cooperation to adapt to the new realities. Economic policies of individual countries and international economic relations both have great relevance to sustainable development. The reactivation and acceleration of development requires both a dynamic and a supportive international economic environment and determined policies at the national level. A supportive external economic environment is crucial.[2]

What is Sustainable Development?

Sustainable development is development that meets the needs of the present, without compromising the ability of future generations to meet their own needs. It can be interpreted in many different ways, but at its core is an approach to development that looks to balance different, and often competing, needs against an awareness of the environmental, social and economic limitations we face as a society. It is a road-map, an action plan, for achieving sustainability in any activity that uses resources and where immediate and intergenerational replication is demanded.

As such, sustainable development is the organising principle for sustaining finite resources necessary to provide for the needs of future generations of life on the planet. It is a process that envisions a desirable future state for human societies in which living conditions and resource-use continue to meet human needs without undermining the integrity, stability and beauty of natural biotic system.

The United Nations World Commission on Environment and Development (WCED) in its 1987 report "Our Common Future" defines sustainable development as Development that meets the needs of the present without compromising the ability of future generations to meet their own needs. The concepts of sustainable development and sustainability derive from the older forestry term "sustained yield", which, in turn, is a translation of the German term "nachhaltiger Ertrag" dating from 1713.[3] Sustainable development could probably be otherwise called "equitable and balanced," meaning that, in order for development to continue indefinitely, it should balance the interests of different groups of people, within the same generation and among generations, and do so simultaneously in three major interrelated areas–economic, social, and environmental.[4]

Benefits of Sustainable Development

From the point of view of neoclassical economic theory, sustainability can be defined in terms of the maximisation of welfare over time. A formal economic analysis then raises the question of whether sustainability has any validity as an economic concept. According to standard economic theory, efficient resource allocation should have the effect of maximising utility from consumption. In an ecological perspective, then, sustainability must involve limits on population and consumption levels.

These limits apply to all biological systems. While humans may appear to evade them for a time, they must ultimately accept the boundaries of a finite planet.[5] In 1992, the United Nations Conference on Environment and Development, the 'Earth Summit', took place in Rio de Janeiro, Brazil. At the time, it was the largest ever international conference held, with over 170 governments represented and a further 2,500 NGOs and 8,000 accredited journalists attending. The central aim was to identify the principles of an agenda for action towards sustainable development in the future. Certainly in the developed world, the substantial media attention given to the serious environmental disturbances surrounding forest in Indonesia, Flooding in the Americas, China and Bangladesh, and typhoons in South-East Asia, for example, brought questions of conservation and ideas of sustainability into the public vocabulary.[6]

As defined by the Brundtland Commission, Sustainable development is development that meets the needs of the present without compromising the ability of future generations to meet their own needs. The Brundtland Commission, formerly also known as the World Commission on Environment and Development was formed in 1983. The rationale was to have an organisation independent of the UN to formulate a global agenda for change that would bring together industrialised and developing nations on a common platform to chart out a course of development that would take into consideration the interrelatedness of people, resources, development and planet. As defined by the Brundtland Commission, Sustainable development is development that meets the needs of the present without compromising the ability of future generations to meet their own needs.

The Brundtland Commission, formerly also known as the World Commission on Environment and Development was formed in 1983. The rationale was to have an organisation independent of the UN to formulate a global agenda for change that would bring together industrialised and developing nations on a common platform to chart out a course of development that would take into consideration the interrelatedness of people, resources, development and planet.[7]

Sustainable development recognises the interdependence of environmental, social and economic systems. It promotes equality and justice through people empowerment. In the political aspect it demands broad based participation and democratic processes. The answer to the question that why sustainable development is important lies in the fact that by providing a new framework for decision-making, issues are considered from a multi-dimensional point of view. Success is measured not simply by the profit generated, but by the triple bottom line of economic prosperity, environmental stewardship and corporate social responsibility.

Besides simply making good common sense, adhering to the principles of sustainable development fulfills compelling business needs as well, including reducing costs and liabilities, enhancing brand image and reputation, increasing customer loyalty, encouraging innovation and stimulating growth and strengthening with our communities.[8]

Sustainable Development in India

There was ready agreement in the literature that sustainable development implies linking what is to be sustained with what is to be developed, but here, too, the emphasis has often differed from extremes of sustain only to develop mostly to various forms of and/ or. Similarly, the time period of concern, ambiguously described in the standard definition as now and in the future, has differed widely. It has been defined from as little as a generation when almost everything is sustainable to forever when surely nothing is sustainable.[9] The United Nations Conference on Environment and Development in 1992 recognised the important role that indicators could play in helping countries make informed decisions concerning sustainable development. At the international level, the Commission on Sustainable Development (CSD) approved its Work Programme on Indicators of Sustainable Development in 1995. The first two sets of CSD Indicators of Sustainable Development were developed between 1994 and 2001. They have been extensively tested, applied and used in many countries as the basis for the development of national indicators of sustainable development.[10]

In 1972, the then Prime Minister of India, Mrs. Indira Gandhi emphasised, at the UN Conference on Human Environment at Stockholm, that the removal of poverty is an integral part of the goal of an environmental strategy for the world. The concepts of interrelatedness, of a shared planet, of global citizenship, and of 'spaceship earth' cannot be restricted to environmental issues alone. They apply equally to the shared and inter-linked responsibilities of environmental protection and human development. Poverty and a degraded environment are closely inter-related, especially where people depend for their livelihoods primarily on the natural resource base of their immediate environment. Restoring natural systems and improving natural resource management practices at the grassroots level are central to a strategy to eliminate poverty. While conventional economic development leads to the elimination of several traditional occupations, the process of sustainable development, guided by the need to protect and conserve the environment, leads to the creation of new jobs and of opportunities for the reorientation of traditional skills to new occupations.[11] Indian cities are urbanising at an unprecedented scale and pace. Over the next few decades, India's urban population is expected to increase significantly, from 377 million in 2011 to 590 million by 2030. The problem is that the country's existing urban transport infrastructure is already over-capacity. This fact coupled with the alarmingly high rate of traffic fatalities, increasing air pollution and greenhouse gas emissions, congestion, and urban sprawl—has created a sense of urgency to improve the quality of life in our cities now for the benefit of future generations.[12] Grassroots and government efforts are making great strides to rectify poverty-related issues; however, the severity of the problem is astonishing. Water tables throughout the country have collapsed, public education is floundering, and HIV infects more people than any other nation in the world. With 30 percent of the population classified as malnourished, common human rights violations, and the rural sectors becoming increasingly poor, India is in need of community-level support.[13]

Sustainable development is a buzz word in natural resources development today. In view of the increased awareness of environmental problems, the accent on sustainable development has grown in recent times, particularly in respect of activities which degrade the environment and affect communities adversely. Mining is one such activity. Minerals and metals have played a crucial role in the development and continuation of human civilisation. Mining or mineral development comprising exploration of the nature's mineral reserves, their extraction from below the earth's crust in solid, gaseous and liquid forms and subsequent processing and recovery of derivative-products for industrial and commercial purposes have been an important human and business activity over the ages. In

India, the movement in support of environmental concerns and sustainable development really started in the early 1980s, partly influenced by international developments but mainly due to the devastating effects of the Bhopal gas tragedy in 1984. The Bhopal tragedy was followed by a number of policy statements and legislations in order to meet environmental challenges. Mineral development involves use of large tracts of land and there are often problems and disagreements around issues such as resettlement, compensation and land rights of the indigenous people. Mining activities can bring benefits to the local communities through creation of jobs, encouragement to business and infrastructure development. Sustainable development has emerged as an important concern for mankind, following intensified damage to environment and socio-cultural integrity that has accompanied accelerated economic development in many regions of the world in post-World War II years.[14]

The effect of climate change on water supply will be negative in almost all the countries. Sustainable city planning should aim at achieving social and environmental equity while improving the lives of the people. For that to happen we need to have a sustainable city form as well as provision and proper management of the services. Waste management practices should be started from the production and distribution stages of economic activities through reuse and recycling. Reuse of things like metals, glass, paper, plastic, textiles, organic waste and water will reduce demand for energy, raw materials, fertilizers and fresh water sources. The two important issues about high-density cities are: (1) the costs and benefits of the form, and (2) how dense should it be and higher than what? National Commission on Urbanisation (NCU) of India (1988) recommended low-rise high density (LRHD) built-form for Indian cities. It explains that such form is less expensive to maintain and has the advantages of security of neighbourhood protection. Transport has an important role in meeting the goals of urban sustainability. One of the challenges of a sustainable urban form is to meet the economic performance objectives and environmental sustainability of a city at the same time.[15]

The key environmental challenges in India have been sharper in the past two decades. The State of the Environment Report by the MoEF clubs the issues under five key challenges faced by India, which are climate change, food security, water security, energy security, and managing urbanisation. Climate change is impacting the natural ecosystems and is expected to have substantial adverse effects in India, mainly on agriculture on which 58 per cent of the population still depends for livelihood, water storage in the Himalayan glaciers which are the source of major rivers and groundwater recharge, sea-level rise, and threats to a long coastline and habitations. Climate change will also cause increased frequency of extreme events such as floods, and droughts.

These in turn will impact India's food security problems and water security. Wary of the threats imposed by climate change and pressures on natural resources, sustainability and environment are increasingly taking centre stage in the Indian policy domain. Along with the national efforts in different sectors, India also recognises that rural areas are equally prone to stress and pressures from natural resource exploitation. In this context, schemes for rural development and livelihood programmes are very relevant.

A vast majority of the works under the Mahatma Gandhi National Rural Employment Guarantee Scheme (MGNREGS) are linked to land, soil, and water. Together with efforts to incorporate sustainability in the rural development process, India is increasingly making efforts to integrate the three pillars of sustainable development into its national policy space. In fact, environment protection is enshrined in our Constitution (Articles 48 A and 51 A [g]). Various policy measures are being implemented across the domains of forestry, pollution control, water management, clean energy, and marine and coastal environment. Some of these are policies like Joint Forest Management, Green Rating for Integrated Habitat Assessment, Coastal Zone Regulation Zone, eco labelling and energy efficiency labelling, fuel efficiency standards etc.[16]

Examine India's socioeconomic development trends and how rethinking development is gaining urgency for shaping sustainable social change. This program examines the diverse factors, internal and global, shaping India's development strategies and patterns. Students gain foundational knowledge of India's past, present, and future development paradigms, economic growth, and social change. The program is based in Jaipur, a bustling hub of NGOs engaged in development projects, social justice initiatives, and political activism.[17] Recently-unveiled federal budget also accords high priority to new and renewable energy. Indian Finance Minister Arun Jaitley has proposed to set up mega solar power projects in Rajasthan, Gujarat, Tamil Nadu and Jammu and Kashmir with a fund of Rs. 500 crores. The government has announced a scheme for solar power driven agricultural pump sets and water pumping stations, for which Jaitley earmarked a sum of Rs. 400 crores in the fiscal plan.

In addition, implementation of the Green Energy Corridor Project is expected to be accelerated in this financial year to boost renewable energy across the country. This churning stems from the growing socio-political realisation in India on the need to take ecological challenges head on. Growing pollution levels (a 2014 WHO report ranked New Delhi as the world's worst city in terms of air pollution), water scarcity and energy crisis have been raising fetters across India. And justifiably so: after all, the country is particularly vulnerable to global ecological variations.

In the last few years, many of its water bodies have dried up and groundwater levels have been depleting due to unplanned urbanisation. There has been widespread damage to natural ecosystems and biodiversity; and land degradation and extreme weather events have severely impacted agriculture.[18]

Education for Sustainable Development is simultaneously a sub-field of education and a conceptual tool to aid policy makers in authoring educational policies that take into account the present environmental, societal and economic challenges. According to the UNESCO, it is based on all levels and types of learning - learning to know, learning to be, learning to live together, learning to do and learning to transform oneself and society.

Education for Sustainable Development is an important pedagogical tool as it is based on the fundamental principle of making an individual see and recognise the interdependence between human beings and each and every unit of ecology. The Brundtland Report of 1987 also made a very important point in this context stating, Sustainable development requires meeting the basic needs of all and extending to all the opportunity to fulfill their aspirations for a better life. The role of ESD, which is based on the three pillars of economy, society and environment, is critical in changing prevalent perceptions and attitudes of people towards self, society and environment.[19]

The Scientific Policy Resolution of 1958 and the Technology Policy Statement of 1983 emphasise self-reliance, as also sustainable and equitable development. Science and Technology Policy of 2003 note that science and technology has unprecedented impact on economic growth and social development. Knowledge has become a source of economic might and power. This has led to increased restrictions on sharing of knowledge, to new norms of intellectual property rights, and to global trade and technology control regimes. Scientific and technological developments today also have deep ethical, legal and social implications'. The Science and Technology system in India consists of central government science and technology departments. The UN Conference on Human Environment in 1972 exerted a major influence on environmental policy in India. The government set up a National Committee on Environmental Planning and Coordination in 1972. The 42nd Constitution Amendment Act 1976, Article 48A (Directive Principles) states that the state shall endeavour to protect and improve the environment and to safeguard the forests and wildlife of the country.

Article 51 A (g) (Fundamental Duties) aims to protect and improve the natural environment including forests, lakes, rivers, wild life and to have compassion for living creatures. The UN Conference on Environment and Development in 1992 and its Agenda 21 influenced pollution prevention and control and natural resource management policies. The Policy Statement for Abatement of Pollution, issued by the Ministry of Environment and Forests in February 1992 admits that the state of the environment continues to deteriorate'and favours a mix of instruments in the form of legislation and regulation, educational programmes and information campaigns. Tradable pollution permits provide incentives for the polluting units to internalise environmental costs in their decision making. They satisfy environmental effectiveness criterion as well as dynamic efficiency. Environmental policy reform based on sound science and public participation can internalize environmental costs in decision making and influence peoples 'behaviour to improve environmental quality. The Planning Commission-National Natural Resources Management System, constituted in 1983, is an apex body and has members from various central government departments which deal with natural resources and environment. In February 2011, the Ministry of Environment and Forests has initiated a major new programme. The Economics of Ecosystems and Biodiversity (TEEB) study of valuing its natural capital and ecosystem services in terms of economic value.[20]

Conclusion

Sustainable development is development that meets the needs of the present, without compromising the ability of future generations to meet their own needs. The concept of sustainable development can be interpreted in many different ways, but at its core is an approach to development that looks to balance different, and often competing, needs against an awareness of the environmental, social and economic limitations we face as a society. It recognises the interdependence of environmental, social and economic systems. It promotes equality and justice through people empowerment. In the political aspect it demands broad based participation and democratic processes.

References

1. Tatyana P. Soubbotina, *Beyond Economic Growth: An Introduction to Sustainable Development*, Retrieved from http://www.worldbank.org/depweb/english/beyond/beyondco/beg_all.pdf
2. See http://sustainabledevelopment.un.org/content/documents/Agenda21.pdf
3. *Sustainable development*, Retrieved from http://en.wikipedia.org/wiki/Sustainable_development
4. Tatyana P. Soubbotina, *Beyond Economic Growth: An Introduction to Sustainable Development,* Retrieved from http://

www.worldbank.org/depweb/english/beyond/beyondco/beg_all.pdf

5. Jonathan M. Harris (2000), *Basic Principles of Sustainable Development,* Retrieved from http://ase.tufts.edu/gdae/publications/working_papers/sustainable per cent20development.pdf
6. Jennifer A. Elliott (2006), *An Introduction to Sustainable Development,* Retrieved from http://190.11.224.74:8080/jspui bitstream/123456789/1061/2/An_ Introduction_ to_ Sustainable_ Development__3rd_edition__Routledge_ Perspectives_ on_ Development_.pdf
7. *Education for Sustainable Development*, Retrieved from http://en.reset.org/knowledge/advancing-sustainable-development-through-education-india
8. Joyashree Roy & Bikram Chatterjee, *Sustainable Development in India? Who Should Do What?* Retrieved from http://www.uttarakhandstat.com/article/01/drjoy/fulltext.pdf
9. Seehttp://www.hks.harvard.edu/sustsci/ists/docs/whatis SD_env_kates_0504.pdf
10. *Indicators of Sustainable Development: Guidelines and Methodologies*, Retrieved from http://www.un.org/esa/sustdev/natlinfo/indicators/guidelines.pdf
11. *Sustainable Development in India: Perspectives,* Retrieved from http://www.moef.nic.in/sites/default/files/wssd/doc4/consul_book_persp.pdf
12. See http://www.wri.org/blog/2013/04/5-keys-sustainable-development-indian-cities
13. See http://fsdinternational.org/country/india
14. Shri Nilmadhab Mohanty & Aarushi Goyal (20120, *Sustainable development: Emerging Issues in India's Mineral Sector*, Retrieved from http://planningcommission.gov.in/reports/sereport/ser/isid_mining per cent20_report1206.pdf
15. Basudha Chattopadhyay, *Sustainable urban development in India: some issues,* Retrieved from http://sa. india environment portal. org. in/files/basudha_paper.pdf

16. *Sustainable Development and Climate Change,* Retrieved from http://indiabudget.nic.in/es2012-13/echap-12.pdf

17. See http://studyabroad.sit.edu/sn/programs/semester/spring-2015/ind/

18. *Sustainable Development: An Agenda for India,* Retrieved from http://www.huffingtonpost.com/samarth-pathak/sustainable-development-india_b_5602482.html

19. *Education for sustainable development*, Retrieved from http://en.reset.org/knowledge/advancing-sustainable-development-through-education-india

20. U. Sankar (2012), *Science and Economics for Sustainable Development of India*, Retrieved from http://www.mse.ac.in/pub/WORKING per cent20PAPER per cent2076.pdf

21. See http://www.brainyquote.com/quotes/keywords/globalisation_4.html

11

Changing Identity of Indian Cinema

Patil Vijay Ramchandra

"The features of globalisation have huge consequences on pandemics. It just connects us so much more closely... And as a consequence, every one of these viruses that passes from animals to humans has the capacity to infect all of us."

—Nathan Wolfe

Introduction

With the end of colonialism, Indian popular cinema emerged as *"India's sole model of national unity"* with an emphasis on *"realist aesthetics"* (Chakravarty, 1993, p. 80). A tension between modernity and tradition, westernisation and indignity, evolved in the cinematic imagination. Out of these dialectical tensions emerged a particular notion of the Indian identity. Through the 1950s and 1960s, directors Like Raj Kapoor and Bimal Roy made films that portrayed the world of underprivileged, and marginalised, and which represented the Indian society as iniquitous and inequitable (Chakravarty, 1993, p. 55). In films such as Awara (1951), Bandini (1963), Do Bigha Zameen (1953), Jagte Raho (1956), Shri 420 (1955), and Sujata (1959), the filmmakers provided a narrative with a socio-political message.

In the 1970s and into the 1980s, Hindi films became catalysts for the nation's homogenising mission, which appealed to the underprivileged by building faith in the *"nation state's protective beneficence"* (Virdi, 2003, p. 109). The underlying assumption was that the (poor) *"angry young man"* was the primary audience of these films. The tremendous success of Zanjeer (1973), a film about a police officer who works outside the bounds of law, introduced the figure of the affected, cynical, violent, rebellious, and urban/worker who was often seen single-handedly fighting rich businesses and ineffectual and corrupt politicians. In Zanjeer and in the evolution of the genre, the world of the "angry, young man" was steeped in crime, unemployment, and poverty:

"It is the articulation of the anguish of the marginalised sector," Kazmi (1998a) writes, *"that largely explains the phenomenon of the angry young man"* (p. 148). It was a device through which Hindi films ensured viewer identification with the working poor and lower middle class sensibilities. Calling it the *"slum's point of view of Indian politics and culture,"* Nandy writes (1998, p. 16), "*There is in the popular cinema same stress on lower-middle-class sensibilities and on the informal, not-terribly tacit theories of politics and society the class uses and the ability to shock haute bourgeoisie with the directness, vigor, and crudity of these theories.*" By calling the slum an *"unintended city"* that forms the *"underground"* of a modern city—the one that provides *"energy, cheap labor, that propels both the engine of civic life and the ambitions of the modernizing elite"*, Nandy (pp. 16-17) argues that the Indian cinema represents the tastes and longings of the slums which dominate the urban public sphere.

The changes precipitated by liberalisation of the Indian economy throughout the 1990s facilitated the growing internationalisation of the production and distribution of Hindi films. With the entry of satellite television, Indian filmmakers began operating in a new media landscape, where a vast range of options, including easy access to Bollywood and Hollywood films, were available to viewers at home. Rajadhyaksha (2003, p. 27) has referred to the shift as the *"Bollywoodisation of the Indian cinema,"* in which the Bollywood culture industry is to be seen as separate and distinct from the actual film production. *"Bollywood is not the Indian film industry or not the film industry alone,"* he writes. *"It might be best seen as a more diffuse cultural conglomeration involving a range of distribution and consumption activities from websites to music cassettes, from cable to radio, from New Delhi to New York."* With liberalisation, the financial equations in Bollywood chases distribution rights for a big budget film roughly doubled in price than that in the Indian market. Television and music rights additionally generated more revenues than the entire production had cost, even before a single ticket was sold. The rise of multiplexes in large metropolitan cities, where the cost of tickets was 10 to 15 times higher than the cost of tickets in family-owned, small-town theaters, increasingly focused film producers on urban and niche audiences who "pay more, buy more" and whose tastes needed to be reflected in the film content (Deshpande, 2001).

According to D'Souza (quoted in Bhattacharya, 2005), a film trade analyst, the days of the *"silver jubilee [a film is running for 25 weeks] are over."* He adds: *"now films target small segments of primary filmgoers who constitute the paying public."* For D'Souza the "paying public" not only can pay for the movie ticket, but has disposable income and attracts advertisers. *"Traditional cinema is in its terminal stages," writes Deshpande, "time is past when people made films for the chavanni [a quarter in Indian currencies] audience."*

In the past 10 years, some of the most popular films such as Black (2004), Dhoom (2004), Dus (2005), Hum Tum (2004), Kabhi Kushi Kabhi Gum (2001), Kaho Na Pyar Hai (2000), Kal Ho Naa Ho (2003), Mohabbatein (2000), Murder (2003), Salaam Namaste (2005), and Yaadein (2001) were top-grossers. All featured westernized themes; foreign locations, actors, and singers; and liberal use of English in the dialogues. Every year, a few films express Indianized themes, such as Gadar (2001), Munnabhai MBBS (2003), Devdas (2002), and Veer Zaara (2004), and do well at the box office. There are fewer and fewer films, however, that do well both in urban and rural areas of India and in the overseas market.

Rang De Basanti (2006), a film shot in Punjab with a British actress in the lead, for instance, is a major hit in metropolitan cities of

Mumbai and Delhi; future plans for the movie include an international premier. Yet Rang De Basanti has done poorly in smaller cities and a town, categorised as 'B' and 'C' film centers, and hasn't found a distributor for most south Indian cities. Box office statistics from India testify to a growing drop in cinema attendance in theaters in smaller towns. Hits like Dhoom or Kal Ho Naa Ho, made close to 80 per cent of their profits from urban multiplexes in India and overseas. In a multiplex in Delhi, a few Hollywood films will play along with Hindi films, but the Hindi films exhibited at these multiplexes are often perceived as urban audience-friendly. Films such as Rang De Basanti, Salaam Namaste, and Nikki and Neal (2005) do well in urban multiplexes, where audiences respond positively to their western themes. Such changes signify a shift in the production, distribution, and consumption of Bollywood films. This article explores ways in which such changes are understood and interpreted by non-elite audiences living in small towns and villages of India.

Ethnographic Audience Analysis

While much work has been done regarding ethnography and audience research especially in cultural studies and international communication, I do not wish to rehash the debates taking place in the academic arena except to say that globalisation requires more such analyses which focus on audiences who are rapidly (and sometimes inadvertently) becoming part of the global mélange. I agree with Parameswaran (2003, p. 311) that abandoning audience ethnography and claiming that *"all that has to be said about audiences has been said"* prematurely closes our understanding of non-western audiences, especially given the reach of corporate globalisation. Ang (2003, p. 367) reminds us that it is *"ludicrous to find definitive and general theoretical answers to know in advance which strategies and tactics different people in the world will invent to negotiate with the intrusions of global forces in their lives."*

In a country like India, which is experiencing what Rajagopal (1996, p. 442) calls *"incomplete modernity"* where *"[modernity] offers a contested and contradictory set of values,"* studies of media reception give us a window into the inner wotion. We need to focus our attention on the hegemonic (and counter hegemonic) acting vast ideological and material fissures. Such ethnography is informed by a method that Kraidy and Murphy (2003) have termed as a *"translocal"* ethnographic method which advocates that ethnography's *"importance lies more in its capacity to comprehend the articulation of the global with the local, than its supposed ability to understand the local in isolation of large-scale structures and processes"* (p. 304). However, scholars, within and outside of India, have conducted textual readings of films (e.g., Kazmi, 1998a; 1999; Shah, 1950; Valicha, 1988), studies of political economy of the film industry (e.g., Pendakur, 2003), or narrative history of films (e.g., Dwyer and Patel, 2002; Gaur, 1973; Gopalan, 2002; Jain and Rai, 2002; Ramachandran, 1984), but only recently have studies of audience reception of particular film texts (e.g., Juluri, 1999; Ram, 2002; Srinivas, 2002), on film-going experiences of audiences (e.g., Derne, 2000; Dickey, 1993), and ethnographies regarding Indian film workers (e.g., Ganti, 2002) begun to emerge. While Bollywood is receiving increased academic attention (e.g., special issue in the journal, South Asian Popular Culture), there have been very few ethnographies about Bollywood audiences in India.

In India it is very difficult to talk about socio-economic class in the traditional way class is understood in western and American sociology. Over the past decade, much has been said about the growth of the Indian middle class as a consequence of the state's economic liberalisation policies (Lakha, 1999). Research suggests that middle class continues to be an elastic term in India, where it includes a vast range of incomes and standards of living (Scrase, 2002). Class is further complicated in Punjab, where the rich do not necessarily cluster and live in urban centers. The green revolution in the 1970s allowed the Punjabi farming community to become wealthy compared to farming communities in other parts of India. The Punjabi farmer, in many villages, is better-off than most middle class families in cities. For the purposes of this study, I have defined the non-elite lower middle class in terms of a particular economic bracket. On average, subjects came from families whose income ranged from 5000 to 10000 rupees (Rs.) per month ($150–$300).

Some subjects' families received support from family members who lived abroad, however, Bollywood Globalisation Non-Elite Audiences 63 and their income could be as high as Rs. 25000 ($600). Most subjects had familial ties to farming communities, which went back generations, and had at least one or several members of their family who continue to be farmers. Several subjects were first-generation college students and, at least one was the first literate woman in her family.

The self-ascription of the subjects was often couched in terms of being lower middle class, rural, and poorer compared to their metropolitan counterparts. In Punjab, Sikh and Hindu families live well-integrated lives in cities and villages. Between 1980–1990, Punjab experienced tremendous sectarian violence between the majority Sikhs and the minority Hindus, but relations have remained peaceful between the two communities during the last 15 years.

Little animosity existed between the two religious groups, who were equally represented among the ethnographic subjects. A number of respondents came from mixed marriages in which each parent followed a different religion. Some subjects were too young to remember the violent decade, but many have heard their parents or grandparents discuss the riots and mass killings.

Some were old enough to remember the days of sectarian massacres, but feel that the situation has changed dramatically. Caste is an important feature of Punjabi society despite Sikhism's objections to caste systems. Villages are divided between the higher and lower castes, although, often, these divisions can just as easily be about class. My respondents came from a mix of high and low castes.

The university had instituted a policy to admit students from lower castes and lower income families to attend college, which allowed for more class and caste integration among the students and the families I interviewed. The Hindu Punjabis identified themselves by their castes more frequently than their Sikh counterparts.

I found it difficult, however, to tell if their caste and religious positions played any role in their consumption or rejection of particular films.

Dream worlds and the Forces of Globalisation

One respondent provided me with a use of metaphor to describe the feelings evoked by the recent films from Bollywood:

Mona: Some movies can be likened to kalpanalok [dream world] where life is absolutely unreal, beautiful, and problem-free. There are nymphets who live in this kalpanalok and we want to see them.

The metaphor of dream world, as described by Mona in the above quote, is part of the construction, consumption, and critique of the Bollywood, S. Rao films by the subjects of this research. While the allusion of reality which we expect in western films is missing from Indian films (so while the storyline and dialogue is usually written in a way that project the spoken in everyday life, the dialogues often interweave with songs and then return to dialogue), the dream world is not about the form of the films (drama-musical) but a recognisable disconnection between the content of the films from the lives of the audiences. Krishan explains the nature of the dream world's distance from his life:

Krishan: They [characters in films] are not connected to our real lives.

Author: In what way?

Krishan: In every way. They move from set to set, from lavish homes to lavish offices and back. Have you noticed they never show the streets? They never show the regular people like us who are walking on the streets or the beggars or the dirt? Most of the time they are not even in India, they are in Mauritius or Vancouver. Their legs are dangling in the sky [Punjabi phrase].

Krishan and others directly referred to the end of the rebellious spirit of earlier "angry young man" films and the narrative scripts that pitched the marginalised against the rich. In the new Bollywood, it is the wealthy who are the heroes. Even the actor who personified the angry young man onscreen in the 70s and 80s films, Amitabh Bachchan, plays in recent films, a multi-millionaire industrialist (in Kabhi Kushi Kabhi Gum) and rector of a wealthy prep school (in Mohabbatein). He has also been seen hosting the Indian version of

"Who Wants to Be a Millionaire?" (Kaun Banega Crorepati?) on TV. "If someone makes a film where the hero is not rich," commented Krishan, *"then they call it an alternative film. Why is a film about a poor man alternative in India? Majority of Indians are poor!"* While escapist films fulfilling material and ideological desires are hardly new to India (Dwyer, 2000), in contemporary Bollywood films, the dreamworld has taken on new meanings and signifiers. Cinematic fantasy of Hindi films has historically revealed a *"collective fantasy, a utopian solution to counteract anxieties such as the emphasis on family, the community and the opportunity for social mobility"* (Dwyer, 2000, p. 72).

Mishra's (2002, p. 29) reference to Bollywood cinema as temples of desire designed to *"accommodate deep fantasies belonging to an extraordinarily varied group of people, from illiterate workers to sophisticated urbanites"* resonates with what Karan Johar (quoted in Khan, 2002), the successful Indian director-producer, says in an interview: *"I try to appeal to as many people as I can."* The new Bollywood dream world, is represented in terms of the material (expensive cars and motorcycles), spatial (foreign locales, beaches, and mansions), and personal (speaking English and wearing designer clothing). The hero's class has acquired high disposable incomes, a jet-setting lifestyle, shopping holidays overseas, and an increasing distance from the everyday reality of lower middle class and rural audiences. Sarbjeet, for instance, reflected my respondents' common failure to connect with rich characters in Bollywood films:

Sarbjeet: There is no connection—his clothes, the cars he drives, the houses, going off to Canada or Switzerland—I cannot relate. Those were one or two films—not every film. Majority of films today have one song set in Switzerland. Everyone is wearing suits that cost thousands of rupees. In earlier films, it used to be 80 per cemt realities, 20 per cent fantasy, now it is 20 per cent reality, 80 per cent fantasy.

The new dreamworld of Bollywood provides the space for the consumable hero (Deshpande, 2001), who is an icon of transnational capital, rampant consumption, and global modernity rather than the embodiment of what Nandy calls the low-brow politics of the slums (p. 6). The consumable hero is a marketable commodity himself/herself, and takes prides in his or her space as a "brand ambassador" for one or several products (Pinto, 2005, p. 5). A star like Shahrukh Khan is "the face" of Pepsi and Santro cars, and Amir Khan the face of Coke and Titan watches. The subjects of this research reported feeling alienated from the rapidly globalising and commercialising dream world of the screen. Talking about a film like Dhoom, an Indianised take on Ocean's eleven, which was doing well at the box offices in the urban centers, Surinder said, *"They must be making these films for someone but it is not for people like me."* Surinder was born in the village of Hoshiarpur, about 35 miles from Patiala. Surinder's father is an indentured laborer, and his brother works as a hired help. Surinder was attending university with the help of state subsidies, and hoped to find a *"government job."* While he liked the *"motorcycle scenes"* in the film, he rejected its social relevance:

Surinder: Where are films about corruption, hatred, unemployment, criminalization of politics? In its place, we have films like this Dhoom which is nothing but an advertisement for foreign motorcycles and expensive sunglasses. Globalisation of the dream world is connected to the materiality of overconsumption and commercialisation. Some subjects critiqued the rampant use of product placement, and others critiqued advertising of brand name items from *"a hero's shoes to his helicopter."*

Rajesh: If you do a little of product placement that is fine but these films go overboard as in Baghban [film made in 2003]. Every scene in that film had either a bottle of Pepsi or a DHL truck or SONY TV. Any social message that films can send to their audiences has gotten lost in Bollywood's drive towards commercialisation.

Shilpa: I haven't seen anything in the Bollywood films that tells us that the system has to change. They spend so much money on making a film but with no message. There is never any emphasis on progressive change.

Meenakshi: Raj Kapoor's films in the 1950s showed poor people living in Bombay's chawls [slums]. Those poor people are still there but they are not in films any longer. Only when they have to show violence or terrorism, they will show the slums. The globalisation of Bollywood films via the constructions of a ubiquitously wealthy and consumption-oriented dream world, these subjects contend, alienates them from these films, and are far too distanced from their everyday lives.

Globalising Indianness

In order to capitalize on the growing market of South Asians abroad, Bollywood producers like Yash Chopra and Subhash Ghai have set up distribution offices in the UK and the U.S. (Pendakur, 2003, p. 44). The outcome is the production of what Shukla (2003, p. 1) has called *"interpenetrating globalism"*: a complicated web of narrative production and structure in which Indian producers and directors make films about Indians who live abroad, and whose lives, filmmakers hope, will appeal to Indians living both in and outside of India. According to Malhotra and Alagh (2004, p. 26) films in the 1990s started providing an ideology of Indian identity that could appeal to Indians in India as well as Indians outside the nation's borders as a project that embraced a nationhood based on common identity. Starting in the mid-1990s, the nonresident Indian, popularly called the NRI, emerged as a disaporic figure in Bollywood films who *"illumines the surprising complementarily of two spheres in operation—home and abroad"* (Shukla, 2003, p. 10). In occupying a category created by the Indian government in the 1970s, he gained meaning from his state of being abroad, and yet he was unproblematically represented as an Indian national.

With the success of early films like Dilwale Dulhania Le Jayenge (1995; frequently referred to as DDLJ) and Pardes (1997), the NRI has emerged as a central narrative figure in films. In DDLJ, the hero, Raj's father (played by Shahrukh Kan) is a rich businessman settled in London. Raj falls in love with Simran (played by Kajol) who is the daughter of a middle class Punjabi immigrant, Baldev (played by Amrish Puri), and the story evolves as Raj tries to convince Baldev to allow him to marry Simran. *"DDLJ told Indians,"* Chopra (2004, p. 92) writes, *"that an Indian is a hybrid who easily enjoys the material comforts of the West and the spiritual comforts of the East."* So, Raj, in his Harley-Davidson leather jacket, and Simran, despite the occasional mini-skirt, are cultural conformists, what Chopra calls the *"strictly, sanitized view of the lives of second-generation NRIs"* (p. 92). In the decade since DDLJ's release, there have been numerous films that depict lives of Indians who live abroad, mostly in the West. As many of the subjects observed, often the protagonists of these films are depicted as rich ex-pats who live upper class lifestyles. Since DDLJ's success, it is not unusual to see films entirely set outside of India and dealing exclusively with the diasporic immigrant experience. As one subject said, *"In older films they used to come back to India but now the film starts and ends in a foreign place."*

The large-scale migration of Punjabis, even from remote villages such as Dosanjh Kalan (whose most famous ex-pat, Ujjal Dosanjh, was a federal minister of Canada), has allowed the subjects of this research to be integrally connected to the diaspora. A number of subjects had friends and families who lived abroad and whose experiences they shared with me. For them, the NRI was not a distant or unfamiliar figure. While they accepted the global movement of South Asians to other parts of the world, they rejected the representation of the globalised Indianness of the films. NRIs in films, they observed, represeerism (the ones living the material dream world) which had little connection to the reality of the lives of most NRIs they knew:

Sarbjeet: Only Punjabi films show what NRIs are really doing like working in gas stations or working in a restaurant like in Des Hoya Pardes. Hindi films don't show how Indians abroad are living.

Sonal: Maybe some Indians like those from IIT [Indian Institute of Technology, an elite engineering school] are living like Shahrukhan in that house, or working for NASA, but my sister is not living like that. She works as a janitor at the New Jersey airport.

The disconnection that these audiences feel from the dream world is further heightened by the differences between subjects' experiences with the diaspora and the diaspora they see played out on the screen. The representation of the diaspora as living an exclusively extrinsic modernity (Raj, 2004, p. 6) represented by the material dream world and an intrinsic traditionality (representing them as more Indian than Indians living in India) is also rejected by the subjects:

Ginny: NRIs are shown as more patriotic, more knowledgeable about Indian culture. In comparison, Indians are shown as more irritated, more dogmatic, they are not as concerned with the society. Everyone here is unhappy, everyone there is happy. Is that possible?

Ginny critiques the conflation in these films of wealth with happiness and the implicit assumption that one could live in another culture and, yet, preserve all the virtues of Indian traditions such as good Indian values and family life (Malhotra & Alagh, 2004, p. 27). Ultimately, such representation of the NRI problematises the identity of the Indians living in India. While valorising the life of the NRI as materially happy and spiritually fulfilled, the films alienate the subjects who feel left behind. These representations create not only material alienation among the subjects by suggesting that the NRI are all rich but also by suggesting they are more Indian than us; subsequently, such alienation results in the rejection of such images. With the exception of DDLJ (perhaps because it was the first film that depicted an immigrant life in popular films), films with NRI themes or with NRI heroes and heroines were not popular among the subjects of this research. No one mentioned Kabhi Khushi Kabhi Gum, Kal Ho Naa Ho, Swades, or other films depicting the lives of NRIs as appealing. One cannot conclude that the subjects are uninterested in the lives of the diaspora, but rather that they don't connect to the Bollywood representations of diasporic Indianness.

If not by the NRI hero, the globalised Indian is represented in Bollywood films by the upper class urban Indian who has enough material wealth to cross national/cultural borders fluidly, travel to exotic locales, and be a modern day hyper consumer. While earlier Indian films represented some modicum of reality where the hero's financial gains would come after a protracted struggle, the globalised Indian figure in contemporary films arrives in the script with ubiquitous wealth and status. Material struggles that affect the day-to-day lives of non-elite, poorer Indians are no longer addressed in these films. Rajadhyaksha has observed that Bollywood *"exports Indian nationalism itself, now commodified and globalized into a 'feel good' version of 'our culture"* (2003, p. 37). While these films continually attempt to populate the world with materially successful Indians who retain traditional Indian values, subjects did not respond favorably to such constructions of Indianness. The globalised Indianness and its many representations found in contemporary Bollywood films did not resonate with the non-elite and rural audiences of Punjab.

Globalisation of Firm Song-Dance

One distinguishing feature of Indian films has always been its music. While the musical lost its dominance as a genre in Hollywood in the early 1960s, largely due to the advent of rock music, India saw no such change. With the advent of talkies, Indian films introduced songs as an important element of the narrative. The main attractions of Hindi cinema for its fans, according to Dwyer and Patel, are the *"sets and costumes, action scenes, presentation of stars, grandiloquent dialogues, and song and dance sequences"* (2002, p. 30). Song sequences are used for several purposes in films. Over the years, directors have worked in different ways to incorporate songs into the narrative. Sometimes a song is diegetically part of the film; other times it is used as a dream sequence, or the lover's fantasy. Sometimes they function to allow an expression of feeling that cannot be articulated otherwise—notably the declaration of love. When music channels like MTV and V on cable and FM radio started broadcasting in India, the Hindi film music gained even more popularity. The music is crucially important economically since the sale of music rights may recover most of the budget of the film. Recently, the film industry has been prereleasing soundtracks for films along with music videos, which are essentially clips of the songs from the film, 2 months in advance. This heightens prerelease interest among audiences.

Since the success of the song Chaiyya Chaiyya in Dil Se (1998), most directors and producers include what is popularly called as an item number, a song and dance sequence, in their films. Hindi films had historically had a version of the item number that would either be set as a cabaret in a nightclub, or feature a courtesan performing a mujra (dance) with qawwali, a specific kind of music attributed to the Muslim Sufi saintstural products separated from the films into which they are inserted. Item numbers have become elaborate song-dance sequences involving up to 100 dancers, usually set in what appears to be a disco, dance club, or a strip club. Many films use foreign dancers. In fact, Yana Gupta, a Czech model, who has found super-stardom in Bollywood, films as an item girl. The dancing style, choreography, and wardrobe for these item numbers are largely influenced by MTV music videos and American hip-hop, salsa, and pop music. Brittany Spears' dance moves from her video, Baby One More Time (1998), for instance, have become highly popular. Several item numbers use Spears' choreography, and dancers wear versions of the sexualized high school uniform Spears wore in the video. Women dominate the coterie of dancers, and some item girls like Malaika Arora, Sameera Reddy, and Yana Gupta have become highly paid stars.

Aisa Jadoo Dalaa Re [the song]? It is just to show her in a small costume because the song had nothing Item numbers attracted the attention of a number of subjects of this ethnography and resulted in lengthy discussions between them and myself. The subjects, no doubt, enjoy film music, and consider it integral to their experience of film viewing. *"I don't understand how people [in the West] sit in the theatre for two hours and watch a film without a single song,"* commented Krishan. *"Our culture is musical,"* says Ginny, *"we have to express some things musically. Not everything can be said in words. Even when a child is born, we say, 'oh listen to him sing', it is music to our ears."* The item numbers, however, are vehemently critiqued by the subjects:

Ruchi: The item girls don't wear anything, almost nothing.

Ruchi: But this is extreme. Helen always had a role in the film. Now we have girls doing item numbers and then you will never see them in the film again. It has become an excuse to show skin. I just saw Khakhee which was a good film but suddenly from nowhere

Lara Dutta shows up and starts dancing and singing to do with the plot of the movie.

Ruchi's critique of the item number is twofold: first, the item numbers have no connection to the narrative of the film and second, they are often used primarily to show skin. The greatest attraction of Hindi films, writes Dwyer, has been to show spaces usually associated with transgressive (non-marital) sexual relations (2000, p. 68). Following strict censorship after independence, when any erotic gesture beyond a gentle embrace was banned by the censor boards, eroticism in Hindi movies became historically contained within the songs. Kasbekar (2001) notes that film songs have always been the venue in which sexual desire was most lucidly expressed. The item numbers, however, makes a clear break from the tradition of song-dance; rather than having some plot function, the item numbers exclusively cater to an "excessive voyeuristic" sexuality (Pendakur, 2003, p. 301):

Ginny: There is too much vulgarity in these songs, the way the dancers dance and sometimes they are wearing nothing but a tiny bikini.

Shiela: Even the music in those songs is filled with vulgar noises.

The overt hypersexualization of the song-dance sequence is a kind of "M-TVisation" of Hindi film music; the song is packaged as a 5-minute video which can advertise the film and be sold as an independent commodity. Observing the changes in the dancing and musical style Lal (1998) writes, *"Whereas in older song-and-dance sequence the erotic had an element of coy and the tentative, today the erotic has in it elements of rank sexuality, brutish pride, and vulgarity. Naked feet adorned by anklets have been replaced with high leather boots and the pelvic thrusts display the hunger of a newly-unleashed sexuality. As in other spheres, in the theatre of sexuality, the Indian adventure with globalisation is on display"*. Websites such as Indiaplaza.com, nehaflix.com, and hindimovies.com, catering to diasporic Indians, sell DVDs containing item numbers from films. Item girls frequently accompany the more established stars in stage shows outside India. Item numbers have become economic necessity for film producers, singers, and music directors who want to market themselves to a global audience, to internationalise the appeal of Hindi film music, and to attract younger, upwardly mobile, city-based audiences. The song-dance sequences have taken on an "international" look, using a multi-cultural dance cast and hip hop-influenced wardrobes. Such tastes and representations are far too alien to the rural and lower middle class audiences. The responses of the subjects suggest a rejection of the images associated with the item numbers, because of their overt sexualization:

Kanwaljeet: I avoid films where I know there are item numbers. That way I know I can go to the film with my brother and not feel embarrassed. The globalising of Hindi films has resulted in cosmetic changes which, while adopting westernized visual styles, provide no room for real transgressions or progressive changes. While items numbers made respondents feel alienated, such discomfort with item numbers is one of many ways in which Bollywood films have become disconnected from the lives of people like Kanwaljeet. Similar to the findings here, Derne's (2005) audience research among the non-elite males in North India have shown that intensification of cultural globalisation in films does not imply that the audiences accept or embrace values that such images represent. Derne, for example, discovered that transnational media have not led non-elite, lower middle class men to *"experiment with new gender arrangements"* and has only *"increased their vigorous defense of local family lives"* (2005, p. 39). The subjects of this research rejected both the hyper sexualization of song-dance and the over commercialisation of the film content.

Resistance and Pleasure of Bollywood

The subjects' critique or rejection of particular kinds of Bollywood films does not imply the rejection of every film produced in Mumbai. Subjects felt they connected to a small number of films such as Astitva (2000), Lagaan (2001), Lakshya (2004), Samay (2003), and Yuva (2004). The film Yuva, while the hero and heroine wore the urbane wardrobes and haircuts, appealed to several subjects because of its representation of college politics and corrupt politicians; Astitva appealed to some subjects because it dealt with the issue of domestic violence, and Lakshya touched them because it showed that a young person needed to focus on his or her goals in life. These films were appealing because they directly confronted the issues that the subjects were dealing with in their daily lives. Some times films can straddle grounds, the aesthetics or look and feel of upper middle class urban and diasporic India as well as having some critical social and political messages. It is possible that the films were appealing also because they mix the feel-good factor of Indian film narratives with social realisms. While subjects designated some films as entertaining and acknowledge that cinema is often about pleasure, they did not want only entertainment. Films that had some social, political, or moral message and had some connection to their lives, the subjects said, appealed to then the most. As Mala said, *"I enjoy some of films and watch them when they are on TV but I don't remember them. I will remember Lakshya for a long time."*

As the subjects have limited disposable income to spend on movies, choosing a special film to make a trip to the theater required some deliberation. With a few exceptions, they frequently chose to go watch a Punjabi over a Bollywood film, although significantly fewer Punjabi films have been released each year. While the subjects lamented the small budgets and lack of technical glitter of Punjabi films, they enjoyed the connections they felt with the characters in Punjabi films. After watching Des Hoya Pardes (2004), which is a story about a Punjabi farmer (Gurshaan) who immigrates to New Jersey to seek political asylum in the U.S., two sisters, Sonia and Shilpi, told me that they thought the story of Gurshaan depicted in the film was the story of their uncle who had left his village of Malwa and made his way to Alexandria, Virginia. As stories about small towns and villages disappear from the Bollywood screen, Punjabi films are beginning to provide that particular cinematic experience. Bollywood producers/directors and small-town viewers and rural audiences are parting ways. In prefiguring the audience (Dornfeld, 1993, p. 229), Bollywood has marginalised people like the subjects of this research as viewers/consumers in the expansion of the liberalised, market-driven economy. The people I spoke to are acutely cognizant of their lives being written out of the film script. More research needs to be done in the diasporic and urban communities in and outside of India also to find the attraction to or rejection of these films (it might be that some of the urban and diasporic audiences reject these films as much as the rural communities of Punjab).

The study of globalisation must address how globalisation is produced, understood, and consumed in various international sites, and globalisation must be analysed as functioning within the larger terrain of interconnected forces (Shome & Hegde, 2002, p. 187). As Bollywood films attempt to connect to the diasporic audiences and focus on the audience as consumer in urban and metropolitan areas, they are leaving other economically and culturally marginalised audiences behind. Much has been written about the elitism among the film society/art society intelligentsia in India who ignore the study of conventional Indian cinema (Vasudevan, 2000). What must also be studied are audiences who are categorised by the Bollywood producers/directors as unprofitable. I contend that the globalising environment of Bollywood films is creating its own elitism constituted by the brand logic of transnational capital which has redefined the meaning of the masses. Bollywood recognises its audiences as the upper middle class diasporic and urban communities whose tastes, values, desires, and consumptions are reflected and re-energised by these films. The masses of the rural, poor, and lower middle class audiences find themselves distanced from the images and dream worlds of Bollywood, and are less and less likely to consume them in the future (Shakuntala Rao, P. 57-74).

References

1. Ang, I. (2003). Culture and communication: Toward an ethnographic critique of media consumption in the transnational media system. In L. Parks & S. Kumar
2. (Eds.), Planet TV: A global television reader (pp. 363–375). New York: New York University Press.
3. Barnouw, E., & Krishnaswamy, S. (1980). (2nd Ed.). Indian film. New York: Oxford University Press.

4. Bhaskar, I. (1998). Allegory, nationalism and cultural change in Indian cinema, Literature & Theology, 12 (1), 50-69.

5. Bhattacharya, R. (August 16, 2005). The trade analyses. Screen. Retrieved August 19, 2005 http://www.screenindia.com/fullstory.php?content_id=10995.

6. Chakravarty, S. (1993). National identity in Indian popular cinema (1947–87). Austin, TX: University of Texas Press.

7. Chopra, A. (2004). Dilwale dulhania le jayenge: The making of a blockbuster. New Delhi: Harper Collins Publishers India & India Today.

8. Derne, S. (2000). Movies, masculinity, & modernity: ethnography of men's film going in India. Westport, CT: Greenwood Press.

9. —.(2005). The (limited) effect of cultural globalisation in India: Implications for Cultural theory. Poetics, 33, 33–47.

10. Desai, J. (2004). Beyond Bollywood: The cultural politics of South Asian diasporic films. New York: Routledge.

11. Deshpande, S. (2001). Hindi films: A rise of the consumable hero. Himal, 4. Retrieved June 22, 2005 http://www.himalmag.com/august2001/essay.html.

12. Dickey, S. (1993). Cinema & the urban poor in south India. Cambridge, UK Cambridge University Press.

13. Dornfeld, B. (1993). Envisioning reception: How public television producers prefigure, approximate, & invoke the transnational audience. In P. Crawford &

14. B. Jafsteinsson (Eds.), The construction of the viewer: Media ethnography & the anthropology of audiences (pp. 229–241). New York: Interventions Press.

15. Dwyer, R. (2000). All you want is money, all you need is love: Sexuality and romance in modern India. London: Cassell.

16. Dwyer, R., & Patel, D. (2002). Cinema India: The visual culture of Hindi film. New Brunswick, NJ: Rutgers University Press.

17. Ganti, T. (2002). 'And yet my heart is still Indian': The Bombay film industry & the (h)indianization of Bollywood. In F. Ginsburg, L. Abu-Laghood, & B. Larkin Bollywood Globalization Non-Elite Audiences 75

18. (Eds.), Media worlds: Anthropology on new terrains (pp. 132–158). Berkeley, CA: University of California Press.

19. Shakuntala Rao, The Globalisation of Bollywood: An Ethnography of Non-Elite Audiences in India, State University of New York, Department of Communication The Communication Review, 10:57–76,2007, Rutledge Taylor & Francis Group file:///C:/ Documents per cent 20and per cent 20Settings/com per cent201.COM1/My per cent20 Documents/Downloads/The per cent 20 Globalization per cent20 of per cent 20 Bollywood....pdf

12

Educational and Health Status of Scheduled Tribes in Andhra Pradesh

Prof D.Pulla Rao

"If the constitutional treaty is rejected it will be back to square one, just at a time when we want Europe to be a more effective force for good in the world, when we need to buttress ourselves against the pressures and insecurities of globalisation."

–Peter Mandelson

Introduction

The Scheduled Tribes are the segregated and isolated communities and are concentrated in the states of Orissa, Bihar, Madhya Pradesh, Andhra Pradesh, Maharashtra, Gujarat and Rajasthan where they constitute about 80 percent of the Scheduled tribe population of India. Even today, widely pervasive reality in respect of tribal communities in India is that most of them are geographically isolated, economically weak, socially ignorant, politically indifferent, culturally rich, behaviourally simple, trustworthy and leading their life in the lap of nature. They are facing problems, which force them to lead a life at bare subsistence level. They are in the situation featured with poverty, deprivation, disadvantages which are difficult to be tackled effectively on their own and making the government in particular and society in general to intervene in a planned manner to solve the miseries of tribes and facilitate development process. A large number of tribal communities continue to be extremely backward and some of them are still in the primitive food gathering stage, where as some others have progressed a little in terms of economic and educational advancement.

The greatest challenge that the Government of India has been facing since independence is the proper provision of social justice to the STs), by ameliorating their socio-economic conditions. STs, Scheduled Castes (SCs) and denotified tribes constitute the weakest section of India's population, from the ecological, economic and educational angles. They constitute the matrix of India's poverty. Though the tribals are the sons of the same soil and the citizens of the same country, they are born and grown as the children of the nature. From the historical point of view, they have been subjected to the worst type of social exploitation. They are practically deprived of many civic facilities and isolated from modern and civilized way of living since so many centuries. On the literacy front, the situation is very discouraging. The literacy rates of tribal population in Visakhapatnam, Andhra Pradesh and at all India level are very less when compared to that of general population. But the encouraging point is the growth rates of literacy for STs are far better when compared to that of general population in the above said areas during the period of 1981-2011census. As a result, the gap between the literacy rates of general population and that of the scheduled tribe population is reducing very slowly.

With regard to female literacy, the results are very disappointing. The female literacy rates for Visakhapatnam, Andhra Pradesh and India are very low when compared to that of the total female literacy rates. But quite interesting aspect is the growth in literacy rates for scheduled tribe population are more when compared to that of general female population. The literacy rates of tribes in Visakhapatnam is 34.34 among this male reported 45.98 per cent and female reported only 22.27 these are very low when compare with state averages 37.04, 47.66, 26.11 per cents for total, male and female literacy rates. The National Health Policy categorically emphasises the urgent need for improving the tribal health especially through detection and treatment of endemic and other diseases specific to tribals. In pursuance of this policy commitment, the Ministry of Health and Family Welfare continued to give focused attention to improve the health conditions of STs by implementing various health care programmes besides relaxing norms with a major objective to attend to the health needs of STs. A separate Tribal Development Planning Cell has been functioning under the Ministry since 1981 to co-ordinate the policy, planning, monitoring and evaluation of the health care schemes for the welfare and development of STs. In India there are 573 scheduled tribe communities and in Andhra Pradesh about 33 of them dwell. In India, the President is empowered by the Constitution to declare a community as a scheduled tribe community.

The growth rates of STs in Andhra Pradesh are 5.47, 2.24, 6.50, 2.79, 1.81 and 1.78 for the years 1951, 1961, 1971, 1981, 1991, 2001 and 2011 census years respectively. Except 1971 and 1991, the decadal growth rate of tribal population was more than the growth rate of general population. From 1951 to 2011 the STs has increased by seven times but for the general population it is only two times. The percentages of STs Population to the total population in Andhra Pradesh are 3.68, 3.81, 5.92, 6.31, 6.59 and 7-00 for the years 1961, 1971, 1981, 1991, 2001 and 2011 census years respectively. There is an increased trend in the percentage of scheduled tribe population to the total population of Andhra Pradesh.

The Data and Methodology

The primary data comprise of collecting information from the selected sample tribal households by way of canvassing a structured schedule among them. In addition, the secondary data are also taken from the Chief Planning Officer of Visakhapatnam District. The primary data has been collected during the months of June and July of 2011.

A Multi-stage random sampling technique is employed to select the sample households. In the first stage, one district viz., Visakhapatnam of Andhra Pradesh has been purposively selected for the study. Then, randomly one mandal was selected from the district, viz., G. Madugula. In the third stage, one village from the mandal was selected i.e., Solabham village. In the fourth stage a sample of 100 tribal households in the sample village were randomly selected and interviewed with a pre-prepared schedule. The schedule contains all range of aspects of socio-economic status.

This paper is addressed to study the literacy levels, dropouts, reasons for dropouts, distance of educational institutions and health characteristics like drinking water facilities, type of fuel used for cooking, gender and age wise classification of diseased persons, health assistance from government authorities, distance to the first-aid facility, awareness about AIDS and so on in the study area. The literacy levels of the head of the households have been presented in Table-1. It is very frightening thing that 81 per cent of the head of the households are illiterates. The literacy per cent of the head of the households is 19 per cent. Among the literates 11 per cent are studied up to secondary level, five per cent studied only primary level of education and only three per cent are acquired higher level of education.

Table-1: Educational Status of Head of the Households in the Sample Area

S. No	Education Level	Number of Persons	Per cent
1	Primary	05	05.00
2	Secondary	11	11.00
3	Higher	03	03.00
4	Illiterate	81	81.00
	Total	100	100.00

Source: *Primary Data.*

The educational levels in the study area have been presented in Table-2. It is clear that the literates in the study area are very low, 19 per cent of the population is educated up to primary level, 20.63 per cent up to secondary level and only 9.30 per cent are obtained up to higher level. About 55 per cent females and 45 per cent males studied at primary school level, 54.95 males and 45.05 females in secondary level and in higher the female per cent is very low with 29.27 per cent and males with 70.73 per cent.

Table -2: Educational Levels of the Sample Population.

S. No	Education level	Male	Per cent	Female	Per cent	Total	Per cent
1	Primary	38	45.24	46	54.76	84	19.05
2	Secondary	50	54.95	41	45.05	91	20.63
3	Higher	29	70.73	12	29.27	41	09.30
4	Illiterates	101	44.89	124	55.11	225	51.02
	Total	218	49.43	223	50.57	441	100.00

Source: Primary Data

The literacy levels in the study area have been presented in Table 3. It is very alarming situation in the study that the literacy levels are 48.98 per cent, among this 54.17 per cent male and 45.83 per cent are female. The total illiterates are 51.02 per cent among them 44.89 are male and 55.11 per cent are females.

Table-3: Literacy Levels in the Study Area

S. No	Literacy level	Male	Percent	Female	Percent	Total	Percent
1	Literates	117	54.17	99	45.83	216	48.98
2	Illiterates	101	44.89	124	55.11	225	51.02
	Total	218	49.48	223	50.52	441	100.00

Source: Primary Data.

Distribution of the drop out children below the age group of 14 years from their education in the sample area has been presented in Table-4. There 32 children who dropped from their education in the study are. Among them 18 girl children are dropped with 56.25 per cent and boys are 14 with 43.75 per cent.

Table-4: Distribution of the Drop Out Children (Below 14 Years Age) from their Education in the Sample Area.

S. No	Drop outs	No of Children	Per cent
1	Boys	14	43.75
2	Girls	18	56.25
	Total	32	100.00

Source: Primary Data.

Table-5 explains the reasons for drop outs from their education in the study area. 21 children with 65.63 per cent are dropped from their education because of their financial problem while 11 children with 34.37 per cent are participating in their household work. So, finally it may conclude that poor economical status leads to more drop outs from schools.

Table-5: Distribution Drop Out Children According to their Reason for not Going to School in the Sample Area.

S. No	Reasons for Drop Outs	No of Children	Per cent
1	Financial	21	65.63
2	Household work	11	34.37
	Total	32	100.00

Source: Primary Data.

Distribution of households according to their available facility for drinking water in the sample area has been presented in Table-6. It is observed that no one having the proper drinking water facility in the study area. Total households are taking unprotected water for their drinking. This type of water facility will reflect the health status.

Table-6: Distribution of Households According to their Available Facility for Drinking Water in the Sample Area

S. No	Water Facility	Number of Households	Per cent
1	Protected	00	00.00
2	Un Protected	100	100.00
	Total	100	100.00

Source: Primary Data.

It is very clear from Table-7 that there is no single household using other fuel than firewood in the study area. That means 100 per cent of the households are using firewood as a fuel for their cooking. This situation is very severe to their health as well as the environment.

Table -7: Distribution of Households According to their Source of Fuel for Cooking in the Sample Area.

S. No	Type of Fuel	Number of Households	Per cent
1	Firewood	100	100.00
2	Kerosene	00	00.00
3	Gas	00	00.00
	Total	100	100.00

Source: Primary Data.

Immunization of the child in the age group of 0 to 5 years has been presented in Table-8. It is observed that there are 21 children in the above given age group. 100 per cent of the children having immunization card among them 85.71 per cent are fully immunized, where as 14.29 are not fully immunized. This may causes them to face some health problems like physically handicapped, mentally disordered and other diseases.

Table-8: Child (0-5 years) Immunization Status in the Sample Area.

S. No	Information about immunization	Yes	Per cent	No	Per cent	Total	Per cent
1	Availability of immunization card	21	100.00	00	00.00	21	100.00
2	Either fully immunized	18	85.71	03	14.29	21	100.00
	Total available children (0-5 years)	21					

Source: Primary Data.

Table-9 explains about the reproductive age women who are in the age group of 15-49 years, especially about their ages at the time of marriage and at the time their first conception in the study area. There are 106 reproductive women in the study area among them 87 are got married at the age of 15-18 years with 82 per cent and only 18 per cent are married after 19 years.

That means still 82 per cent of the women in the study area are married below the age of 18 years.

Table-9: Distribution of Reproductive age (15-49 Years) Women in the Sample Area.

S. No	Age	Age at Marriage	Per cent	Age at first Conception	Per cent
1	< 15	04	03.77	00	00.00
2	15-18	83	78.30	26	24.53
3	19 and above	19	17.93	80	75.47
	Total	106	100.00	106	100.00

Source: Primary Data.

Gender wise distribution of diseased persons in the sample area has been presented in Table-10. Out of 462 total populations in the study area the percentage of diseased persons are 29 with 131 members, among them 54 per cent are male and 46 per cent are female diseased persons.

Table-10: Gender Wise Distribution of Diseased Persons in the Sample Area.

S. No	Gender	No of persons	Per cent
1	Male	71	54.19
2	Female	60	45.81
	Total	131	100.00

Source: Primary Data.

It is evident from the Table-11, 81per cent of the diseased persons are in the productive age group and remaining 19 per cent are unproductive. The disease prevalence rate in the age group of above 60 years is very less. It is not because of their good health it is because of their size in the total population.

Table-11: Age Wise Distribution of Diseased Persons in the Sample Area.

S. No	Age	No of persons	Per cent
1	Up to 14	22	16.79
2	15-60	106	80.91
	60 and above	03	02.40
	Total	131	100.00

Source: Primary Data.

Distribution of sample population according affected diseases in the study area has been presented in Table-12.

It is observed that 52.67 per cent of the diseased persons are effected from fever while 36.64 per cent from malaria and 10.69 per cent from dengue.

Table -12: Distribution of Sample Population According Affected Diseases.

S. No	Type of Disease	No of Persons	Per cent
1	Fever	69	52.67
2	Malaria	48	36.64
3	Dengue	14	10.69
	Total	131	100.00

Source: Primary Data.

Distribution of diseased persons whether they consults the doctor has been presented in Table-13. It is predominant that 69.47 per cent of the diseased persons are consults the doctor and still 30.53 per cent are not consulting the doctor for their treatment in the study area.

Table-13: Distribution of Diseased Persons Whether Consults the Doctor for their Treatment.

S. No	Opinion of Diseased Persons	No of Persons	Per cent
1	Yes	91	69.47
2	No	40	30.53
	Total	131	100.00

Source: Primary Data.

The expenses levels of the diseased persons in the study area have been presented in Table-14. It is evident that nearly 50 per cent of the diseased persons are spending Rs. 1,001 to Rs. 3,000 for their treatment, 14 per cent are spending more than Rs. 3,000 and 35.88 per cent are spending below Rs. 1,000.

Table-14: Distribution of Diseased Persons According to their Expenditure for their Diseases.

S. No	Level of Expenditure	No of Persons	Per cent
1	Below 1,000	47	35.88
2	1,001-2,000	32	24.43
3	2,001-3,000	34	25.95
4	3,001 and above	18	13.74
	Total	131	100.00

Source: Primary Data.

Table-15 explains the opinion of the sample households regarding to the government medical services. It is observed that 74 per cent of the households expressed their opinion that they have the medical officer's visit in the study area. 87 per cent are opinioned that they are getting sufficient services from the government health centers. Regarding the medicine 91 per cent are opinioned that they are getting sufficient medicine from the government health centers. That means the performance of government health centers in the study area is good.

Table-15: Opinion of the Sample Households Regarding to the Government Medical Services.

S. No	Name of the Service	Yes	Per cent	No	Per cent	Total	Per cent
1	Visit of the medical officer	74	74.00	26	26.00	100	100.00
2	Sufficient Services provided	87	87.00	13	13.00	100	100.00
3	Sufficient Medicine provided	91	91.00	09	09.00	100	100.00
4	Un necessary tests	21	21.00	79	79.00	100	100.00

Source: Primary Data.

The awareness about AIDS in the sample population has been presented in Table-16. It can see from the table 68 per cent are heard about the disease and 52 per cent are known the causes and symptoms of the AIDS. It may conclude that the government has to take more awareness programmes about the disease because nearly

50 per cent of the households do not know the causes and symptoms of the AIDS.

Table-16: Awareness about the AIDS in the Sample Population

S. No	Knowledge about AIDS	Yes	Per cent	No	Per cent	Total	Per cent
1	Heard about AIDS	68	68.00	32	32.00	100	100.00
2	Causes	52	52.00	48	48.00	100	100.00
3	Symptoms	52	52.00	48	48.00	100	100.00

Source: Primary Data.

Distance to the medical centers will have an effect on the health status of the households. It is observed that from Table- 17, about 19 per cent of the households they don't have any medical center blow the 16 Kms and 81 per cent nearer to medical centers with distance of 10 Kms. It may negatively affect the health of the households in the study area.

Table -17: Distance to the Medical Center to the Sample Households.

S. No	Distance in km	No of Persons	Per cent
1	10	81	81.00
2	16	19	19.00
	Total	100	100.00

Source: Primary Data.

Conclusions

We have mainly discussed about the educational and health characteristics like literacy levels, health conditions and availability of health and educational facilities. Literacy levels in the study area are very unfavourable to the development. It is 81 per cent for heads of the households and 51 per cent of total population are illiterates. Still 55 per cent of the female population is illiterates. Drop outs are also high with 32 number of children among which 14 boys and 18 girls. The availability of infrastructure facilities is very poor in the study area. There is no proper drinking water facilities in the study area still they are drinking unprotected water. All the households are using firewood as a fuel for their cooking. The school and the health facilities are located at a far of place, more than 10 Kms. from their village.

Still 83 per cent of the women are getting marred below the 18 years age and only 19 per cent are getting married at 19 years and above. There are 21 children who are below the five years age group, among them 18 children are fully immunised. The disease prevalence is more in male with 54 per cent and female with 46 per cent. Productive age group people are affected more from diseases (with 80 per cent). Fever and malaria are the main diseases which are affecting the sample population. 69 per cent of the diseased persons are consulting the doctors and they are spending about Rs. 3,000 on treatment. It is good for people's health point of view almost all people they are aware about AIDS, causes and symptoms of disease.

Policy Implications

After studying the educational and health status of scheduled tribes the present study proposes some comprehensive strategies for the development of scheduled tribes of the study area in particular and in India in general.

1. This study brought out that STs are the most backward in the human development indicators. So human development projects for STs are recommended particularly health, education, drinking water and hygienic living conditions.
2. The education promotes the human development, especially women education. But in the study area both general and female literacy rates are very low. So, proper educational facilities need to be provided for the development of STs.
3. Tribal people are at risk with regard to their health as the disease prevalence rates are high in this region. So suitable situational measures have to be adopted to treat the scheduled tribes, like mobile health units, training a couple in each village in first aid who can motivate them to use modern medicine and make them to approach trained doctor as gender differentials are noticed in the study area.

4. The expenditure on food is more in the study area and very negligible on other things like education and health. Though the respondents are spending more on food their intake levels are not up to the stipulated levels. So, it is suggested that government has to provide more income generation programmes and enable them to take nutritive food.

5. Good governance is the key factor in delivering goods and services to the needy. The delivery system must be made perfect without any leakages. The beneficiary must receive 100 per cent of the benefits targeted to him.

References

1. Ali A (2003): "Health Status of Tribals in India", Published in Adak (Ed.) "Demography and Health Profile of the Tribes", Anmol Publications, New Delhi.

2. Aparna Mitra and Pooja Singh (2008): "Trends in Literacy Rates and Schooling among the Scheduled Tribe Women in India", International Journal of Social Economics, Vol. 35, No. 1/2, pp. 99-110.

3. Basu SK (1993): "Health Status of Tribal Women in India", Social Change, Vol. 23(4), pp. 19-39.

4. Meera A, Nangia P and Roy TK (2003): "The Reproductive Behaviour of Tribal Women in Madhya Pradesh", Published in Adak (Ed.) "Demography and Health Profile of the Tribes", Anmol Publications, New Delhi.

5. Pandey GD and Tiwari RS (2003): "A Study of Socio-cultural Factors affecting Reproductive Health among the Primitive Tribes of Madhya Pradesh", Published in Adak (Ed.) "Demography and Health Profile of the Tribes", Anmol Publications, New Delhi.

6. Pulla Rao D (2013): Educational status of Scheduled Tribes in Andhra Pradesh: A study in Visakhapatnam and West Godavari Districts, *International Journal of Informative and Futuristic Research (IJIFR),* Volume 1, Issue 1, September, 2013. (Online Journal).

7. Pulla Rao D (2013): Demographic and Health status of Scheduled Tribes in Vizianagaram District of Andhra Pradesh, *ESRI Journal*, Vol. 4, No. 1, January, pp. 37-45.

8. Pulla Rao D (2012): Food and Health status of Scheduled Tribes in Visakhapatnam District of Andhra Pradesh, *The Dawn journal*, Vol.1, No.1, January, pp.29-43.

9. See http://www.brainyquote.com/quotes/keywords/globalisation_5.html

13

Women Empowerment: A Way of Economic Development

N.G. Pendse & Sukanta Sarkar

"In its current form, globalisation cannot be sustained. Democratic societies will not support it. Authoritarian leaders will fear to impose it."

–John Sweeney

Introduction

Women constitute almost half of the population in the world. But the hegemonic masculine ideology made them suffer a lot as they were denied equal opportunities in different parts of the world. The rise of feminist ideas has led to the tremendous improvement of women's condition through out the world in recent times. Access to education has been one of the most pressing demands of theses women's rights movements. Women education in India has been a major preoccupation of both the government and civil society as educated women can play a very important role in the development of the country.[1] For centuries women were not treated equal to men in many ways. They were not allowed to own property, they did not have a Share in the property of their parents, they had no voting rights, they had no freedom to choose their work or job and so on.[2] Women play an important role in all the fields of development. Socially economically if she is strengthened then she will create wonders. Women contribute directly and indirectly for the economic development. Though the nature has given the genetic power of reproduction especially to the women, the socio-economic status of women is so poor and the incidence of poverty is more on woman only. Empowering women is the only solution for all questions. Hence it is essential to study the past and present position of women and suggest measures for their upliftment.[3]

More than half a billion women in developing countries have no reasonable income, no health care and no security. Extreme poverty is female and means hunger, disease, foreshortened or no education, no ownership and no secure access to water and energy. Women also have limited opportunities owing to isolation, exclusion from decision-making processes, low mobility, overwork and violence. Unequal gender relations are generally to the advantage of men, although many current impoverishing mechanisms also work to their detriment. Gender equality seeks human dignity for women and men, recognising that gender roles and identities are flexible and influenced, among other things, by social status and ethnicity. A gender approach takes account of specific risks to men and women and supports strategic partnerships between the sexes. Empowerment of women is nevertheless important as a means of establishing equality between the sexes.[4]

Empowerment refers to increasing the economic, political, social, educational, gender, or spiritual strength of an entity or entities. Empowerment is the process of obtaining these basic opportunities for marginalised people, either directly by those people, or through the help of non-marginalised others who share their own access to these opportunities. It also includes actively thwarting attempts to deny those opportunities. Empowerment also includes encouraging, and developing the skills for, self-sufficiency, with a focus on eliminating the future need for charity or welfare in the individuals of the group. This process can be difficult to start and to implement effectively. Many of the barriers to women's empowerment and equity lie ingrained in cultural norms. Many women feel these pressures, while others have become accustomed to being treated inferior to men.[5] The past three decades have witnessed a steadily increasing awareness of the need to empower women through measures to increase social, economic and political equity, and broader access to fundamental human rights, improvements in nutrition, basic health and education. Along with awareness of the subordinate status of women has come the concept of gender as an overarching socio-cultural variable, seen in relation to other factors, such as race, class, age and ethnicity. In recognition of the importance of establishing gender equality around the world, the United Nations Development Fund for Women (UNIFEM) was established as a separate fund within the United Nations Development Program (UNDP) in 1984. At that time, the General Assembly instructed it to ensure women's involvement with mainstream activities.[6]

It is basically the creation of an environment where women can make independent decisions on their personal development as well as shine as equals in society. Women want to be treated as equals so much so that if a woman rises to the top of her field it should be a commonplace occurrence that draws nothing more than a raised eyebrow at the gender. This can only happen if there is a channelised route for the empowerment of women. The crimes against women fly directly against orchestrating women empowerment in India. The United Nations Development Programme constituted eight Millennium Development Goals (MDG) for ensuring equity and peace across the world. The third MDG is directly related to the empowerment of women in India. The MDGs are agreed-upon goals to reduce certain indicators of disparity across the world by the year 2015.[7]

Despite many international agreements affirming their human rights, women are still much more likely than men to be poor and illiterate. They usually have less access than men to medical care, property ownership, credit, training and employment. They are far less likely than men to be politically active and far more likely to be victims of domestic violence. Evidence demonstrates that, in economies where gender equality is greater in terms of both opportunities and benefits, there is not only higher economic growth but also a better quality of life. Addressing gender inequalities and empowering women are vital to meeting the challenge of improving food and nutrition security, and enabling poor rural people to overcome poverty. Women are major players in the agriculture sector, in household food and nutrition security, and in natural resource management. They account for 43 per cent of the agricultural labour force in all developing countries and up to 50 per cent in Eastern Asia and sub-Saharan Africa. They work along the value chain in their own enterprises, in family activities and as employees, and undertake a wide range of activities, often utilising their own knowledge systems. They also engage in a mix of non-farm activities, as part of their strategy to diversify their livelihood options, and are responsible for the majority of household tasks.[8]

What is Women Empowerment?

Women Empowerment is the ability of women to exercise full control over their actions. This means control over material assets, intellectual resources and even over their ideologies. It involves, at the psychological level, women's ability to assert them which has, so far, been constricted by the 'gender roles' assigned to them especially in a culture like India which resists changes.[9] Empowering women to participate fully in economic life across all sectors is essential to build stronger economies, achieve internationally agreed goals for development and sustainability, and improve the quality of life for women, men, families and communities.

The private sector is a key partner in efforts to advance gender equality and empower women. Current research demonstrating that gender diversity helps businesses perform better signals that self-interest and common interest can come together.[10] Women's empowerment is a flow rather than a stock variable manifesting into various outcomes and well being is a necessary but not sufficient condition for the former, i.e. well-being going through various pathways like gaining resources, autonomy and agency. These pathways denote expansion in capabilities in a way which brings changes in the lives of individuals; people who are previously denied power are now being empowered.[11]

Women's empowerment is a new phrase in the vocabulary of gender literature. The phrase is used in two broad senses i.e. general and specific. In a general sense, it refers to empowering women to be self-dependent by providing them access to all the freedoms and opportunities, which they were denied in the past only because of their being women.

In a specific sense, women empowerment refers to enhancing their position in the power structure of the society. The word women empowerment essentially means that the women have the power or capacity to regulate their day- to- day lives in the social, political and economic terms which enables them to move from the periphery to the centre stage.[12]

Importance of Women Empowerment

Women's empowerment is very essential for the development of society. Empowerment means individuals acquiring the power to think and act freely, exercises choice and fulfill their potential as full and equal members of society. As per the United National Development Fund for women (UNIFEM), the term women's empowerment means: (a) Acquiring knowledge and understanding of gender relations and the ways in which these relations may be changed; (b) Developing a sense of self-worth, a belief in ones ability to secure desired changes and the right to control ones life; (c) Gaining the ability to generate choices exercise bargaining power; (d) Developing the ability to organise and influence the direction of social change, to create a more just social and economic order, nationally and internationally.

Women Empowerment is a global issue and discussion on women political right are at the fore front of many formal and informal campaigns worldwide. The concept of women empowerment was introduced at the international women conference at NAROIBI in 1985. Education is milestone of women empowerment because it enables them to responds to the challenges, to confront their traditional role and change their life. So that we can not neglect the importance of education in reference to women empowerment India is poised to becoming superpower, a developed country by 2020.[13]

Women's Empowerment Principles

The Women's Empowerment Principles are a set of Principles for business offering guidance on how to empower women in the workplace, marketplace and community. They are the result of collaboration between the United Nations Entity for Gender Equality and the Empowerment of Women (UN Women) and the United Nations Global Compact.[14] The Women's Empowerment Principles offer guidance to companies on how to empower women in the workplace, marketplace and community. They are the result of collaboration between the United Nations Global Compact and the United Nations Entity for Gender Equality and the Empowerment of Women (UN Women) and are adapted from the Calvert Women's Principles. The development of the Women's Empowerment Principles included an international multi-stakeholder consultation process, which began in March 2009 and culminated in a launch on International Women's Day in March 2010. The seven Principles are:

1. Establish high-level corporate leadership for gender equality
2. Treat all women and men fairly at work – respect and support human rights and nondiscrimination
3. Ensure the health, safety and well-being of all women and men workers
4. Promote education, training and professional development for women
5. Implement enterprise development, supply chain and marketing practices that empower women
6. Promote equality through community initiatives and advocacy
7. Measure and publicly report on progress to achieve gender equality.[15]

Women Empowerment in India

Economic empowerment is the capacity of women and men to participate in, contribute to and benefit from growth processes in ways which recognise the value of their contributions, respect their dignity and make it possible to negotiate a fairer distribution of the benefits of growth. Economic empowerment increases women's access to economic resources and opportunities including jobs, financial services, property and other productive assets, skills development and market information. Women's economic participation and empowerment are fundamental to strengthening women's rights and enabling women to have control over their lives and exert influence in. It is about creating just and equitable societies.

Women often face discrimination and persistent gender inequalities, with some women experiencing multiple discrimination and exclusion because of factors such as ethnicity or caste. The economic empowerment of women is a prerequisite for sustainable development, pro-poor growth and the achievement of all the millennium development Goals. Gender equality and empowered women are catalysts for multiplying development efforts. Investments in gender equality yield the highest returns of all development investments. Women usually invest a higher proportion of their earnings in their families and communities than men. A study in Brazil showed that the likelihood of a child's survival increased by 20 percent when the mother controlled household income.[16]

The subject of empowerment of women has becoming a burning issue all over the world including India since last few decades. Many agencies of United Nations in their reports have emphasised that gender issue is to be given utmost priority. It is held that women now cannot be asked to wait for any more for equality. The position and status of women all over the world has risen incredibly in the 20th century. It has been very low in 18th and 19th centuries in India and elsewhere when they were treated like 'objects' that can be bought and sold. For a long time women in India remained within the four walls of their household. Their dependence on men folk was total. A long struggle going back over a century has brought women the property rights, voting rights, equality in civil rights before the law in matters of marriage and employment.[17] The completion evaluation of the IFAD-supported Tamil Nadu Women's Development Project in India took place in late 1999. The project had aimed to bring about the social and economic betterment of women. The core mechanism was the women's self-help groups, which were set up with both financial (saving and lending) and community action objectives. At the time of the evaluation, a total of 5207 of these groups had been formed, almost double the established target. The evaluation noted that, at least in the latter phases, the project acted not as just "a credit-cum-subsidy project, but as a genuine process of empowerment." The evaluation concluded that such *empowerment lay in the interaction between the social and economic aspects of the project.*[18]

After Independence the Constitution of India guarantees equality to women by introducing (Article 14, 15 (1) and 16) which ensure rights of women that is no discrimination by the State, equality of opportunity etc. Not only the above mentioned Articles but also during the 73rd and 74th Amendments (1993) to the Constitution of India provided for reservation of seats (at least onethird) in the local bodies of Panchayati Raj Institutions and Municipalities for women. Another Constitutional Amendment (84th Constitutional Amendment Act, 1998) reserving 33 per cent seats in Parliament and State Legislatures is in the pipeline. But even after 66 years of our independence, women are still one of the most powerless and marginalized sections of Indian society.[19] Women's agency is an important constituent of women's empowerment. It can be said to be operative when results into a fundamental shift in perceptions, or inner transformation'so that women should be able to define self interest and choice, and consider themselves as not only able, but entitled to make choices.[20]

The United Nations Development Programme (UNDP) in India is committed to the promotion of gender equality and social, economic and political inclusion. The mandate is derived from the fact that inequality, based on wealth, region, ethnicity and gender is a fundamental concern for human development. Inherited disadvantage in opportunity due to gender, social group and location is wrong for intrinsic reasons as it violates basic principles of human rights. UNDP aims to advance social inclusion by promoting positive relationships among groups and individuals within communities so that all identify with, belong to, and are not isolated by stereotyping and labeling. Economic inclusion is ensured by creating sustainable livelihoods to reduce gaps in income that force people into poverty and political inclusion is promoted by ensuring that the structures and processes are in place so that everyone has a voice in the planning and decision-making that affects their quality of life.[21]

Empowerment for women in India requires a crosscutting approach and one which addresses the diversity of social structures that govern women's lives. Identity politics in India is a very critical political instrument, which is both used and abused throughout political and social institutions. There are numerous social movements fighting for the rights of the marginalised, such as the Dalit rights movement, the tribal rights movement, etc. These movements have achieved many gains in assuring representation of the traditionally marginalised communities into mainstream society. Women's rights within these movements are largely unarticulated and thus reinforce inequalities within the very structures from which they are demanding inclusion. Empowerment approaches for women is not only about providing services, but also about recognising their lived realities of multiple layers of discrimination that hinder their access to services.[22] Innovations to change social norms can be catalytic because women's empowerment requires the transformation of inequitable gender attitudes, behaviours and harmful practices, such as child marriage, female genital cutting as well as restrictions on women's mobility and their rights to education, health, work and civic participation.[23] India has ratified various international conventions and human rights instruments committing to secure equal rights of women. Key among them is the ratification of the Convention on Elimination of All Forms of Discrimination against Women (CEDAW) in 1993. India has ratified the convention with two declaratory statements and one reservation. Both the declarations relate to marriage.[24]

Women Empowerment through Education

Education as means of empowerment of women can bring about a positive attitudinal change. It is crucial for the socio-economic and political progress of India. The Constitution of India empowers the state to adopt affirmative measures for prompting ways and means to empower women. Education significantly makes difference in the lives of women. These can be direct or indirect. Education increases the economic, social and political opportunities available to women. It leads to direct economic benefits in the form of higher lifetime earnings for women. The society and community also benefit from the higher productivity of its labour force. Education increases womens knowledge about controlling fertility and access to family planning services and often encourages them to delay the age at which they marry. Education is important because literacy has become a tool of evaluating a person whether one can read or write. Illiteracy has become a very pejorative word in our society.[25]

In addition to education, employment can also be an important source of empowerment for women. Employment, particularly for cash and in the formal sector, can empower women by providing financial independence, alternative sources of social identity, and exposure to power structures independent of kin networks. Women education in India plays a very important role in the overall development of the country. It not only helps in the development of half of the human resources, but in improving the quality of life at home and outside. Educated women not only tend to promote education of their girl children, but also can provide better guidance to all their children. Moreover educated women can also help in the reduction of infant mortality rate and growth of the population.[26] Education is considered as a potent instrument through which processes modernisation and social change come to existence. Education exposes people to new thoughts and ideas and provides necessary skills.[27]

In recent decades, the Government of India has instituted some educational programmes such as the National Literacy Mission, and the Sarva Shiksha Abhiyan in an effort to combat the scourge of illiteracy in the country. The rate of illiteracy is particularly high in rural areas, especially among socially marginalised minorities, women and people from lower castes. Pursuant to the objectives of the NPE, 1986, the Mahila Samakhya Scheme was started in 1989 to translate the goals enshrined in the NPE into a concrete programme for the education and empowerment of women in rural areas particularly those from socially and economically marginalized groups. The MS scheme recognises the centrality of education in empowering women to achieve equality. The Mahila Sanghas or women's collectives at the village level provide the women a space to meet, reflect, ask questions and articulate their thoughts and needs and make informed choices. The ILO promotes women's economic empowerment and gender equality as key development goals – as asserted in international labour Conventions and by the Millennium Development Goals. There is also evidence that women's empowerment and gender equality can contribute to increased economic growth.

National Mission for Empowerment of Women

The National Mission for Empowerment of Women (NMEW) was launched by the Government of India on International Women's Day in 2010 with the aim to strengthen overall processes that promote all-round Development of Women. It has the mandate to strengthen the inter-sector convergence; facilitate the process of coordinating all the women's welfare and socio-economic development programmes across ministries and departments. The Mission aims to provide a single window service for all programmes run by the Government for Women under aegis of various Central Ministries. In light with its mandate, the Mission has been named Mission Poorna Shakti, implying a vision for holistic empowerment of Women. The National Resource Center for Women has been set up which functions as a national convergence center for all schemes and programmes for women. It acts as a central repository of knowledge, information, research and data on all gender related issues and is the main body servicing the National and State Mission Authority.[28]

Millennium Development Goals

Gender equality and women's empowerment are central to UNDP's strategy for achieving the Millennium Development Goals and bringing about transformational change. UNDP works to ensure that women have a real voice in governance institutions at all levels, that they have equal participation in public dialogue and influence the decisions that will determine the future of their families and communities. These strategies are integrated into UNDP's work on poverty reduction, HIV, democratic governance, crisis prevention and recovery, energy and environment to achieve sustainable human development.[29] Eliminating gender differences in access to education and educational attainment are key elements on the path to attaining gender equality and reducing the disempowerment of women. In recognition of the pivotal role of education in development and of persistent gender inequalities in access to education, the elimination of gender disparity in primary education is one of the Millennium Development Goals.[30]

The Millennium Development Goals are eight international development goals that were established following the Millennium Summit of the United Nations in 2000, following the adoption of the United Nations Millennium Declaration. All 189United Nations member states at the time (there are 193 currently) and at least 23international organisations committed to help achieve the following Millennium Development Goals by 2015:

(a) To eradicate extreme poverty and hunger;

(b) To achieve universal primary education;

(c) To promote gender equality and empower women;

(d) To reduce child mortality;

(e) To improve maternal health;

(f) To combat HIV/AIDS, malaria, and other diseases;

(g) To ensure environmental sustainability, and

(h) To develop a global partnership for development.

As of 2013 progress towards the goals was uneven. Some countries achieved many goals, while others were not on track to realise any. A UN conference in September 2010 reviewed progress and concluded with the adoption of a global plan to achieve the eight goals by their target date.

New commitments targeted women's and children's health and new initiatives in the worldwide battle against poverty, hunger and disease. The MDGs were developed out of several commitments set forth in the Millennium Declaration, signed in September 2000. Although there has been major advancements and improvements achieving some of the MDGs even before the deadline of 2015 the progress has been uneven between the countries. In 2012 the UN

Secretary-General established the "*UN System Task Team on the Post-2015 UN Development Agenda*", bringing together more than 60 UN agencies and international organisations to focus and work on sustainable development.[31]

National Policy for Empowerment of Women

The principle of gender equality is enshrined in the Indian Constitution in its Preamble, Fundamental Rights, Fundamental Duties and Directive Principles. The Constitution not only grants equality to women, but also empowers the State to adopt measures of positive discrimination in favour of women. India has also ratified various international conventions and human rights instruments committing to secure equal rights of women. Key among them is the ratification of the Convention on Elimination of All Forms of Discrimination against Women (CEDAW) in 1993. The goal of this Policy is to bring about the advancement, development and empowerment of women. The Policy will be widely disseminated so as to encourage active participation of all stakeholders for achieving its goals.

Specifically, the objectives of this Policy include: (i) Creating an environment through positive economic and social policies for full development of women to enable them to realise their full potential; (ii) The *de-jure* and *de-facto* enjoyment of all human rights and fundamental freedom by women on equal basis with men in all spheres – political, economic, social, cultural and civil; (iii) Equal access to participation and decision making of women in social, political and economic life of the nation; (iv) Equal access to women to health care, quality education at all levels, career and vocational guidance, employment, equal remuneration, occupational health and safety, social security and public office etc.; **(v)** Strengthening legal systems aimed at elimination of all forms of discrimination against women; (vi) Changing societal attitudes and community practices by active participation and involvement of both men and women; (vii) Mainstreaming a gender perspective in the development process; (viii) Elimination of discrimination and all forms of violence against women and the girl child; and (ix) Building and strengthening partnerships with civil society, particularly women's organisations.[32]

Protection of Women from Domestic Violence Act, 2005

The Protection of Women from Domestic Violence Act 2005 is an Act of the Parliament of India enacted to protect women from domestic violence. It was brought into force by the Indian government from October 26, 2006. The Act was passed by the Parliament in August 2005 and assented to by the President on 13 September 2005. Primarily meant to provide protection to the wife or female live-in partner from domestic violence at the hands of the husband or male live-in partner or his relatives, the law also extends its protection to women living in a household such as sisters, widows or mothers. Domestic violence under the act includes actual abuse or the threat of abuse whether physical, sexual, verbal, emotional or economic. The Act seeks to cover those women who are or have been in a relationship with the abuser where both parties have lived together in a shared household and are related by consanguinity, marriage or a relationship in the nature of marriage, or adoption; in addition relationship with family members living together as a joint family are also included. Even those women who are sisters, widows, mothers, single women, or living with the entitled to get legal protection under the proposed Act.

Domestic violence or domestic abuse typically occurs between people who are in an intimate relationship. Most often the abusers are husbands, ex-husbands, boyfriends or intimate partners. Domestic violence includes physical, emotional and sexual abuse. Both men and women can be victims of domestic abuse, but females are most often the victims. Domestic violence is one of the most common forms of violence and happens in most societies all over the world. A survey report that was taken showed on the inspection that most of the protection officers got the complaints of domestic violence which can take many forms and variations and can happen once in a while or all at the same time. Domestic violence can be Psychological Abuse, Social Abuse, Financial Abuse, Physical Assault or Sexual Assault. Violence can be criminal and includes physical assault or injury (hitting, beating, shoving, etc.), sexual abuse (forced sexual activity), or stalking. Sexual violence particularly needs to be recognised as a form of cruelty not only because of its high prevalence within marriage but also because the definition of rape within Sec 376 IPC specifically excludes marital rape as an offence. [33]

Compulsory Registration of Marriage Act, 2006

The Supreme Court of India has ordered the compulsory registration of all marriages in India, irrespective of the religion of the couple getting married. It has given states and union territories that have not yet enacted the rule, in accordance with its 2006 orders, a deadline of three months to frame rules to implement the compulsory registration. A Bench of Justices Arijit Pasayat and P Sathasivam passed the order on October 25, based on a petition filed by a divorced woman, Seema, seeking directions for making marriage registrations compulsory. The Bench reiterated that marriages should be compulsorily registered *"in respect of persons who are citizens of India, even if they belonged to various religions"*. The court directed the states and central government to notify the procedure for compulsory marriage registrations within three months. This can be done by amending the existing rules or by framing new ones. Objections from the public shall be invited for one month thereafter, the court said. When the Indian government enacts a comprehensive statute on the issue, it shall be placed before the apex court for its scrutiny, the Bench added. The age and marital status (unmarried, divorced, widowed) of the couples shall be clearly stated in the registration form, the court said. An officer appointed under the rules shall be authorised to register marriages and the consequences of non-registration of marriage or filing a false declaration shall be provided for in the rules, the Bench stated. The court agreed with the National Commission for Women that compulsory registration of marriages would help tackle various women's rights infringements such as child marriage, ensuring a minimum age in accordance with the law, marriage without the consent of both parties, bigamous unions, and a woman's right to live in her marital home and receive maintenance.

In India there are only four statutes for the compulsory registration of marriages — the Bombay Registration of Marriages Act, 1953 (applicable to Maharashtra and Gujarat), the Karnataka Marriages

(Registration and Miscellaneous Provisions) Act, 1976, the Himachal Pradesh Registration of Marriages Act, 1996, and the Andhra Pradesh Compulsory Registration of Marriages Act, 2002. In July 2007, the apex court clarified that the order was meant to cover all religions, after that though some states had framed rules in compliance with the court's 2006 order, they had done so only for Hindu marriages and not other religions. The apex court also noted that in five states, provisions exist for voluntary registration of Muslim marriages. These states are Assam, Bihar, West Bengal, Orissa and Meghalaya.[34]

The Rajya Sabha passed a bill to make registration of marriages, irrespective of religion, mandatory under the Registration of Births and Deaths Act, 1969, which currently only regulates registration of births and deaths. The amendment to the bill seeks to amend the Act to include the registration of marriages within its purview. The Registration of Births and Deaths (Amendment) Bill, 2012, which was passed by voice vote, defines marriage to include marriage solemnized between a male and female belonging to any caste or religion. It also includes re-marriage. Marriages already registered under the Anand Marriage Act, state laws or any other existing laws are not required to be registered under the Bill. The Supreme Court had rendered this judgment in 2006 that the law once passed in Parliament must be placed before the court for scrutiny. Noting that there were enormous benefits of registering marriages, the minister said people should not be penalized for not doing the registration. There is enough leeway in the Act and state governments are free to make rules. The Bill is not quasi-judicial power for determining whether marriages are valid or invalid, he said in response to the debate on the bill. The amendment bill will benefit women as the registration certificate would provide evidential value in matrimonial and maintenance cases and prevent unnecessary harassment meted out to them. It will also provide evidential value in matters of age of parties, custody of children and right of children born out of such marriages[35]

Sexual Harassment of Women at Workplace (Prevention, Prohibition and Redressal) Act, 2013

The Sexual Harassment of Women at Workplace (Prevention, Prohibition and Redressal) Act, 2013 is a legislative act in India that seeks to protect women from sexual harassment at their place of work. It was passed by the Lok Sabha (the lower house of the Indian Parliament) on 3 September 2012. It was passed by the Rajya Sabha (the upper house of the Indian Parliament) on 26 February 2013. The Bill got the assent of the President on 23 April 2013. The Act came into force from 9 December 2013. The Act uses a definition of sexual harassment which was laid down by the Supreme Court of India in Vishaka v. State of Rajasthan (1997). Article 19 (1) g of the Indian Constitution affirms the right of all citizens to be employed in any profession of their choosing or to practice their own trade or business. Vishaka v. State of Rajasthan established that actions resulting in a violation of one's rights to 'Gender Equality' and 'Life and Liberty' are in fact a violation of the victim's fundamental right under Article 19 (1) g. The case ruling establishes that sexual harassment violates a woman's rights in the workplace and is thus not just a matter of personal injury. The Bill was first introduced by women and child development minister Krishna Tirath in 2007 and approved by the Union Cabinet in January 2010. It was tabled in the Lok Sabha in December 2010 and referred to the Parliamentary Standing Committee on Human Resources Development. The committee's report was published on 30 November 2011.

The Criminal Law (Amendment) Act, 2013

The Criminal Law (Amendment) Act, 2013 is an Indian legislationpassed by the Lok Sabha on 19 March 2013, and by the Rajya Sabha on 21 March 2013, which provides for amendment of Indian Penal Code, Indian Evidence Act, and Code of Criminal Procedure, 1973 on laws related to sexual offences. This new Act has expressly recognised certain acts as offences which were dealt under related laws. These new offences like, acid attack, sexual harassment, voyeurism, stalking have been incorporated into the Indian Penal Code. Section 370 of Indian Penal Code (IPC) has been substituted with new sections, 370 and 370A which deal withtrafficking of person for exploitation. If a person (a) recruits, (b) transports, (c) harbours, (d) transfers, or (e) receives, a person, by using threats, or force, or coercion, or abduction, or fraud, or deception, or by abuse of power, or inducement for exploitation including prostitution, slavery, forced organ removal, etc. will be punished with imprisonment ranging from at least 7 years to imprisonment for the remainder of that person's natural life depending on the number or category of persons trafficked.

A new section, 376A has been added which states that if a person committing the offence of sexual assault, "inflicts an injury which causes the death of the person or causes the person to be in a persistent vegetative state, shall be punished with rigorous imprisonment for a term which shall not be less than twenty years, but which may extend to imprisonment for life, which shall mean the remainder of that person's natural life, or with death."

Certain changes has been introduced in the CrPC and Evidence Act, like the process of recording the statement of the victim has been made more victim friendly and easy but the two critical changes are: 1. the 'character of the victim' is now rendered totally irrelevant, and 2. there is now a presumption of 'no consent' in a case where sexual intercourse is proved and the victim states in the court that she did not consent.

Constrains for Women Empowerment

There are several constraints that check the process of women empowerment in India. Social norms and family structures in developing countries like India, manifests and perpetuate the subordinate status of women. One of such norms is the continuing preference for a son over the birth of a girl child, which is present in almost all societies and communities.

The hold of this preference has strengthened rather than weakened and its most glaring evidence is in the falling sex-ratio. The root cause of this type of attitude lies in the belief that male child inherits the clan in India with an exception in Meghalaya. Women often internalise the traditional concept of their role as natural, thus inflicting an injustice upon them. Poverty is the reality of life for the vast majority of women in India. It is another factor that poses challenge in realising women's empowerment. Indian women are facing some major constraints like lack of confidence, socio-cultural barriers, motivational factors, knowledge in Business Administration, awareness about the financial assistance, exposed to the training programs, identifying the available resources etc.[36]

Since women are much more likely to be constrained by marriage and child bearing and rearing than men. Among women, employment varies greatly by marital status. Women who are divorced, separated, deserted, or widowed are much more likely to be employed than currently married women; never married women are least likely to be employed. Women's employment is likely to be affected by residence, since agricultural work, which accounts for most employment in rural areas, is typically more compatible with women's other responsibilities as well as with low levels of education and skill development. Women who have no education are much more likely to be employed than women with education, irrespective of education level. However, it is notable that employment, after first declining with years of education, increases in every marital category for women with the highest level of education (12+ years). Employment declines sharply by wealth for women, irrespective of marital status.

Conclusion

Despite many international agreements affirming their human rights, women are still much more likely than men to be poor and illiterate. They usually have less access than men to medical care, property ownership, credit, training and employment. They are far less likely than men to be politically active and far more likely to be victims of domestic violence. Empowering women to participate fully in economic life across all sectors is essential to build stronger economies, achieve internationally agreed goals for development and sustainability, and improve the quality of life for women, men, families and communities. The private sector is a key partner in efforts to advance gender equality and empower women. Current research demonstrating that gender diversity helps businesses perform better signals that self-interest and common interest can come together. Women's empowerment is very essential for the development of society. Empowerment means individuals acquiring the power to think and act freely, exercises choice and fulfill their potential as full and equal members of society.

Empowerment for women in India requires a crosscutting approach and one which addresses the diversity of social structures that govern women's lives. Identity politics in India is a very critical political instrument, which is both used and abused throughout political and social institutions. There are numerous social movements fighting for the rights of the marginalised, such as the Dalit rights movement, the tribal rights movement, etc

References

1. M. Suguna, Education and women empowerment in India, *International Journal of Multidisciplinary Research,* Vol.1 Issue 8, December 2011, Retrieved from http://zenithresearch.org.in/images/stories/pdf/2011/Dec/zijmr/15_ VOL per cent 201_ ISSUE8_ ZEN. pdf
2. *Women Empowerment : A Challenge of 21st Century*, Retrieved from http://www.rmttc.com/images/new_pdf/concept_paper.pdf
3. Dr. Ravi N. Kadam, *Empowerment of Women in India- An Attempt to Fill the Gender Gap (June, 2012)*, Retrieved from http://www.ijsrp.org/research_paper_jun2012/ijsrp-June-2012-95.pdf
4. *Gender equality and empowerment of women: Policy document*, Retrieved from http://www.entwicklung.at/uploads/media/PD_Gender_Equality_19032010_Web.pdf
5. *Empowerment (2014),* Retrieved from http://en.wikipedia.org/wiki/Empowerment
6. Augusto Lopez-Claros, Women's Empowerment: Measuring the Global Gender Gap, Retrieved from http://www.weforum.org/pdf/Global_Competitiveness_Reports/Reports/gender_gap.pdf
7. *Women Empowerment in India – A Burning issues,* Retrieved from http://www.womenempowermentinindia.com/
8. *Gender equality and women's empowerment Policy*, Retrieved from http://www.ifad.org/gender/policy/gender_e.pdf
9. Dr. Shruti Singh, *Women Empowerment in Modern India*, Retrieved from http://www.themenplattform-ez.de/wp-content/uploads/2012/07/SSRN-id2361581.pdf

10. *Women's Empowerment Principles,* Retrieved from http://www.unwomen.org/en/partnerships/businesses-and-foundations/womens-empowerment-principles

11. Tulika Tripathi, *Women's Empowerment: Concept and Empirical Evidence from India,* Retrieved from http://www.cdedse.org/ws2011/papers/Tulika per cent20Tripathi.pdf

12. Dr. Dasarathi Bhuyan (2006), Empowerment of Indian Women: A Challenge of 21st Century, *Orissa Review*, Retrieved from http://odisha.gov.in/e-magazine/Orissareview/jan2006/engpdf/Empowerment_of_India.pdf

13. M. Suguna, Education and women empowerment in India, *International Journal of Multidisciplinary Research*, Vol.1 Issue 8, December 2011, Retrieved from http://zenithresearch.org.in/images/stories/pdf/2011/Dec/zijmr 15_ VOL per cent 201 _ISSUE8 _ZEN. pdf.

14. *Women's Empowerment Principles*, Retrieved from http://weprinciples.org/

15. See https://www.unglobalcompact.org/issues/human_rights/equality_means_business.html

16. *Women's economic empowerment*, Retrieved from http://www.oecd.org/development/povertyreduction/50157530.pdf

17. Puja Monda, *Essay on Women Empowerment in India.*

18. *India: Women's empowerment,* Retrieved from http://www.ifad.org/gender/learning/role/labour/in_tamil.htm

19. Dr. Shruti Singh, *Women Empowerment in Modern India*, Retrieved from http://www.themenplattform-ez.de/wp-content/uploads/2012/07/SSRN-id2361581.pdf

20. Tulika Tripathi, *Women's Empowerment: Concept and Empirical Evidence from India*, Retrieved from http://www.cdedse.org/ws2011/papers/Tulika per cent20Tripathi.pdf

21. See http://www.in.undp.org/content/india/en/home/ourwork/womenempowerment/in_depth/

22. Reecha Upadhyay, *Women's empowerment in India: An Analytical Overview,* Retrieved from http://asiafoundation.org/resources/pdfs/women sempower mentindiabriefs. pdf

23. Anju Malhotra Jennifer Schulte Payal Patel Patti Petesch, *Innovation for women empowerment and gender equality*, Retrieved from http://www.icrw.org/files/publications/Innovation-for-Womens-Empowerment.pdf

24. See http://www.aicte-india.org/downloads/woman_ empowerment.pdf

25. *The Concept and Profile of Women's Empowerment in India,* Retrieved from http://shodhganga.inflibnet.ac.in/bitstream/10603/8562/9/09_chapter per cent204.pdf

26. M. Suguna, Education and women empowerment in India, *International Journal of Multidisciplinary Research*, Vol.1 Issue 8, December 2011, Retrieved from http://zenithresearch.org.in/images/stories/pdf/2011/Dec/zijmr/15_ VOL per cent 201_ ISSUE8_ ZEN. pdf

27. Mukut Kr. Sonowal, *Impact of Education in Women Empowerment: A Case Study of SC and ST women of Sonitpur District, Assam,* Retrieved from http://caesjournals.org/spluploads/IJBASS-2013-008.pdf

28. *National Mission for Empowerment of Women*, Retrieved from http://www.nmew.gov.in/index.php

29. See http://www.in.undp.org/content/india/en/home/ourwork/womenempowerment/overview.html

30. *Gender Equality and Women's Empowerment in India,* Retrieved from http://dhsprogram.com/pubs/pdf/OD57/OD57.pdf

31. *Millennium Development Goals*, Retrieved from http://en.wikipedia.org/wiki/Millennium_Development_Goals

32. *National Policy for Empowerment of Women,* Retrieved from http://www.wcd.nic.in/empwomen.htm

33. See http://www.legallyindia.com/Blogs/Entry/domestic-violence-act-2005-a-boon-or-blight-to-the-society

34. *Compulsory marriage registration in 3 months: SC to states*, Retrieved from http://infochangeindia.org/women/news/compulsory-marriage-registration-in-3-months-sc-to-states.html

35. *The Time of India (Aug 14, 2013),* Marriage registration to become mandatory, Retrieved from http://times of india. india times. com/india/Marriage-registration-to-become-mandatory/articleshow/21814554.cms

36. Pankaj Kumar Baro & Rahul Sarania, *Employment and Educational Status: Challenges of Women Empowerment in India, Pratidhwani the Echo,* Retrieved from https://www.thecho.in/files/RAHUL-SARANIA.pdf

37. Read more at http://www.brainyquote.com/quotes/keywords/globalisation_5.html # I1Adsm 4 pYHcVjRGL.99

38. Mahila Samakhya, Retrieved from http://www.archive.india.gov.in/sectors/education/index.php?id=16

39. Women's social and economic empowermentand gender equality, Retrieved from http://www.ilo.org/wcmsp5/groups/public/—ed_norm/—relconf/documents/meetingdocument/wcms_164291.pdf

40. *Sexual Harassment of Women at Workplace (Prevention, Prohibition and Redressal) Act, 2013*, Retrieved from http://en.wikipedia.org/wiki/The_Sexual_Harassment_ of_ Women_ at_ Workplace_(Prevention,_Prohibition_and_Redressal)_Act,_2013

41. *The Criminal Law (Amendment) Act, 2013,* Retrieved from http://en.wikipedia.org/wiki/Criminal_Law_(Amendment)_Act,_2013.

14

Sustainable Landscape Management in Bangladesh

Prof Mohammed Ataur Rahman

"If the constitutional treaty is rejected it will be back to square one, just at a time when we want Europe to be a more effective force for good in the world, when we need to buttress ourselves against the pressures and insecurities of globalisation."

— Peter Mandelson

Introduction

Earth surface is not always smooth. Landscape is a large part of the land surface distinguished from others by specific features. According to the European Landscape Convention (ELC) 2007 Article 1 Landscape is an area, as perceived by people, whose character is the result of the action and interaction of natural and/or human factors. The term "landscape" is defined as a zone or area as perceived by local people or visitors, whose visual features and character are the result of the action of natural and/or cultural factors. Recognition is given to the fact that landscapes evolve through time and are the result natural and human activities. Landscape should be considered as a whole and natural and cultural components are taken together but not separately. Landscapes may be quite varied within a geographical zone. Landscape may be of two types: Natural and Man-made. However, at the present time, there are virtually no natural landscapes left: human activities leave their mark everywhere. Almost every landscape contains a village, city or other community, fields, land where trees have been cut down, roads, bridges, and many other features reflecting human activity (Astanin and Blagosklonov 1983). Often unwillingly, man instigates many considerable changes in the landscape. As we change the earth's appearance, we must not permit it to become ugly and we must preserve and manage the landscapes; this is as important as preserving monuments of history, architecture and the arts.

Landscape management is an integral part of natural conservation vis-à-vis proper land utilisation for production of food and other essentials managing the land resources like water, soil and biodiversity. Management of landscape requires collective ideas, compromising the need of existence of all, as well as, fulfillments of the needs of human being and long-term foresee ness to assess any detrimental effects by manmade activities directly or indirectly. Learning to measure how landscapes perform in delivering food, biodiversity and livelihood outcomes is anticipated to endow management systems with the capacity to sustain these multiple functions while reducing or reversing the degradation of natural resources. Landscape managers recognise producers of crops, livestock, fish and forest resources as stewards of ecosystems and biodiversity. Therefore, knowledge about designing and managing landscape is utmost essential to manage the natural resources and go forward with development. As the nature has its own laws and change is universal none can protect changing. But still it is true that human being is the supreme creation on the earth and all other creations are supporting the natural system for the betterment of human being.

There might be a lack of understanding or feelings of ill competitions for his existence or dominance, human being often plays biased activities with the natural resources. The quick manmade change of landscape is one of them. To secure the lives, livelihoods we need to manage natural systems wisely and logically it is essential to conserve and maintain the significant or characteristic features of a landscape, which is greatly valued on account of its distinctive natural or cultural configuration. Such protection must be active and involve management measures for preservation of significance. For framing proper planning, more particularly in those most affected by change and badly damaged areas like suburbs, peri-urban and industrial areas, floodplains and coastal areas, there needs a systematic study on overall changes due to steadfast increase of population and significant industrialisation during the last century.

Methodology

The work has been started in 2008 with a self-funded initiative to collect information from different sources like research publications, government and public research institutions, offices, books and journals, periodicals and also from the news media. Physical investigations were made visiting most of the country meeting people of different ages and categories. Photographic documentations were made in support of the observation studies. Many changes are also shared from the author's own experiences of his life time, different work places, and during the visits in different places of the country. Comparisons are also made by revisiting the site observation. Since, there are marked changes of landscape were found but not scientifically documented or studied as it was less understood or overlooked in the past, so little data is available. However, this comprehensive study was done with care and involving much labour giving utmost importance on its scientific needs.

Physiography and Landscape of Bangladesh

Bangladesh is a tropical monsoon country located between 20°34′ and 26°38′ North latitudes and 88°01′ and 92°41′ East longitudes. It is a part of the Ganges and Brahmaputra delta which lies to the south foothills of the eastern Himalayas; and west to the Arakan and Lusai folding ranges and in the south, the Bay of Bengal (Fig 1). Hundreds of rivers and tributaries from the upper north, northwest and eastern zones travel towards the Bay. There are few hillocks in the central zone of Bhawal and Madhupur, Lalmai and some high flats in the Barendra region. Besides these, there are scattered patches of hills and hillocks which are mainly the extensions of Himalayas and Lusai-Arakan ranges; but most of the rest areas are alluvial plains, flood plains, deep and shallow depressions or wet lands through which the rivers and streams are flowing.

Geologically, Bangladesh is a part of the Bengal Basin and its prominent tectonic elements are Indian platform, Bengal Foredeep, Arakan Yoma folded system, and the Sub-Himalayan Foredeep. Other features are Rangpur Saddle, Dinajpur slope, Hinge Zone, Barisal High and Troughs of Sylhet, Faridpur and Hatiya. The floor of the Bengal Basin consists of quaternary sediments deposited by the Ganges, the Brahmaputra and Meghna rivers, known together as the GBM river system, and their numerous tributaries and distributaries.

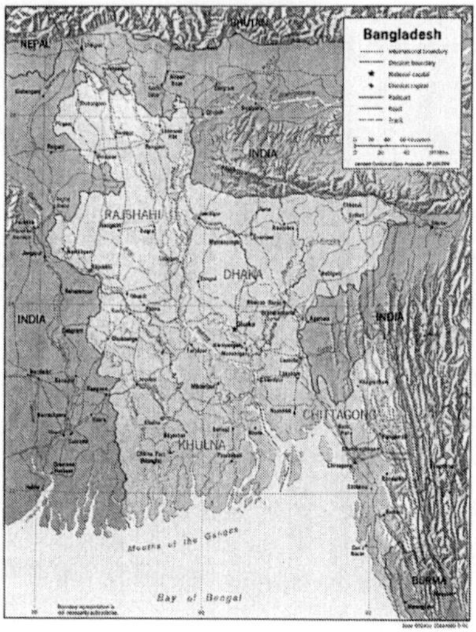

Fig. 1 Physical Sketes Map of Bangladesh: Source http:// en.wikipedia.org

The sediments are washed down from highlands on three sides of the basin, particularly from the Himalayas, where the slopes are steeper and the rocks less consolidated. Over 92 per cent of the annual runoff generated in the GBM catchment area flows through Bangladesh, although it comprises only about seven per cent of the total catchment (Coleman 1969). The physiography of Bangladesh can broadly be classified into three major forms:

1. **Hills** about 12 percent; occupy the Himalayans ranges, Chittagong hills and the low hills and hillocks of Sylhet and are derived from tertiary rocks and unconsolidated tertiary and Pleistocene sediments.
2. **Old alluvial** soils eight per cent; Madhupur and Barind tracts, formed on the old alluvium of the Pleistocene epoch, with reddish and brownish in color, lies in between Rajmahal and Tripura Hills (Rashid 1991).
3. **Recent alluvial** soils 80 per cent; are found in the Gangetic alluvium, Teesta silt, Brahmaputra alluvium and coastal saline tracts. The coastal saline tract is a part of the active flood plain, but subject to flooding with saline water at high tides. This tract includes the southern parts of the old Khulna, Barisal and Patuakhali districts and the islands and coastal areas of Noakhali and Chittagong regions.

A few large depressions, locally known as bheels, also called Haors are mainly found in Greater Mymensingh and Sylhet, besides these, Chalan in Greater Pabna and Rajshahi, Chanda bheel of Faridpur, Dakatia bheel of Khulna are important. Many bheels are actually ox-bow lakes of old river beds, but tectonic subsidence is also regarded as one of the causes of the origin of basin. The overall topography of Bangladesh is flat, with local relief ranging between one and two meters. At least 20 percent of the area of the country consists of low lying tidal plains, with elevations of less than 3 meters above sea level. Due to flat terrain, rivers have extremely low gradients e.g., 4-5 cm/km for the Ganges, 6-10 cm/km for the Brahmaputra and only 3 cm/km for the Meghna (Rashid and Pramanik 1990).

According to the landscape, different habitats are created for flora and fauna due to long run adaptation. The hilly eastern zones: Chittagong and Sylhet are mostly covered by mixed forest with deciduous and evergreen plants. These forests maintain the huge biodiversity with the forest dwelling characteristics of moving and survival in the undulated and steep hills. The diversified plants and animals are adaptable for searching water and food and having the unique behaviours of survival and regeneration. The featured examples are flying frogs, pitchers plants and orchids. Flying frogs can make their wet nests with plant leaves and lay eggs there; pitcher plants can catch insects and digest and the orchids ere epiphytes collects water and nutrients from the air. There are hundreds of examples of special adaptation according to habitats and these cannot survive outside these habitats.

Landscapes provide safety against adverse conditions like cyclones, storms, droughts and floods etc. Undulated surface keeps the natural systems moving and provides increased surface area. Nature has its own laws and change is universal; still human often governs the natural systems and their biased activities accelerated the changes including landscape. The hills of the north, northeast and southeastern region strongly limits the intensity of tropical cyclones; the mangroves of the Sundarbans protects the coastal zones and provides habitats for huge biodiversity vide; the central Madhupur and Bhawal Sal forests of Madhupur Tracts act as screening lung and the strong trees protect the central region from tornadoes and the Sal forests are usually termed as the lung of the Dhaka megacity. There are many trees viz. Palmyra palm, Fishtail palm, coconut and areca nut and bamboos are traditionally grown in the wind prone zone to protect the structures from cyclone and tornadoes. Traditionally the floodplains are maintained digging ponds and raising earth for homestead and protect the houses and plants and animals from floods. The wet bodies act as catchments holding excess surface water thus there is a nice natural and traditional defense mechanism has been established which is very helpful for developing a DRR policy (Rahman and Rahman 2013).

Traditionally Managed Landscapes

Although it has been referred in many books and articles that Bangladesh is a country with flat topography but it is not absolutely true. Besides the hills and the depressions the whole country along with the floodplain is gently undulated and a gradient has always been maintained towards the elevated zones upward and gently down towards the low-lying depressions like bheels, hoars and rivers. With the exception of some restricted khas land of the hills and hillocks, and water-bodies: rivers, hoars and lakes people used to manage the land for traditional farming by terracing making blocks along the slopes with Ails or raised boundaries to facilitate water holding and for demarcation of ownership of the land. In broader sense the flatlands are of two types, flood free high flats and flood prone lands occasionally gets inundated during the wet monsoon. However, in a specific locations a few terms are often used like: Bheeta, Tek, Bandh, Kanda (Kandi), Baied, Kuri, Duba, Bheel, Haor etc.

Before nineteenth century people used to made their homes in the flood free zones however, with the increasing population people started to use the flood prone of flood plains for habitation by managing the flood plains with simple technique raising some with earth area excavating large ponds and Dighies. These duel functional water-bodies used to serve the needs of water as well as fish-farming and the excavated earth for raising the homesteads above the flood level providing the scope for growing trees for food, timber and fuel etc. This unique multipurpose floodplain management is rare in any other regions of the world. Large ponds with area above one acre are termed as Dighi; above 10 acres is Sagor and smaller ponds of area less than an acre are called Pukur. A few examples are Khanjali Dighi, Deba, Raja Pukur, Durgasagar and many more etc. *(Wikipedia and Banglapedia)*. An area of 1,469 km^2 manmade ponds is in Bangladesh [22, 23] Akonda 1989 and Khan 1994]

Most of the ponds were excavated during nineteenth centuries and before. These ponds are used as fresh water sources for domestic purposes, bathing, swimming and fish production etc. (Rahman 2004). Ramsagar is the largest manmade water-body in Dinajpur. The huge pond was named after Raja Ramnath who excavated it to supply drinking water to the people living in the surrounding villages. It is said that there was a continuous drought and famine in this part of the country from 1750 to 1755 AD. About 1.5 millions labours worked for digging the Ramsagar and the total expense amounted is about 30,000 Taka. The water area of Ramsagar measures 1079 m along-south and 1926 m along east-west.

Approximate depth of the tank is 9.5 m. The tank is surrounded by 10.75 m high embankments. Beyond the embankment the surrounding is a large plain area having some undulating landscape (Banglapedia). It has been observed that, almost all of the ponds of Mymensingh city used get dry in the dry season with the lowering water level of the Brahmaputra river which lies in the north and east boundaries of the city. But the water level of large pond of Ananda Mohan College does not go down; after investigation it has been found that there are four deep ring wells in the mid zone those were made during the excavation of the pond in the then British period in 1920s. These wells were connected with the ground water table and thus helping to keep the water level of the pond up. These wells are also helping in recharging of the ground water.

In the coastal floodplains the houses are usually made on wooden platform on raised earth, excavating two or three ponds in each and every home. The flood plains were nicely conserved by digging deep ponds for multipurpose uses. Excavated earth used to meet the purpose of house building on raised landscape and the houses were designed to facing the south.

Traditionally many activities are adopted to control erosions of rivers and ponds. Bamboo clumps are established along the rivers and also homesteads to control erosion, as well as, to protect from the tornados especially the Nor'wester. Bananas are used to plant along the periphery of the newly excavated ponds to control erosion of the banks. Homesteads of the flood free or flood plains used to have a small forest groove and other vegetations for multipurpose uses for supplying foods, fruits, vegetables and spices; bamboos, timber and fuels; fence and hedges; medicinal plants dyes, oils and cosmetics and ornamental purposes etc.

These are primarily grown to fulfill the demand of plat products for household needs as well as shelterbelt for protection of structures from tornado, cyclonic storms, and erosion control and for shade. There are about two hundred plants species are of economic and environmental values are grown in a standard village home (Rahman 2004).

Reasons for Changing Landscape

Due to geographical position and tectonic movements like earthquake, folding, land sliding, erosion and sand deposition, the whole country possessed an undulating landscape maintaining a natural gradation from the high elevation to low-lying areas and ultimately to the Bay of Bengal. These undulations facilitate discharge and storage of surface and seepage water and adaptations of lives with special behaviours for different locations. However, as the change is universal gradual succession is also following with the changes. Some changes are very slow takes thousands of years; some are quick e.g. earthquakes, volcanic eruption, folding and land sliding etc. The biggest change in the recent past caused by the Assam earthquake (magnitude 7.5 Richter) on April 2, 1762, had changed the course of the Brahmaputra and opened Jamuna due to tectonic uplift of the Madhupur tract. The old Brahmaputra which was a mighty river passed through Jamalpur and Mymensingh and met Meghna near Bhairab Bazar but this river almost remains dry in most of the period except wet monsoon (Wikipedia).

However, there are some distinct manmade changes which have significant effects on the landscape. Human biased changes are of course for their interest, but it has been observed that many of these changes are not always behaving positively for the mankind as well as for the benefits of other lives. Some changes may have given short time benefit but in long run they become detrimental for the human itself. The most important examples are the Farakka barrage and Kaptai dam on the Ganges and the Karnafuly respectively. Farakka barrage diverted water from the Ganges to the Hooghly but the down-stream in Bangladesh have been seriously affected due to low water flow in the Padma resulted many distributaries drying up, salinity intrusion, declining mangroves and spawning anadromous fishes and reptiles (Satter 1996, Hebblethwaite 1997, Adel 2013). The Kaptai dam has caused permanent watershed in the hill catchments destroying a huge tropical rain forests (Ahmed 2008). As the changes are universal, there are always welcome but properly management of the changes is essential.

Two monsoon weathers viz. the northeast and southwest monsoons distinctly appear with a short dry winter and a long hot and wet season. During the wet monsoon, every year a huge quantity of sand and clayey minerals with organic materials comes down from the upper hilly areas through the streams and rivers. During the last two centuries a huge timber extraction and deforestation were done in the Eastern Himalayan zones of Assam, Meghalaya, Cachar and Sylhet for timber extraction as well as for cultivation of tea and some other plantation crops; the Arakan-Lushai and Chittaging Hill Tracts forests had also been exploited in the name of establishment of plantation forest with teak and some other fast growing exotic species like pines, eucalyptus and Acacias. Thus the world's famous Dipterocarpus zone starting from Arunachal to Chittagong had been destroyed and many wild animals and birds have lost their habitats and are rare (Rahman 2012).

The low lying areas usually are called bheels, haors, baors and lagoons etc. used to flood with water due to monsoon rain. The excess runoffs usually pass through the streams and rivers finally to the Bay of Bengal. As the most of the floodplains are very vulnerable to floods due to three to four days' continuous downpour, the main flat lands, mostly the agricultural land is very prone to serious damages of agricultural crops and livelihoods. Bheel and haors were calculated 239,977 ha in 1976 that represents 1.66 per cent of the total area of the country and an area of 10,750 ha has been decreased since 2010 (Hasan *et.al.* 2013). Before1965 AD, i.e. prior to Indo-Pak war the landscape of Bangladesh was very different that of the today's landscape. After the mass migration of Hindu population and quick development of road transportation system the major changes occurred. Moreover, Green Revolution added changing the landscape. The overall result is a quick change of landscape and loss of land area due to landfills of the big ponds, Dighis and water bodies. On the other hand, many homestead forests were cleared for extension of agricultural land (Rahman 2004, Dasgupta 2005).

During that period, HYV IRRI rice was introduced in Bangladesh. As the IRRI rice is irrigation and fertilizer dependent, water from the lagoons and the bheels was drawn for irrigation and the partially dried water bodies were used for paddy cultivation. For dry season irrigation, dams were constructed across the rivers and streams to use as water sources. Upstream dams made by the neighbouring country, India to pump out water from the major rivers the Ganges and Brahmaputra which resulted low water flow in dry season and spillage of excess water in the wet monsoon. Excess water of rainy season and the melted water of Himalayan glaciers flooded the river basins and raised the basins; silts fill the catchments, lagoons, bheels and haors etc. The water flow of Brahmaputra has been changed and the old Brahmaputra has lost its direction. The saline water of the Bay of Bengal entered further inside of the country up to Chandpur and Faridpur as the fresh water flow has been obstructed at the up streams. Subsoil water table has been declined due to introduction of deep tube well irrigation for high yielding cereal crop production (Zahid A. and Ahmad S.R.U. 2013)

Among the four types of forests and woodlands, the remnants of the hills and hillocks of Chittagong, Chittagong Hill Tracts Greater Sylhet and some parts of the northern districts: Greater Mymensingh and Dinajpur are seriously destroyed due to illegal logging, agricultural extension and replacement with exotic plants like Teak, Mulaccana, Acacia spp, Eucalyptus and some plantation crops like tea, rubber and oil palms and some fruit-crops e.g. pineapple, banana, guava and lemons etc. For monocroping with timber or other plantation crops, during clear felling, logging and transportation the hills were seriously eroded; many shade loving plants lost their habitat; deciduous teak and Gamar caused drying up of moist hills, water table declined and ultimately most of the perennial streams of the hills lost their flow and thus many wild animals also lost their habitat and rarely available or not exist at all now.

Sal Forests of Madhupur Terrace is in the central region, Lalmai of Comilla and some small forests of Dinajpur are vanishing due to urban, industrial and agricultural expansion. These Sal forests once were very rich with many flora and fauna. Some exotic species like Acacia, Eucalyptus and some plantation crops like, rubber and oil palms and some fruit-crops e.g. pineapple, banana, guava and lemons etc are being planted replacing Sal forests. But due to change of habitats the Bhawal and Madhupur forests has already been destroyed and many industries mainly garments and apparels, medicine, etc., institutes like universities, poly-techniques, administrative offices, agriculture research institutes, markets, tourists spots and different workshops has already replaced the huge and unique Sal forests although once it was considered as the lung of the Dhaka city. The Modhupur Terrace has the unique characteristics with red soil containing fine clayey silts, up to seventy feet deep but very little water holding capacity during the dry winter. Thus the root systems of Sal trees are superficial but with strong coppicing root network and the trees are deciduous. Trees are very strong and extremely durable and can withstand in strong winds of tropical cyclones and tornadoes. But they do not withstand in prolong water-logging and in stagnancy.

Plain-land Forests usually the homestead forests and some small woodlands and bamboo groves scattered through out the plains. Traditionally each and every rural home has a small forest grove with bamboos and many types of fruits and timber plants usually to fulfill the needs of timber, fuel-wood, fruits, palms and nuts and also to protect the homes from storms and cyclones. These homestead forests are usually established in the North and Northwest corner of the homes. Most of the homesteads of the flood-pains have the traditional homestead forests established on the raised land excavating large deep ponds in every rural home (Rahman 2004). These forests create a micro-climate with shade and habitats for wild animals as well as shade loving plants. These small forests also are the place for kucha latrine usually shifted one place to another after one or two years and the filled pits with the feaeces become a fertile place for growing tree crops and it is a unique wary of utilising human waste. Thus the rural homes were the unique example of short-cycled biomass and water recycling. But now-a-days the rural tradition are in the verge of extinction with so-called modernisation and the kuccha houses and latrines are being replaced with pacca brick-cement-concrete houses and losing the land as well as soil fertility.

These are usually the mangrove forests of Sundarban, coastal islands Chakuria Sundarban. A huge mangrove plantation project from Mirershari, Sitakund to Teknaf was undertaken but most of the plantations were destroyed by establishing ship breaking and shrimp farming projects. Although the great Sundarban Forest has been declared as a World Heritage Site but due to expansion of shrimp farming, agriculture and tourisms it is squeezing alarmingly. Due to creation of pockets in large areas of Sundarbans, the huge tropical cyclones of 2007 and 2009 the Sidr and Aila respectively gutted the coastal regions seriously. Moreover, illegal logging, hunting and poaching of wild animals the whole biodiversity of Sundarban is under a great threat. Moreover, unplanned thick plantations along the coastal embankments with Acacias and Rain-trees acted as protecting shield rather than windbreaks which increased the wind-speed of the tropical cyclones like Sidr-2007 and Aila-2009 while passed the huge cyclonic wind through the narrow pockets like rivers or weak zones and seriously impacted by killing lives and damaging infrastructures of inner coastal regions (Rahman 2013).

Impacts of Landscape Change

The change of landscape due to above reasons has definitely caused serious impacts on: Habitat and land area; Navigation system; Climate; Agriculture; Rural infrastructure; Migration; Loss of Biodiversity, and Socioeconomic condition. Due to rapid industrialisation and urbanisation a massive change of landscape has been observed after the independence in 1971. The rural infrastructures and economy had been collapsed during the famine of 1973 and 1974 due to flood and economic restriction from the USA and Arab countries. The most affected areas were northern districts e.g. Rangpur, Dinajpur, Bogra, Jamalpur, Mymensigh and Dhaka. Many people migrated to the cities and townships for work. Some were also migrated to the Chittagong Hill Tracts (CHT) where they took shelter there they maintained their livelihoods by extracting forest resources. Moreover, they introduced flat land agricultural practices changing the hilly tropical forest landscapes in many areas of CHT.

After 1975, unplanned canal digging program for irrigation and flood control has affected the landscape, badly. Nevertheless, new homes for the increased population and extension of cities and townships, and industrial expansion in the suburbs have also changed the landscape significantly. More interestingly, many high areas of Dhaka like Uttarkhan, Kurmitola, and Uttara etc. once were flood free zones, but as the new buildings are constructed and the catchments and lagoons are being filled up and the water flow to the main rivers have mostly been obstructed. The drainage system is so poor that even the hundred years old trees are dying due to continuous stagnancy of surface water. The whole scenario is very alarming. People are constructing buildings with raised floor and the roads are become waterways in the monsoon. Many roads get damaged during flying of vehicles in water-logged conditions and the areas are getting worst every year. The similar situation has been observed in most of the townships of Bangladesh.

Detailed Study and Description of Impacts of Landscape Changes

Habitat and Land Area

Deforestation

According to the landscape phytogeographical regions were formed after thousands of years' adaptation and succession. These were: North and Northeast tropical mixed forest region; Eastern Hill Tracts Tropical Mixed Forest region; Sal Forests of Bhawal, Modhupur, Dinajpur and Lalmai regions; Mangrove or Littoral Forests region; Swamp Forests regions; Wet land or Aquatic region; Flood Plains and flatlands; and Flood free and Homestead regions. The vegetations of the regions have specialised characteristics for their individual habitats. However, within a region there may be different sub-zones where plants grow with their own habit. The hills have high and low water-table zones. Many plants serve as pulling agent to keep water table up. The wild banana (*Musa paradisica*), bamboos, zingibers, canes, arums and ferns are important species holding the water tables up and this water is the main source of flow of the perennial streams and springs. Many water perennial water bodies are still exist on the high hills of Chittagong Hill Tracts e.g. Debotar Pukur and Boga Lake of Bandarban.

Specific characters and requirements are more important for their survival. There is a close interdependency between the flora and fauna of a region in prevailing climatic conditions both for seasonal and periodic. For example, from a humid climax forest if the tall trees are removed, the underlying high humid flora viz. ferns, arums and cannas will gradually abolished likewise, the tree climbing dwellers especially the apes and primates e.g. baboon and monkeys and tree frogs will also leave that region. Due to human interventions, most of the forests of the east and northeastern regions have lost tall forest trees due to illicit extraction and also for replacement plantations or cultivation with different crops e.g. pineapple, tea, rubber, arums, lemons, etc. In many cases, tillage, terracing, monocrop cultural practices and pesticidal uses of chemicals etc. are being followed which have caused excessive erosion, loss of humus, low humidity due to less transpiration, land sliding, and loss of biodiversity. Many perennial streams are now flow less in the dry season i.e. from November to April.

On the other hand, most of the catchments are brought under paddy cultivation and the basins are being raised for extension of land of the foothills. Often dams are made across the streams and rivers to facilitate irrigation. Obstruction of such natural flow causes change of dry weather flora and diverted the streams and continuous siltation has raised the catchments basins. Some of the upstream dams and embankments often burst during heavy rainfall and cause serious damages to the crops, structures and lives (Khalequzzaman 2012). Plants those are habituated with dry weather root elongation system have also suffered in the blockage condition of stagnant water due to the dams and embankments.

A large dam was made in Kaptai for hydroelectric power generation which created a huge water body in the catchments of the Chittagong Hill Tracts disturbing the natural beauty of the hill forests. The erosion, land sliding, and squeezing of foothills by extending the flatland agriculture and obstruction of natural water flows reduces the great landmass area. It is really a great loss for the nation and of course for natural habitat. CEGIS (2008) reported that 156,780 ha land was lost due to erosion along the Jamuna, Ganges and Padma rivers during the period 1973-2008. About 15 km sea beach of Cox's Bazar is at high risk of erosion, especially the Shrimp hatchery, Himchari, Kalatoli, Motel and Hotel zone, Diabetic Hospital areas etc. The one half of the village, Kolatoli has already been lost to the sea due to erosion as the unplanned discharge of water to the sea from 55 nos. shrimp hatcheries. (The Daily Ajker Deshbidesh October 16, 2008).

Navigation system

The rivers of Bangladesh mark both the physiography of the nation and the life of the people. About 700 in number, these rivers generally flow south. The larger rivers serve as the main source of water for cultivation and as the principal arteries of commercial transportation. Rivers also provide fish, an important source of protein. Flooding of the rivers during the monsoon season causes enormous hardship and hinders development, but fresh deposits of rich silt replenish the fertile but overworked soil. The rivers also drain excess monsoon rainfall into the Bay of Bengal. Thus, the great river system is at the same time the country's principal resource and of course for easy transportation.

The profusion of rivers can be divided into five major networks. The Jamuna-Brahmaputra is 292 kilometers long and extends from northern Bangladesh to its confluence with the Padma. Originating as the Yarlung Zangbo Jiang in China's Xizang Autonomous Region (Tibet) and flowing through India's state of Arunachal Pradesh, where it becomes known as the Brahmaputra, it receives waters from five major tributaries that total some 740 kilometers in length. At the point where the Brahmaputra meets the Tista River in Bangladesh, it becomes known as the Jamuna. The Jamuna is notorious for its shifting sub-channels and for the formation of fertile silt islands (*chars*). No permanent settlements can exist along its banks. The second system is the Padma-Ganges, which is divided into two sections: a 258-kilometer segment, the Ganges, which extends from the western border with India to its confluence with the Jamuna some 72 kilometers west of Dhaka, and a 126-kilometer segment, the Padma, which runs from the Ganges-Jamuna confluence to where it joins the Meghna River at Chandpur. The Padma-Ganges is the central part of a deltaic river system with hundreds of rivers and streams-some 2,100 kilometers in length flowing generally east or west into the Padma.

The third network is the Surma-Meghna system, which courses from the northeastern border with India to Chandpur, where it joins the Padma. The Surma-Meghna, at 669 kilometers by itself the longest river in Bangladesh, is formed by the union of six lesser rivers. Below the city of Kalipur it is known as the Meghna. When the Padma and Meghna join together, they form the fourth river system—the Padma-Meghna—which flows 145 kilometers to the Bay of Bengal. This mighty network of four river systems flowing through the Bangladesh Plain drains an area of some 1.5 million square kilometers. The numerous channels of the Padma-Meghna, its distributaries, and smaller parallel rivers that flow into the Bay of Bengal are referred to as the Mouths of the Ganges. Like the Jamuna, the Padma-Meghna and other estuaries on the Bay of Bengal are also known for their many *chars*. A fifth river system, unconnected to the other four, is the Karnaphuli. Flowing through the region of Chittagong and the Chittagong Hills, it cuts across the hills and runs rapidly downhill to the west and southwest and then to the sea. The Feni, Karnaphuli, Sangu, and Matamuhari—an aggregate of some 420 kilometers-are the main rivers in the region. The port of Chittagong is situated on the banks of the Karnaphuli. The Karnaphuli Reservoir and Karnaphuli Dam are located in this area. The dam impounds the Karnaphuli River's waters in the reservoir for the generation of hydroelectric power.

During the annual monsoon period, the rivers of Bangladesh flow at about 140,000 cubic meters per second, but during the dry period they diminish to 7,000 cubic meters per second. Because water is so vital to agriculture, more than 60 per cent of the net arable land, some 9.1 million hectares, is cultivated in the rainy season despite the possibility of severe flooding, and nearly 40 per cent of the land is cultivated during the dry winter months. Water resources development has responded to this dual water regime by providing flood protection, drainage to prevent over-flooding and water-logging, and irrigation facilities for the expansion of winter cultivation. Major water control projects have been developed by the national government to provide irrigation, flood control, drainage facilities, aids to river navigation and road construction, and hydroelectric power. But, interestingly no initiatives have been taken to improve the navigation system of the country.

Before 1960, most of the rivers were used for navigation for transportation. Shamvuganj, Barmi, Bhairab, Narayanganj, Chandpur, Dewanganj, were famous for rice and jute business where the goods were transported by river routes throughout the year. The sustainable transportation by sailing boats was eco-friendly and less costly. But today the old Brahmaputra, Narsunda, Kachamatia, Kangsha, Mogha Rivers, etc. remain dry except for a few months of the wet monsoon. In many rivers, permanent settlement with houses and villages are established in the chars. Due to withdrawal of water from upstream of the Padma (the Ganges), Brahmaputra and Tista, Gomti, Titas and Kushiara etc. by the neighboring country, the mighty rivers become dry and flow-less or run with a very little water flow in the dry winter. The navigation system during the dry season is mostly affected.

Due to low water flow, the river basins and the chars are cultivated; irrigation is being done making dams and Ails (raised surroundings) which again help further obstruction of water flow during the wet season. This causes heavy siltation and thus helps rising of river beds, which again disrupts the navigation system. However, due to abnormal behaviour with the earth, the earthquake caused some changes of the landscape, Narsunda, Gopla and Kalankini rivers lost their flows due the depressions and raising of river basins in the early nineteenth century. Over the last two decades, Bangladesh has used coastal afforestation and polderisation to stabilise and protect newly accreted lands from tidal and storm surges. Polders are mainly designed to provide protection against tidal intrusion with the main objective of increasing agricultural production; however, they also provide protection against floods and storm surges. A sudden increase in the construction of embankments took place after 1960. The initiative, called the Coastal Embankment

Project (CEP), involved the construction of some 5,107 km of embankments to form 123 polders and protect an area of 1.5 million hectares. It has been estimated that 957 km are sea dykes.

Sea dykes are perceived to provide protection against storm surges and anticipated sea-level rises due to climate change. Drainage in these polders is provided at low tide by means of flap gates mounted in sluice structures, usually located where natural drainage channels (Khals) cross the embankment alignments. The objective to increase agricultural productivity was achieved with great success for the first 10 to 15 years, until drainage congestion became serious in some areas, thus necessitating an integrated approach (Ali 2002). As a result, the Coastal Embankment Rehabilitation Project started to incorporate elements of internal water management, land-use inside the polder, and social use of the embankment and foreshore. Despite criticisms over drainage problems, the polders have resulted in higher agricultural returns by excluding saline tidal flooding. Communications have also been improved. Polderisation has contributed considerably to alter and new land-use in coastal Bangladesh. This institutional structure was operational during 2002–2006 and contributed to the preparatory operationalization of ICZM in Bangladesh (Islam 2006b).

However, the poldered projects of the coastal region in the saline zone represent the detrimental effects of present-day flood control and drainage (FCD) system. Since the land is not graded, most of the low-lying areas inside many poldered projects have been turned into waterlogged areas though there were numerous controlled structures for flood control and drainage. The channels outside and inside the compartments get silted up gradually. Moreover, the outfalls and inlets are also choked up due to rapid sedimentation and water-logging creeping gradually to other elevated areas. As a result, human activity creates an irreversible change in the hydrological regime of the channels.

Climate

Although direct relation with the climate and landscape is yet to be documented but the change of landscape reduces the depth of water bodies but spreads over a large area in the wet monsoon.

However, in the dry season water bodies dry up quickly and the temperature of this region falls sharply which increased the maximum and minimum temperature of hot and cold seasons. It affects the overall climatic conditions and a reason for changing the vegetation. It is true that the deep water bodies reflect less heat to the atmosphere. Deep rivers, Bheels, Dighis, ponds and lakes are helpful for cooling effect of atmosphere. On the contrary, shallow water bodies spreading in wider area, gets heated very quickly and emits temperature to the atmosphere especially in the summer and autumn. It has been observed that, in the August and September fishes die in shallow water bodies in the sunny days. Sometimes, water temperature exceeds 55°C and emits heat to the atmosphere, which is another reason for global warming. Therefore, deep water bodies are to be restored immediately by landscape management, which will also help in conservation of surface water table.

Agriculture

Agriculture is one of the worst sufferers of changed landscape of Bangladesh. The frequent floods during the wet monsoon and severe drought in the dry season are causing huge crop loss of the country. As the temporary water reservoirs e.g. Bheels, Hours, lakes, ponds are being filled or the basins are being raised by siltation the water holding capacity of these reservoirs have been decreased and floods become a common factor every year. The natural water flows and outlets of the catchments viz. stream, rivers and tributaries have also been obstructed by dams, roads and highways the quick discharge of water delays and most of the agricultural crops get damaged.

The floods of 1974, 1984, 1987, 1988, 1999, 2000, 2002, 2003, 2004, 2005, 2006, 2007 and 2008 are the common examples. The flood of 1988 during August-September inundated 89,000 sq. km. areas of 52 districts of the country and caused loss of 1517 human lives and in 1998 flood with unprecedented duration of 65 days inundated 53 districts covering about 100,000 km² area and it took lives of 918 people. But the fact is flood becomes a common occurrence which has been causing agricultural loss of hundreds of million tons of crops. Drought is another severe natural phenomenon which at some intervals visits Bangladesh and causes disastrous crop failures. In 1979, the country was hit by a severe drought, which was termed by many as the worst in the recent past (Nawaz and Shah 2011). As the surface water holding capacity has drastically been decreased due to changes of landscape, a continuous rainless period of about two to three months causes serious damages to many crops. Mere dependency on irrigation can not solve the problem any more.

Crop selection has now become a difficult task for the farmers. Due to introduction of high yielding varieties many of the food and drought resistant crops have already been lost on the other hand creepers and climber vegetables of the monsoon can not withstand in floods. Irrigation dependent cropping system in the dry weather season had been introduced in mid-sixties of the last century with high yielding IRRI rice and wheat. The consequences of this system are: land leveling, terracing, drains and canals for maintaining gradation for irrigated water flow by disturbing the landscape and natural undulations. Due to deep tube well irrigation, the subsoil water table has been receded and there arises a great crisis of surface water. Not only this, withdrawal of arsenic contaminated subsoil water by the deep tube wells, causing severe threat to lives, as well as, agriculture.

Due to extension and development of the cities, hundreds of houses are being constructed every year. Most of the lagoons and Jheels have been brought under housing in Dhaka city. The rivers around the city are also squeezed and discharge of water has become difficult. As a result many of the areas flooded even after one to two hours' heavy rainfall. Actually land filling is done by dredging sands from the rivers and also collecting earth from the city adjacent areas destroying the undulating hills of the north and from the agricultural soil of the surroundings. The agricultural and forest land have been reducing every year. The same situation has been observed in other cities and townships. Moreover, the most important construction material the bricks are made burning clayey soil mixing with cement and sand. There are hundreds of such brick fields which are producing millions of bricks every year. The brick fields are also a reason for changing landscape and for deduction of agricultural lands of the country.

Rural Infrastructure

Due to changes of the landscapes, the infrastructure of the rural areas has been changed dramatically. Repeated floods, cyclones, storms and droughts affect the rural economy. Damages of crops and lives and changes of cropping system as a whole and destroyed the rural infrastructures. Repeated and prolong flooding situation, the houses especially the mud wall, bamboo and straw thatched houses are being collapsed. The poor villagers used to suffer for food, drinking water and for shelter. Domestic animals viz. cows, goats, chickens, dogs and cats etc. die for food and shelter. Stored foods and feeds, seeds, clothing etc. get deteriorated; transportation and communication systems have also been collapsed. Field crops like paddy, vegetables, seedling stocks and spices are also affected. Millions of hungry people cry for food and shelter every year. As the rural economy is agriculture-based, and most of the people live in floodplains, landscape management is a vital point for rural infrastructure. Therefore, a proper management is utmost essential to preserve the rural infrastructures.

Migration

Since, the rural economy has been collapsed; thousands of hungry people migrate to the cities for works i.e. for food and shelter. The uncertainty of crop production due to flood and drought, the dependency on high input dependent cropping culture the marginal farmers suffer more. Most of the land is grabbed by the rich who has turned the cultural practices more mechanised; as a result, a huge manpower becomes workless. The gap between the poor and rich is widening day by day and more people have become landless. This caused illiteracy, poverty and sickness and the scenery is really very pathetic. The youths and the child labours are being gathered in the townships during the last three to four decades. Some youths have managed to migrate to the Middle East, Malaysia and western countries for work opportunities. The child labourers are being engaged for domestic helps, garment, furniture and lather industries. Many more are still workless and street beggars. Human trafficking to the Middle East and western countries are still going on. In many cases the migrant workers are being cheated by dishonest human traffickers. However, this migration has often created labor crisis for agriculture in the rural areas.

Loss of Biodiversity

Bangladesh is a transitional zone of flora and fauna, because of its geographical settings and climatic characteristics. It was very rich in aquatic, terrestrial and amphibians and anadromous flora and fauna. Both flora and fauna are threatened by the loss of habitats resulting from increasing human population (SoE Report 2001). Moreover, its monsoon climate has four distinct seasons and phases of land. The seasons are Wet monsoon, Post wet monsoon, Dry monsoon and Pre-wet monsoon. With these phases biodiversity and their adaptation vary significantly.

Table: Landscape, Biodiversity and Adaptation of some important crops.

Crops	Landscape	Adaptation
Rice: Aus	Uplands/Charlands	***Cropping period:*** pre-monsoon-wet-monsoon, drought resistant, grows with rising temperature, seeds do not require soaking prior to sowing in the dry soil, film water is sufficient for germination and initial growth; with the increasing temperature and rainfall grows well, flowers at long days in June and harvesting time is July, ripens well in the rainy days.
Rice: Jhumia	Hills/Hillocks	***Cropping period:*** pre-monsoon to wet monsoon, grows well in the marginal soil of the hill slopes where no standing water, usually mixed cropping with chili, sesame, rosella, maize and creeper and climber plants like cucumber, gourds etc. Most of the Jhumia are sticky. Ripen with the increasing rainfall.

(cont...)

Rice: Amon	Flood Plains	Cropping period: wet monsoon to post-wet monsoon; needs water soaking for germination, transplants in wet soil with standing water, vegetative growth needs high temperature and humidity; flowering starts in the short-day usually October and ripens in November. Late season rainfall hampers crop production with poor pollination, and ripening delays.
Rice: Boro	Lowlying catchments/ Wetlands	Cropping period: Dry monsoon to pre-wet monsoon, Fully water dependent and can not tolerate dry stress, continuous irrigation is essential, low temperature and humidity usually do not hamper growth. With the rising temperature it ripens in April. Hail stone and glacier melted river floods cause damage of the crop.
Jute	Uplands and flood free plains	Cropping period: Pre-monsoon to wet-monsoon crop, seeds do not require soaking usually sown in March and early April, dry stress tolerant but early heavy rainfall and hail stone are detrimental to growth and can not tolerate water logging. But in the increasing monsoon rainfall in July water-logging do not effect the growth and maturation of jute as special adaptation with adventitious root system helps growth. Harvesting time is usually August to early September, needs water for rottening and high intensity sun light requires for drying jute. Therefore optimal seasonal condition according to adaptation is highly essential. Plants are deep rooted.
Sugarcane	Uplands and flood free plains	Cropping period: pre-monsoon to late post monsoon or early dry monsoon; Long vegetative period. March is the best time for planting, ramming is required to prevent moisture loss in the initial stage. Early heavy rainfall and water logging is detrimental, but with the increasing temperature and rainfall

(cont...)

		grows quickly in May and June, then during the wet monsoon it can tolerate temporary water logging with adventitious roots from the nodes. Again heavy rainfall in the post wet monsoon and cyclonic storm cause damage to crop. Sucrose accumulation increased with the recession of monsoon rainfall and the peak achieves in late October to December.
Maize	Uplands and flood free plains	Cropping period: Late February and March to May and June; No seed soaking is required, grows well with increasing temperature and occasional rainfall. Dry stress tolerant and adapted to high temperature. Adventitious roots support growth.
Corms/yams	Uplands	Cropping period: March to September; some yams are harvested in the following season, do not withstand in water-logging condition, high temperature, rainfall and humidity helps better growth and yield.
Arums/Taro	Uplands/Flood plains	Cropping period: March to August/ September; some arums are harvested in the following season, can withstand in water-logging condition, high temperature, rainfall and humidity helps better growth and yield. Stem, stolons and bulb and leaf and leaf-sheaths are edible. Very good crop for wet season and a good calorie food.
Rhizomes: Ginger and Turmeric	Uplands	Cropping period: Ginger: April to October/ November and y turmeric in the dry winter; both do not withstand in water-logging condition; high temperature, rainfall and humidity helps better growth and yield. Turmeric is partial shade loving; earthing up required in July.
Country beans	Uplands and flood free plains	Cropping period: Late May and June to October up to March even in the following year if proper pruning is done in the late March. It has a long vegetative period over

(cont...)

		the wet monsoon. Can not tolerate water logging, therefore, in the homesteads they are grown on the earth-mound usually made with the dry soil-boulders collecting from the clayey loam field. These traditional mounds are coated with fresh cow-dung to protect from erosion. The inter-boulder space breaks the capillary action and thus prevents the country beans from water logging during the heavy monsoon rainfall. The climber country beans are traditionally supported with bamboo tops with branches for vertical spreading of the climber with maximum surface area for more inflorescence. The stem does not have any tendrils but can rotate anticlockwise around the support.
Cucumber	Uplands and flood free plains	Cropping period: May and June to July up to November. Can not tolerate water logging, therefore, in the homesteads they are grown on the earth-mound usually made with the dry soil-boulders collecting from the clayey loam field. These traditional mounds are coated with fresh cow-dung to protect from erosion. The inter-boulder space breaks the capillary action and thus prevents the country beans from water logging during the heavy monsoon rainfall. Traditionally vertical support is preferred, but horizontal trellis is also used. The stem possesses tendrils which help in climbing.
Pumpkin	Uplands and flood free plains	Cropping period: Late February and March to June and July September to April. Creeps over ground, horizontal trellis and also on the roof of the thatch house. The stem possesses tendrils which help in climbing. During creeping over the ground tendril used convert into adventitious roots and obtain water and nutrients from the ground.

(cont...)

Gourds: Snake gourd, Bitter gourd, Sponge gourd and Ridge gourd etc	Uplands and flood free plains	Cropping period: May and June to July up to November. Can not tolerate water logging, therefore, in the homesteads they are grown on the earth-mound usually made with the dry soil-boulders collecting from the clayey loam field. These traditional mounds are coated with fresh cow-dung to protect from erosion. The inter-boulder space breaks the capillary action and thus prevents the country beans from water logging during the heavy monsoon rainfall. Traditionally vertical support is preferred, but horizontal trellis is also used. The stem possesses tendrils which help in climbing.
Lathyrus,	Flood plains	Cropping period: Post wet-monsoon-Pre-wet-monsoon: sown in September and harvests in Pre-wet-monsoon in March and April; water soaked seeds are sown at the recession of monsoon rainfall usually as a mixed crop in the Amon rice fields. After the harvesting of rice the remaining straws support the creeper Lathyrus to grow well, spreads quickly in the early winter with the due and fogs. Flowers and the pods ripen in the early pre-wet monsoon in March. As a legume crop, it improves the soil fertility and adds biomass. Some tendrils of the compound leaf end help holding the supports for creeping and climbing.
Mung beans, Black grams	Uplands	Cropping period: Sown in September and harvest in November/December. No water-soaking of seeds; Leguminous increase soil fertility by nitrogen fixation; creeps freely or with the support of rice straws.
Sweet potato	Upland/ Clarland	Cropping period: stolon cuttings are planted in the sandy loam soil in late September; grow well especially along the riverside char-lands; harvests in Pre-wet monsoon. Does not require watering and the potato has very good storage capacity and good for transportation. In the uplands this creepers grow all over the year and their leaves are very nutritious and are used for curry.

(cont...)

Mustard	Floodplains/ Uplands	Cropping period: usually seeds are sown in Pre-monsoon October and November after single plough; does not like rain and can not tolerate water logging; besides the oil seeds, thinned out plants, leaves and flowers are used for delicious curry preparation. Plants are deep rooted
Onion/Garlic	Floodplains/ Uplands	Cropping period: Sown in the post monsoon October and November and harvests in the pre-monsoon time usually in the March and April. Green leaves and flowers are used for curry in the winter.
Radish	Upland/Flood free plains	Cropping period: Sown in the post monsoon October and November and the swollen root crops are usually harvested in the dry winter and early pre-monsoon time. However, the leaf vegetables are harvested immediately two to three weeks after germination. Low or no watering is required. Plants are deep rooted
Ground nuts	Charlands	Cropping period: Sown in the post monsoon October and November and harvests in the dry winter and early pre-monsoon time. Special behavior flowering above the ground and after pollination, the ovary or pod enters into the ground, the sandy soil. Plants are deep rooted
Millets/ Pannisetum	Uplands	Cropping period: sown at the end of February, drought resistant, no need for watering; with sporadic rainfall and increasing temperature grow well. Small grains. Harvests in April.
Sesame	Uplands	Cropping period: Two types: Long Day Plants are sown in the end of February and March and harvest in May and the Short Day Plants Sown in September and October and harvest in November and December, drought resistant, Attract honey bees, a very good barrier crop. Plants are deep rooted.

(cont...)

Tea	Hills/Valleys	Cropping period: Perennial deep rooted trees, kept as bushes after pruning. Rhizosphere is more than one meter humus rich sandy loam. Usually triple store Partial shade loving and grows well under high humidity and rainfall. Does not like high intensity light of the autumn i.e. of post monsoon for that reason needs shade trees. Water logging is harmful.

Therefore, every season has distinct crops with specialised characteristics. It is evident that, the soil microflora also varies season to season and thus a unique biodiversity with adaptation with landscape has been prevailing here. Many fishes e.g. Koi (*Anabas testudineus)*, Magur (*Clarias gariepinus*), Taki (*Channa punctata*), Shol move against the water current during pre-wet monsoon, but in Post wet monsoon they move along the water current. Some fishes have only three months' life in wet monsoon but their laid eggs hatches in the next wet monsoon. The landscape "Bayed" is unique place for such fishes.

Due to change of landscape the vegetation has been changed in most of the areas. Natural Forest area squeezed from 17 per cent to six percent. Rural homestead forests have also been reduced to a great extent, as a result, the primary habitat for biodiversity affected badly. Many species and varieties of plants and animals have lost their habitat, food and shelter which have caused a huge loss of biodiversity. Human's biased cultural practices patronised to extend high yielding crops neglecting the less yielding or valuable ones without considering their indirect benefit for the natural environment.

Irrigation dependent cropping culture has almost destroyed the dry season crops. Moreover, changes of landscapes have also changed the eco-niches. As a result, the pest and diseases are more; indiscriminate use of chemical pesticides has affected the microbes, insects, annelids, amphibians, reptiles and birds etc. Most of the beneficial insects like bees, flies and ants which directly help pollination become rare and many crops are affected.

Excess uses of fertilizers and pesticides have also affected the nitrogen, sulfur and phosphorus fixing organisms, mycorrhiza (root-fungal symbionts) and aquatic plants and animals.

Socio-Economic Condition

Quick change of landscape due to human activities; unplanned development of road transformation, industrialisation and urbanisation, expansion of agricultural land, introduction of unsustainable cultural practices, destruction of hills and water bodies, deforestation and neglects of navigation etc., as whole affected the socio-economic system and the rural economy and infrastructure have been collapsed. Although many economists are trying to introduce formula for improvement of mass poor population but in fact they have neglected the natural laws, as a result, a tiny portion of the population has made their fortune but the economic condition of the rest, further deteriorated.

People have lost their social bindings, respects and relationships. Many are underfed and deprived from education and health service. The numbers of needy people or street baggers have abnormally been increased.

Extra input dependant agriculture, seed technology and mechanised system etc. have taken away the marginal farmers from the field. Only the rich and the middlemen are harnessing the benefits. The gap between rich and poor is widening further day by day. Of course Bangladesh is one of the most densely populated countries; per capita land is very low, still then land use is very poor as the landscape management was not maintained properly.

From the high rising building of Dhaka city it is very difficult to realise the sufferings of common and marginal farmers who are the innocent victim of poor landscape management for which they are facing so many problems.

The whole economy has become donation and aid dependent. However, in the name of sustainable management, a huge amount of aid money has been mishandled by so called experts and environmentalists; only writing project reports, doing workshops and seminars and highlighting the problems but not for their solution. Some of such organisations are now economic boom and operating commercial institutes in the name of helping the poor.

Landscape Management

The present situation has become a multi-directional and multidimensional problem with manifold crises like food, shelter and energy etc.; the basic needs of mass population. It is really difficult to get out from the octopus of the rich. But nature has its own laws; we have to work from the individual, family members, zonal and regional community towards the awareness and for an effective solution. For managing the landscape, the primary functions are: Preservation of natural undulations and topography; Protection against further disturbances of the landscapes; Identification of the causes of detrimental changes and effective measures to reduce them; Appropriate agricultural practices; Protection of existing water bodies and excavation of large and deep water bodies; Protection and conservation of woodlands and homestead forests; Control of top soil erosion; To minimise irrigation dependent cropping culture; Shelterbelts with appropriate plant species; Proper planning for urbanization; and Development of navigation system.

Preservation of Natural Undulations and to Pography

To manage the landscape the primary task is to protect the natural undulations and topography. It is a great advantage that our hilly regions are in high rainfall areas and they were rich with natural forests. The Chittagong Hill Tracts, Chittagong, Sylhet, and Northern areas of greater Mymensingh and Dinajpur have an average rainfall of 2000 mm. Most of the rainfall (about 80 per cent) occurs in the wet monsoon i.e. from June to August. So, during this season, the top soil should be protected by reestablishing forests with indigenous species. The catchments should also be protected to hold the runoff. For immediate protection, bamboo should be planted in the open and erosion prone areas.

Other mixed sun loving forest trees e.g. Black Siris, Dipterocarpus, Bohera, Amloki, Haritoki, Nageshwar, Agar, Jackfruits and citruses etc. should be established in open and sunny uplands. Canes and Murtas can be planted in partially shaded and wet areas. They are also very helpful for preventing erosion.

After establishing the primary flora, the secondary ones i.e. the partially shade loving plants should be established. Chapalish, Gamari, Toon or Rangi, Kao, Pitraj and Awal etc. are the ideal species for secondary plantations. Under-storey plants like wild banana, Cana, Cyperus, Screw pine (Keya), arums and ferns etc. are to be allowed to grow which will help top soil protection. The Sal forests of Bhawal, Madhupur, Lalmai and Dinajpur should be protected. They are mostly deciduous forests and rich with diversified flora and very important for soil and water conservation.

Protection against Further Disturbances of the Landscapes

Prior to any further change of landscape, scientific study for long term effects on the environment should be done. At any cost natural undulations should be maintained for greater interest of the mankind. It is the natural laws through which many adaptations are being made to acclimatise with the prevailing climatic and environmental conditions. Everything for the well-beings of the lives on the earth and human being is the ultimate beneficiary. The accumulative and vice versa cooperation and recycling of earth's ingredients are the nature's phenomenon of continuation of lives on earth. Therefore, every species has the right to survive on the earth and to contribute to the natural cycles.

The hill forests are the beauties of nature and an inclusive part of ecosystem. Although most of the hill forests are indiscriminately exploited, the remaining must be protected and to be allowed them for regeneration. Planned afforestation with indigenous species will certainly create a habitat for animals as well. Some forest plants and bamboos have good capacity to protect top soil erosion, land sliding and they can also rejuvenate the land by increasing porosity. During construction of bridges across the rivers, the quantity of water of the highest rainfall should be brought under consideration and after keeping sufficient water discharge capacity, the bridges are to be constructed. For discharging excess water, there should be additional water discharging bridges on both the flood plains of either side, to be constructed. Although river erosion is a very common factor but this can easily be minimised. The most important factor behind the erosion of rivers in the downfall areas is obstructions of natural flows, particularly of the central mainstream. In such cases, dredging is essential and it should be done when the water current remains the highest, and should be started from the down stream and of course, in the central mainstream.

Identification of the Causes of Detrimental Changes and Effective Measures to reduce them

Among the important causes of landscape changes, human disturbances are most significant. Deforestation, unplanned urbanization, agricultural and industrial extension, construction of roads and highways, obstruction of natural flows, raising of catchments' basins, cutting of hills and hillocks, dams and embankments for water storage for irrigation and hydroelectric power generation, changes of agricultural practices, etc. are described earlier. Mining, disposal of wastes from the cities and townships for earth filling and earth cutting for filling the water bodies or to raise low lying areas are also important factors.

Therefore, proper care should be taken to taken and long term planning should be made for any development work. Management of landscape should always get priority.

Deforestation

Forests are of course the primary sources of building materials, fuel wood, foods and medicines; rational exploitation and regeneration of forest resources should be given utmost importance. Care should be taken to maintain the under storey and herbaceous flora. These are essential for soil and water conservation and keeping the forests cool and humid.

Most of the wild animals, including earth dwellers find their habitat and thus maintain a unique biodiversity. Watersheds are important for aquatic flora and fauna. An eco-niche is created among the terrestrial and aquatic lives. These are also important for keeping the springs and perennial water flows alive throughout the year. Clear felling must not be done in our tropical climax natural forests. Once these forests are cleared, it is difficult to get back the high water tables and many species loss their habitat.

Unplanned Urbanization

As the rural economy and infrastructure have been collapsed people are gathered to the cities and townships for better lives. Urban population is increasing at an alarming rate. For their shelter, the cities are expanding. Since most of the cities and townships do not have master plan, people used to construct houses as per availability and capacity of land and money respectively. They seldom bother for wider roads, drainage system and waste disposal facilities. Moreover, low lying areas and catchments are being used for building construction for houses and industries after land filling. In the same way, the hills are also being cut for residential and industrial construction purposes. There is significant increase in urban and industrial areas in the country and form 1976 to 2000 it has expanded 47,495 ha and from 2000 to 2010 the increment was 87,616 ha (Hasan *et.al.* 2013).

A huge accumulation of sand gravels and concrete in the urban construction and mega-structure, the current demand is around 18 million tons a year (Kabir 2013) and for each ton of cement, the building industry needs about six to seven times additional tons of sand and gravels (USGS, 2013b). Furthermore, the volume being extracted is having a major impact on rivers, deltas and coastal and marine ecosystems, results in loss of land through river or coastal erosion, lowering of the water table and decreases in the amount of sediment supply. Extraction has an impact on biodiversity, water turbidity, water table levels and landscape and on climate through carbon dioxide emissions from transportation. Despite the colossal quantities of sand and gravel being used, our increasing dependence on them and the significant impact that their extraction has on the environment, this issue has been mostly ignored by policy makers and remains largely unknown by the general public (GEAS 2013).

Moreover, disposal of wastes is a great concern for blockage of drainage system and also for health. This is not only creating problems for heath and drainage system but huge recycleable materials are being lost every day. The poor or narrow water discharge system creating water logging situation in many parts of the cities and townships. Wet season water table is getting up and many plants are dying due to continuous water logging. Roads are inundated and get deteriorated which is caused life miserable for the city dwellers, especially in the wet season. To overcome the situation, at least 100 years' master plan is required for every city. The master plan should have sufficient water discharge facilities, large water reservoirs or lagoons, waste disposal or recycling facilities, wider sewerage system, urban forest parks and recreation facilities etc. For all constructions, plantations and transportations systems etc. there should have safety rules and regulations. Immediate measures should be taken for awareness the various problems for safe and healthy urban life.

Agricultural and Industrial Extension

Agricultural and industrial extension is often changing the landscape. Flat land agricultural practices are done by leveling the undulated lands, by land filling the water bodies especially the reservoirs e.g. Dighies, ponds and lagoons etc. These cultures should immediately be stopped. Rather large deep reservoirs are to be excavated. These reservoirs are essential for mitigating the water crisis of the dry season and also for holding excess water of the wet reason to reduce the incidences of floods.

Construction of Roads and Highways

Construction of roads and highways should be made very carefully that, under no circumstances landscape is disturbed. However, the newly constructed highway and railway line from Gazipur to Sirajganj across the low lying floodplains of Bhuapur, Tangail and Gazipur by controlling the Dhaleswary which has already been lost its dry season flow. Sufficient water discharge outlets should be kept for flowing excess rain or upstream waters through the flood plains. In the flood plains and riverine areas eco-friendly transportation system using wind and water current should get preference. However, roads and highways are essential for quick transportation so after a thorough survey of landscape, elevation and quantity of precipitation roads and bridges are to be planned.

Obstruction of Natural Flows

The detrimental effects of obstruction of natural flows are described earlier. Many dams and embankments were made in the up streams but most of them are vulnerable to burst now, there it is strictly recommended not construct any dams for any reason on the up streams. The dams are to be inspected regularly and appropriate measures should be taken to protect them. Obstruction of natural flows often diverts the streams and rivers, causes loss of new areas. Sometimes, river beds rise due to siltation.

Rising of Catchments' Basins

Many basins of the catchments have been raised due to poor foreseeness of human beings. As a result, many aquatic flora and fauna are being lost. Care should be taken against filling of catchments especially by land filling and dumping of garbage in the catchments.

Cutting of Hills and Hillocks

Cutting of hill and hillocks for industrial establishment in Chittagong is causing a great land area loss and exposure of the rocky stratums. Some folded ranges in Cox's Bazaar are being cut for residential accommodation. Moreover, digging hard rocks of the coast line of Cox's Bazaar has been dug for shrimp culture which will long run effect the coastal belt vulnerable to sea current erosion. Hill cutting may cause land sliding, fault during earth quake. Earth cutting is also being done in the gas fields but it is a dangerous activity.

Excellent landscapes are to be found on sea shores, where many spas and recreation zones are located. The places where wide clean sea beaches are located near green coastal forests and shrubbery are of particular value. Beaches are important part of resorts, and it is a shame when they are destroyed due to negligence in human economic activities. The wearing away of the shore by the surf is a continuous process is a continuous process, but it assumes threatening proportions and requires protective measures only when man interferes unwisely. The building constructed after destroying the plates/ stratums of the folding ranges and the discharges of water from the shrimp projects are destroying the wonderful fine-grained beach. This destruction will move the shore line to inland and wash away large amounts of land mass. The cost of restoring what had been destroyed and recreating the beaches is incomparably higher than the profits obtained from shrimp cultivation and tourism.

Beaches are needed not only for recreation. They are the best natural defenses against the shore being washed away by the sea waves. Now, the unregulated earth cutting and water disposal from the beaches and under water coastal slopes should be banned immediately. Dams and embankments are for water storage for irrigation and hydroelectric power generation. In last half a century cascades of hydroelectric power plants have been built with reservoirs after constructing large dams all over the world. Considerable amount of water have been accumulated in the reservoirs. These reservoirs help solve energy problem, irrigate agricultural land, improve water transport, water supply to the cities and townships, improve fisheries and form the basis of recreation and tourist zones. But there are many negative aspects e.g. inundation of large area at the upper zone reducing potential agricultural production of forest area

Changes of Agricultural Practices

After the Green Revolution and with the advancement of hybridization technology many agricultural practices have been changed. Many crops are nonresponsive to photoperiods and can be grown throughout the year after climatic manipulation. Thus the genetic diversity is reducing day by day, as a result, plants are becoming more dependent of manipulated nursing rather than natural and seasonal adaptation.

Appropriate Agricultural Practices

To manage the landscapes appropriate agricultural practices can play a vital role. Many experts opined that without disturbing the landscape it is impossible to feed the huge population but the opinion is still controversial. Kerala of India, a unique example which is very much successful without changing landscape for agriculture. They are using every square meter of land with highest productivity in the world. Simply they are following the right cultural practices planting right plant at right place. Crop never dictates the land there but the crops are chosen according to their habit and habitat. They are also adopting multiple and multi-tier cropping culture. We need to switch back to our crop rotation cultivation practices with cereals, legumes, millets, sugarcane and seasonal and dry season crops. Mixed cropping with barrier crops, utilisation of water bodies with water tolerant rice, fish, mollusks and other aquatic plants and animal culture etc. should immediately be adopted. Irrigation depended cropping culture must be reduced.

Protection of existing water bodies and excavation of large and deep water bodies

Surface water bodies play a very critical role in water conservation, agriculture and household water uses. As water is indispensable material of lives its uses should be respected. Crisis of fresh water will create unfavourable condition of living. Water maintains gradation and always moves towards lower level. High water tables of the upper regions help flow of water to lower region. The main sources of water are the rainfall and melting glaciers and some precipitations in the form of dew and fog. Water from these sources absorb by the soil excess comes down as run off to the catchments and other reservoirs then overflows to the further down to the lakes and then to the sea.

In the undulated plains the reservoirs are the ultimate ready sources of water. The vegetations, crops and rural and urban lives get water from those sources. If these sources are destroyed, the whole ecosystem will suffer especially in the dry season. Hundreds of such deep (minimum five meter from the ground level) ponds and Dighies were excavated in this region earlier in the eighteenth and nineteenth centuries. The best examples are the Ramsagaor of Dinajpur, Dighies of Natore, Mymesingh, Gouripur, Kishoreganj,

Feni and Chittagong, and in many Jaminder Baries throughout the country. Except some char and hills, every rural home had a pond till the mid-sixties of twentieth century. These excavated Dighies and ponds were utilised for fish and aquaculture and of course for drinking, bathing and household uses.

Evaporation from these sources keeps the weather cool and humid. The surface water bodies also help keeping the subsoil water table up. However, now-a-days ponds have been excavated for fish and shrimp cultures in many areas of Mymensigh, Khulna and Chittagong. But these are very shallow (only 1.5 to 2.0 meter deep) which have very little effect in conservation of water and for drinking and household uses. As earlier mentioned shallow water bodies have a negative effect in cooling the atmosphere. Moreover, in the coastal areas excavated shallow water bodies for shrimp culture increase salinity. So, it is strictly recommended that ponds and Dighies must be deep (not less than 5 meter) for conserving and utilisation of surface water for day to day uses. The dug earth will also help for raising landscape with increased surface area.

Protection and Conservation of Woodlands and Homestead Forests

Supplying food, feed, fuel and fibre to 9 billion people in 2050, without depleting the earth's natural resources is a critical challenge for the coming years. Increasingly, farmers, extracting industries, tourists' facilities and expanding populations have competing claims on scarce land and water resources. Many areas in the world are progressively threatened by issues such as water shortages, soil depletion, climate change, and poverty and food insecurity. These issues are often interrelated. In many threatened areas the public and private organisations- be it NGO's, governments, farmers or companies - do not share information, nor work effectively together to manage the natural resources under stress (IDH Report).

It is essential to protect and conserve the existing woodlands and homestead forest. These are good sources of biodiversity especially for the benefit of cropping culture. Most of the pollinating agents e.g. insects bees, butterflies, birds find their safe habitat. Many mammals, reptiles and amphibians viz. wild cats, rabbits, lemurs, jackals, mongoose, rodents, porcupines, bats, snakes, lizards, tortoises, frogs and earthworms etc. create good eco-cycles in these small but biologically and ecologically rich habitats. They help direct or indirectly to the natural environment and crop production. Homestead forests are highly productive as the short-cycle recycling of biomass is easier. Moreover, all members' participation can be ensured there. Not only these, traditional knowledge for utilisation of the resources are still available. Rural people know what to grow where and how to use them. Some of the ethnic societies like the Monipuris are still maintaining their traditional practices for their livelihoods and also for Medicare with herbal plants and also use animal extracts for curing diseases. These homestead forests keep the environment cool, work as wind breaks to protect from strong winds, storms and cyclones. These vegetations also protect erosion as they are usually designed for that purpose.

Control of Topsoil Erosion

To control topsoil erosion of the hills and undulated lands effective measures should be taken immediately. The following measures are suggested to control topsoil erosion: Avoid clearing vegetation of the top hills especially of the high rainfall regions of Sylhet and Chittagong, Chittagong Hill Tracts. For cultivation of plantation crops e.g. tea, rubber, timber, fruits etc., weed suppression measures can be taken by adopting slashing and mulching techniques. No herbicidal application is recommended in the hills. Natural bamboos of top hills must be persevered. Natural bamboos, wild bananas, canes wild turmeric, ferns etc. can hold the soil and keep the water table up. They are also important for preserving birds, reptiles and rodents. Crops viz. tea, rubber must not be planted on the step hills with more than 57 per cent. Terracing and boxing methods can be followed for plantation. Windbreaks, shelter belts and hedge plantations should be raised. Terraces should be of 1 meter to 1.5 meter wide along the contour with 20 per cent inward slope and must not be continuous. All terraces should be discontinued after every 10 to 12 meters leaving a small bund of about one meter.

Drainage practices are not recommended on the hills. Sometimes drainage practices make the hills more vulnerable to land sliding especially where the depth of rhizosphere is shallow and water table is high. Plantation should be done along the contour following quincunx planting method. This facilitates holding of soil and reduces the speed of runoff. To control runoff speed of the gullies, hard-rock palettes or stones or concrete slabs should be placed in the pits. All tillage cultivation practices on the hills should be banned. Plants or crops those do not allow undergrowth or underlying vegetation should not be preferred in the hilly zones.

To Minimise Irrigation Dependent Cropping Culture

Irrigation is one of the important cultural practices of modern agriculture. Early Egyptian and Mesopotamians adopted irrigation and cultivated the Nile and Tigris and Euphrates basins and turned desert into cropping lands by managing the landscape. However, in our condition, irrigation can also help to improve crop production but management of landscape is more important. For landscape management, it requires short- and long-term planning. Earlier, in Bangladesh irrigation was done for Boro rice cultivation utilising the water from the natural reservoirs like Bheels and Haors etc., without obstructing the natural flows like stream and rivers.

But today dams and embankments are being made across the rivers and streams to store water in the upstream and water is being used for irrigation to grow more food especially the high yielding IRRI rice and other vegetable crops. For storage of water in the upstream, sometimes permanent dams are often constructed which obstruct natural flows, increase siltation, changes the flora and fauna and soil ecosystem. Gradual siltation raises the basin and creates impediments to the soil. Moreover, most of the dams and embankments are very vulnerable to washout during heavy and continuous rainfall which often causes huge damage and loss of lives, structures and crops in the down streams. Use of subsoil water by deep tube well drilling is another bad practice of modern agriculture. Due to pulling out of subsoil water, the water table often gets down below and there creates drying up of surface water bodies like ponds, dighies, rivers and canals etc. This again makes the lives miserable due to shortage of water for daily uses. Moreover, Arsenic contaminated subsoil water creating serious health hazards to human and animals.

The other impacts are loss of biodiversity especially the huge drought tolerant crop varieties. The Aus, millets, sorghums and many pulses are rarely cultivated now. These are being replaced with HYV IRRI and some hybrid vegetable crops. These irrigation dependent crops are usually very prone to pest and diseases and extra input dependent. Need huge chemical fertilizers and pesticides and thus tertiary problems arise i.e. the effect of indiscriminate use of chemicals to soil, water, air and lives including microbes. Therefore, conventional irrigation practices in our tropical monsoon area should immediately be controlled; otherwise, the ongoing biological systems will collapse.

Shelterbelts with Appropriate Plant Species

As Bangladesh enjoys two distinct monsoon weathers: Southwest and Northeast monsoons, during the transitional weather conditions low pressure depressions create in the Bay of Bengal which turn into cyclonic storms and cause serious damages of lives and structures. Moreover, localised cyclones due to heating up of the terrestrial areas damage structures, lives and crops. Bangladesh has also long coastal belts (740 km) in the south and western face of greater Chittagong. Tidal upsurge with high speed often inundated the coastal areas, damage structures, lives and crops, especially during the transitional monsoon cyclonic storms.

To protect local, coastal and regional areas from storms, cyclones, torrnadoes and tidal upsurges it is essential to reduce the wind speeds by planting appropriate tree species those can withstand in the high speed wind and break the wind speeds. Naturally grown halophytic plants e.g. Sundri (*Heritiera minor*), Geoa (*Excoecaria agallocha*), Goran (*Ceriops sp.*), Kankra (*Bruguiera gymnorhiza*), Khamo (*Rhizophora mucronata*), Baen (*Avicennia officinalis*), Keora (*Sonneratia apetala*) and Kulsi (*Aegiceros majus*) etc. have the special adaptation for withstanding in the Littoral zones with clayey alluvial soil, tides and strong salinity and winds. There are several palm species e.g. Golpata (*Nipa fruticans*), Hital (*Phoenix paludosa*), Coconut (*Cocos nucifera*) and cane (*Calamus tenuis*) and some swamp elephant grasses (*Typha angustata* and *T. elephantiana*), *Alpinia allughas* and screw pine (*Pandanus facicularis*) etc. have the soil binding capacity and control erosion. They also reduce the speed of tidal upsurges. Moreover they maintain a gradual hierarchy and reduce the speed of the strong winds. Most of the palms can withstand at a speed more than 250 km/hour. They can easily break strong wind flow and reduce the speed.

Selection of species is a very important task to manage the landscape especially in the Littoral zones where high water table persists most of period. High water table do not allow root penetration at sufficient depth of the earth. Therefore, shallow rooted mesophytic plants suffer from strong winds of cyclones and tornadoes. On the contrary, palms viz. coconut, areca nut, fishtail palm and Palmyra and date palms should be preferred in those areas. However, to maintain a functional and productive plantation other mesophytic species like Jam (*Syzyzium jambos*), Jhau (*Casuarina equisetifolia*), Gab (*Diospyros peregrina*), Dephol (*Garcinia mangostana*) etc. should be planted in a large scale. Moreover, shallow rooted trees must not be planted near the structural buildings, bridges and roads and highways but keeping a safe distance of 15 to 20 meter according to the height of the canopy.

Proper Planning for Urbanisation

Urbanisation is an inevitable process which occurs because of various factors. The rapid industrial development speeded up the process. At present about 35 million people live in the urban areas of Bangladesh; if the growth rate of urban population remains the same then by 2020 this population will be more than 120 million of total population 200 million of the country. This situation is really a great concern to the nation. Increased population need more space for housing and the agricultural land will squeeze further.

Scientific and technological progress and the urbanisation process raise the level of cultural and daily services for the population, the comfort of housing, and general prosperity. The urban way of life has many advantages, and they are preferred by many people. But urbanisation also involved many serious shortcomings, above all air pollution and deterioration of the climate. The principal sources of air pollution in the cities are industry and motor transport. Polluted city is more opaque, reduces solar energy, and sometimes caused poisonous gas to occur. The hurried way of life and constant nervous tension, the stress experienced by the inhabitants of big cities, combined with little physical exertion, polluted air and the long time spent indoors have caused an increased in nervous, heart, lungs, liver, metabolism, and other diseases.

The basic shortcomings of life in cities have to do with deficiencies in man's biological environment. Efforts are therefore being made to reduce pollution and make the elements of nature in cities as close as possible to the natural environment. The main factor here is the planting of greenery. Greenery plays a major role in cities. Trees and shrubs trap as much as 72 per cent of the suspended dust and up to 60 per cent of the sulfur dioxide. They regulate air temperature and humidity, enrich the air with oxygen, and emit phytoncides killing microorganisms. In the hottest weather, the air temperature among green plants is 4 to 8°C lower than among buildings. Plants help man to fight noise in the cities. Tree foliage absorbs up to 26 per cent of the sonic energy which falls on it. A Street lined with trees is five times quieter than one without trees. Experts estimate that for an optimal urban life there must be about 50 m^2 of greenery per person and another 300 m^2 in recreational forest zone. Plants not only create a favorable microclimate in the city and improve the sanitary condition of the air, but are also an important part of the urban landscape. Plants have beneficial effect upon man's nervous system. The whole range of the colors in nature reduces nervous tension, soothes negative emotions and contributes to positive ones. That is why the most serious attention should be given to protecting and increasing greenery in cities.

Plants have many functions to fill: they must fight noise, dust, harmful gases, excessive solar radiation and humidity. They must be decorative and improve the architectural and aesthetic appearance of the city, and, most importantly, form a favorable microclimate. The largest mass of greenery in a city is the city park. The size of the parks ranges from 100 to 1000 hectares. Large cities have several central and local parks. City parks should be viewed as ecosystems capable of existing and developing with some help from man. Wild flowering and fruit plants should be raised and the biocenoses are to be strengthened with increased variety of trees and shrubs (Astanin and Blagosklonov 1983). All industrial enterprises should have purification plants or effluent treatment plant (ETP). Greenery should be established between the factories and the industrial areas.

Houses are to be built at a certain distance from each other, so that the sunlight and air can reach the lower as well as the upper storeys. The plan should be based on socio-economic principle, which of the regulation of territorial development and population size to create a healthy environment and maximum facilities for the population. Large cities with population more than one million should have a multiple structure instead of the traditional single centre. Up to a million people will live in each zone. Within each zone, there should be a relative balance between manpower and jobs, and the population must have all the necessary facilities. People can thus be able to work, live and relax within each zone. This will dramatically reduce transport flows, and save a tremendous amount of social time enabling the working people to devote extra time to study, homework, sport, relaxation and entertainment. We must value and preserve the landscape.

Streets should be wide enough and greenery ensuring plenty of air, light, power transmission lines and traffic safety etc. Smooth street surfacing, replacement of auto rickshaws by buses, banning of heavy-duty vehicles from the main streets, prohibiting unnecessary horn signals, and radiobroadcasts in the streets- all play an important part in noise abatement. Last but not least in noise abating are town planning measures which include making streets sufficiently wide, locating housing at a distance from the roadways, and planting greenery. All the living room and bedrooms windows open on to the side away from the busy street. Rapid urban growth makes it increasingly difficult to provide city residents with a place to relax the natural conditions and an active recreation in natural environment has a particular appeal for urban residents. Therefore, the need for special recreation zones grows correspondingly. Serious attention has to be paid to recreation sites, the restriction of human activities in the suburbs and planning of tourist itineraries. Moreover, cities like Dhaka, Chittagong and Sylhet etc. will be overpopulated, unhygienic and in the wet season the road transportation system will be collapsed by rainwater. Many of the cities including Dhaka have already been experienced the situation. In most of the areas, the roads act as canals for discharging surface runoff of the wet monsoon.

Since most of the cities and townships are situated on the bank of rivers, the outlets of the drainage system are river. However, quick and rapid expansion of urban areas and illegal encroachments has narrowed the water flow and its subsystems. Moreover, lack of proper urban planning has aggravated the situation further; narrow roads, drains and sewerage systems, and lack of proper and sufficient garbage disposal facilities made the township very unsuitable for dwelling. Drains are often getting blocked and rivers are silted. Sometimes upstream floodwater enters the cities and townships for which although embankments with sluice-gates were constructed but in most of the cases they are not functional. Moreover, the embankments are occupied illegally by the slum dwellers and musclemen. Some hazardous industries viz. tanneries, dyeing, chemicals and detergent manufacturing, brick kilns etc. are established within the city areas which are disposing and discharging hazardous chemicals, gases and dusts to the air, water bodies and soil. They are causing health hazards to flora and fauna including microbes and human being. Therefore, a proper planning of a city is utmost essential. There should have a master plan for at least 100 years future plan for every city or township.

Development of Navigation System

It is a very difficult task at the moment but still very important. Since most of the natural systems have been disturbed and increasingly siltation process is progressing, these need experts and policy makers' immediate attention to halt diversion and obstruction of the natural flows. Dredging of the rivers is one of the best options and this should be started from the down stream in June and July and gradually advance towards the upstream. This will provide moving of silt along with the water-flow faster. Excavation of canals especially across the flood plains connecting two or more water bodies or rivers systems in the coastal zone will improve the navigation system. All roads and highways should keep sufficient clearance under the bridges to pass the sailed boats, cargos, steamers and launches. Permanent structures must not be built on the charlands of the rivers as the river-flow often changes their course especially early and mature state.

Many rivers have been narrowed down due to agricultural extension, urbanization, narrow bridges and by road linkages which must be widened and deepened by re-excavation. Most importantly, it is essential to re-excavate the wet-bodies especially the bheels or lakes where water remains throughout the year. Usually these bheels are connected with the rivers either as distributor or tributary. If these are disconnected by siltation, earth filling or encroachments, it must be revived by excavation. For wetland and river restoration and maintenance policy must be updated and a national policy should be made considering the prevailing situation.

Conclusion

Landscape Management in Bangladesh is a very complex task. Geographical location, changes of direction of the rivers, heavy siltation, high population, frequent weather and climate extreme events are very influential factors. With a huge population the small land area has been affected by many crises like encroachments and land grabbing, land filling, crossroad transportation systems disturbing the natural water flows, trans-boundary withdrawal of water by construction of dams and embankments, deforestation in and immediate neighboring countries especially from the eastern Himalayan and Burmese ranges and also urban-industrial expansion. The administrative systems are also complex: cooperation and coordination is poor especially with the research and scientific bodies to the policy makers. More interestingly enough the policy makers favour short-term benefits rather than the long-term future. Since the gradation of the land is very low, it is very difficult to protect the country from floods especially in the wet monsoon. The fragile river system of the flood-plain is under tremendous mismanagement; there is a little care for keeping their continuous flow, as a result, most of the river has lost their dry-season flow; narrowing or diverting water flow due to unplanned bridges for the roads and highways, extended industrial or urban construction and agriculture have obstructed and messed up with high siltation that flattened and nearly vanished most of the catchments. Cutting of hills and hill forests for industrial and agricultural expansion has created serious problems in many areas of Chittagong, Chittagong Hill Tracts, Cox's Bazar and Sylhet threatened with land sliding, erosion and increased risk of earthquake.

Although there are some laws and ordinances for hills and wet bodies but is of no planning for overall landscape management, as a result, implementation of existing laws is practically impossible. The central Madhupur terrace, the Sal Forest has already been vanished and replaced with industries, government and non-government institutions, urban and agricultural expansion, rubber and pineapple plantations and tourism spots etc. The remaining hills and hill forests of Tetulia, Panchagar, Sherpur, Mymensingh, greater Sylhet Comilla, Chittagong and Chittagong Hill Tracts are under the threat of flat-land agriculture. Traditional ponds are the unique system to hold the access water, act as reservoirs and source of water for domestic use as well as for aquaculture, and provide increased land area. Therefore, an immediate landscape planning at national and regional level is required to save the valuable ecosystems from further destruction.

Recommendations

- A national landscape plan should immediately be prepared for sustainable and long-term management of the country to mitigate the human induced disasters.
- Hills, catchments and wet-bodies, forests, floodplains, croplands and urban and rural-settlements should be brought under the landscape management plan.
- Wet-bodies should be restored to increase the water holding capacities of the rains and glacier melted surface waters.

- Management and excavation of traditional ponds for floodplain management and to mitigate the surface water crisis should be given priority. For recharging the ground water-tables large water bodies or ponds should have ring wells.
- Regional cooperation should be strengthen for sustainable landscape management and sharing forests, wild-lives, water-flows of rivers, glaciers and watersheds, migratory birds and animals etc.
- For a sustainable landscape management the status of the soil must be conserved; cement-concrete structures usually reduce or destroy soil, therefore, this should carefully be looked into during the urban and industrial expansion and even in the rural pacca structures.
- Humus rich top soil must not be used for making bricks.
- During construction of roads and highways along or across the water-flows, the flows of water in any season must not be obstructed, rather sufficient clearance should be ensured to pass the water even in the wet monsoon.
- Unplanned urbanisation and industrialization must be stopped.
- Windbreaks and shelterbelts should be established in a scientific way - these must allow wind to pass but not protect as a windshield.
- Safe and set back distances should be maintained during plantations as well as construction.
- Erosion and accretion of land should be managed following hydrological laws of water flows and siltation.
- Respect the traditions and evaluate their scientific values and integrate them into conventional practices to ensure sustainability.

Reference

1. Adel MM 2013 Farakka Barrage, the greatest ever riparian bluff for upstream water piracy. Academia Journal of Environmental Science 1(3): 036-052.
2. Ahmed AIMU 2008 Underlying Causes of Deforestation and Forest Degradation in Bangladesh Global Forest Coalition, The Netherlands Report http://vh-gfc.dpi.nl/img/userpics/File/

UnderlyingCauses/Bangladesh-Report-Underlying-Causes-Workshops.pdf accessed on January 3, 2014.

3. Ali, M.L. 2002. An integrated approach for the improvement of flood control and drainage schemes in the coastal belt of Bangladesh. Delft, Wageningen University and International Institute for Infrastructural, Hydraulic and Environmental Engineering. (Ph.D. thesis).
4. CEGIS (Center for Environmental and Geographical Information Services) 2008. Prediction of river bank erosion along the Jamuna, Ganges and the Padma Rivers, UNDP, Dhaka, Bangladesh, 66
5. Colman JM 1969 Brahmaputra River: Channel Process and Sedimentation, Sedimentary Geology B129-239.
6. Dasgupta S 2005. The Challenge of Farming Systems in Bangladesh in the Post Globalisation Period; Food, Agriculture, and Rural Development Policies in a Globalizing World, GLO 2005 http://www2.hcmuaf.edu.vn/data/pvhien/theme_1.pdf accessed on 11 January 2014.
7. European Landscape Convention (ELC) 2007: Landscape Institute http://www.landscapeinstitute.org/policy/European Landscape Convention.php Accessed on January 1, 2014.
8. GEAS 2013. Sand, rarer than one thinks, UNEP Global Environmental Alert Services March 2013.
9. Hasan, M.N.; Hossain, M.S.; Bari, M.A. and Islam, M.R., 2013. Agricultural land availability in Bangladesh. SRDI, Dhaka, Bangladesh, 42pp.
10. Hebblethwaite G. 1997. The Impact of Farakka Barrage upon Bangladesh. B.Sc. Thesis. Newcastle University, UK.
11. IDH Report: Sustainable Land and Water Program http://www.idhsustainabletrade.com/sustainable-land-and-water-program accessed on 4 March 4, 2014.
12. Islam, M.R. 2006b. ICZM initiatives and practices in Bangladesh. In: R. Krishnamurthy & Co-workers, eds. Integrated coastal zone management (ICZM) — the global challenge. New Delhi, Research Development Services.

13. Kabir MA 2013: Cement Makers Coming of Age: The Daily Star November 23, 2013 http://archive.thedailystar.net/beta2/news/cement-makers-coming-of-age/ accessed on 29 March 2014.

14. Khalequzzaman M, 2012 Flood Control in Bangladesh through Best

15. Management Practices; SAARC Workshop on Flood Risk Management in South Asia; 9-10 October 2012, Islamabad, Pakistan.

16. KRÄNZLIN, I.: Pond Management in Rural Bangladesh. System Changes, Problems and Prospects and Implications for Sustainable Development. (= Basler Beiträge zur Geographie 46) Basel, 2000, 213 S.

17. Nawaz, F. and Shah, M.N.N. 2011: Mechanisms and Challenges of Disaster in Bangladesh African Journal of History and Culture Vol. 3(7) pp 104-112, 2011

18. Rahman MA, 2004: Model Rural Homestead farming- A Real Example of Crop Diversification *In* Plantation Crops and Organic Farming Research Articles Series:-1 Some Environmental Problems and Their Solutions Touhid Publications, Dhaka, Bangladesh pp. 19-43.

19. Rahman, M.A. and Rahman S. 2013. Natural and Traditional Defense Mechanisms to Reduce Climate Risks in Coastal Zones of Bangladesh: IGBP-APN Write a Paper Workshop; Global Environmental Change and Sustainable Development in the Asia and Pacific SIDs Least Developed Countries, 26-30 August 2013, Windsor Suites Hotel Sukumbhit, Bangkok, Thailand.

20. Rashid H 1991 Geography of Bangladesh, The University Press Limited, Dhaka Bangladesh

21. Rashid H and Pramanik MAH, 1990. Visual Interpretation of Satellite Imagery for Monitoring Floods in Bangladesh. Springer-Verlag, New York Inc. USA..

22. Sattar A 1996 Farakka Bangladesher Bhagyo Zekhane Bondi, Padma, Jamuna Prakashani, Dhaka, Bangladesh.

23. SoE Report 2001: State of Environment Reports: Bangladesh 2001Regional Resource Centre for Asia and the Pacific (RRC.AP) at Asian Institute of Technology http://www.rrcap.ait.asia/pub/soe/bangladeshsoe.cfm accessed on 5 January 2014.

24. USGS, 2013b. Sand and gravel (construction) statistics, in: Kelly, T.D., Matos, G.R., (Eds.), Historical statistics for mineral and material commodities in the United States. U.S. Geological Survey Data Series 140, Reston.

25. Zahid A. and Ahmad S.R.U., 2013. Groundwater Resources Development in Bangladesh; Contribution to Irrigation for Food Security and Constraints to Sustainability http://fpd-bd.com/wp-content/uploads/2013/05/H039306.pdf Accessed on 27 March 2014

26. http://www.fao.org/fileadmin/templates/agphome/documents/PGR/SoW1/asia/BANGLADE.PDF

27. Read more at http://www.brainyquote.com/quotes/keywords/globalisation_5.html#I1Adsm4pYHcVjRGL.9

15

Anxiety Level among the Married Women

Prof Farzana Alim and Mariyam Fatima

"I measure the progress of a community by the degree of progress which women have achieved."

— B. R. Ambedkar

Introduction

India has embarked on an ambitious strategy that integrates reproductive, maternal, newborn, child and adolescent health (RMNCH+A) to address the major causes of mortality among women and children. The RMNCH+A strategy are holistic in design encompassing all interventions aimed at Reproductive, Maternal, New Born, Child and Adolescent Health under one broad umbrella. Rolled out by Government of India in 2013 the strategy focuses on the Strategic Life Cycle Approach and is based on the Continuum of Care Concept. The strategy promotes and provides for inter-linkages between different interventions at various stages of the life cycle and facilitates linking of child survival to other inventions such as reproductive health, family planning, maternal health. The strategy has a sharp focus on adolescents, recognising nurses as 'pivots' for service delivery and potentiates expanding focus on child development and quality of life.

The strategy is built on the need for prioritising high impact interventions across the five thematic areas in specifically identified geographical locations across the country. A review of available data very well establishes the fact that the country has huge inter-state and inter-district variations as far as health indices are concerned. Poor performing blocks and pockets also exist in the good performing states of the country. Corroborating with available evidence, Government of India has identified 184 High Priority Districts (HPDs) in the country for focused interventions to accelerate the progress towards achieving Millennium Development Goals 4 and 5 and also the health related targets enlisted in the 12th Five Year Plan. To facilitate the process of reaching the set goals and targets, Government of India has also prioritised high impact interventions across the thematic areas of reproductive, maternal, newborn, child and adolescent health as identified in the "5x5 matrix".

Objective of the Study

The main objective of the study is to identify the gap assessment under RMNCH+A Programme of Delivery points.

Methodology

The study was conducted in Chhatarpur district of Madhya Pradesh, as Chhatarpur is one of the high priority district in Madhya Pradesh in terms of high maternal mortality rate and infant Mortality rate in the country. A supportive supervision checklists designed by MPTAST (Madhya Pradesh Technical assistance and support team) in consultation with GOI (Government of India) was used as a tool to identify the gaps related to infrastructure, human resource, Drug, diagnostics, consumables, protocols, IEC, Records & registers, skills & trainings, level of awareness.

Result and Discussion

Besides district hospital, there are 10 Community health centers, 36 Primary health centers and 192 sub health centers in the district. In total there are 34 designated delivery points in the district.

Facility Gap Assessment

An assessment was done at 3 sub centers, 28 Community Health Center/Primary Health Center and three First Referral Units in the district. Based on detailed analysis of Gap Assessment findings, following are the Major Gaps Identified (Table.1).

Geographical Challenges

Inter facility distance is one of the major challenges in the district. Average distance of a sub-center from PHC is around 28 Kms, Average distance of a PHC and CHC is 57 Kms and FRU is 70 kms from district hospitals. Delivery points are also not distributed evenly in the district (Figure.1).

Table-1: Major Gaps Identified at Delivery Points

S. N.		Sub Center (n = 3)	PHC (n = 28)	FRU (n = 2)	District Hospital
1.	Location of Health facilities	28 Kms. (Average distance from PHC)	57 Kms. (Average distance from district HQ)	75 Kms. (Average distance from district HQ)	——
2.	Human Resource				
	Gynecologists	—	—	100%	-
	Anesthetist	—	—	100%	-
	Pediatrician	—	—	100%	-
	Medical Officers Vacancy	-	18%	—	-
	ANM Vacancy	30%(for second ANM)	—	—	——
	Staff Nurse / GNM		29%	25%	—
	LHV / HA Vacancy	-	28%	-	-
	Lab. Technicians Vacancy	—	43%	50%	-
	Pharmacist Vacancy	—	53%	50%	—
	RMNCH+A counselor	-	100%	100%	100%

3.	Training Gap				
	Emergency Obstetric Care Training	——	——	50%	—
	Life Saving Anesthesia Training	——	——	100%	—
	Basic Emergency Obstetric Care Training	——	60%	50%	—
	Skill Birth Attendant	100%	—	—	—
	Manual Vacuum Aspiration	—	80%	—	—
	Integrated Management of Neonatal Childhood Illness	—	100%	-	—
	Facility based-Integrated Management of Neonatal Childhood Illness	—	100%	100%	100%
	Navjat sishu suraksha karikaram	100%	30%	-	-
	Post partum insertion uterine contraceptive device	-	100%	100%	100%
4.	Infrastructure Gap				
	Poor condition of Building	—	21%	-	-
	24X7 Electricity Supply	33%	18%	-	-
	24X7 Water Supply	33%	29%	-	-
	Staff Quarter	67%	82%	-	-
	Labor Room in Good Condition	-	21%	50%	
	New Born Care Corner	100%	36%	50%	-
	Sick New born Care Unit	-	-	100%	-

	New Born Stabilization Unit	-	54%	50%	-
	Waste Management Mechanism	67%	54%	—	—
	Functional Blood Bank / Storage Unit	—	—	100%	—
5.	Essential Equipments Gap				
	Blood Sugar testing Kit	33%	-	-	-
	Neonatal and Adult Resuscitation Kit	7%	39%	-	-
	Radiant Warmer		31%	-	-
	Suction Apparatus	-	11%	-	-
	Manual Vacuum Aspiration Equipment	-	82%	-	-
	Operation Theater Table/Anesthesia Machine/ Multichannel Monitor/Pulse-oximeter	-	-	50%	-
5.	Drugs and Supplies Gap				
	Oral Contraceptive Pills	-	14%	-	-
	Emergency Contraceptive Pills	-	21%	-	-
	Sanitary Napkins	67%	21%	-	-
6.	Service Delivery Gap				
	Additional expenditure for Mother	57%	50%	-	-
7.	IEC Material display Gap	25%	29%	—	—

Human Resources

Availability of adequate human resource required at the facilities is another major gap in the district. 18 per cent of PHCs are without a medical officer, at 100 per cent of the First Referral Unit specialist post is vacant. Second Auxiliary Nurse Midwife is not available at 30 per cent of the Sub-center designated as delivery point. Lady Health Volunteer is not available at 28 per cent of the PHCs. Another important human resource gap is vacancy of Lab Technician, Pharmacist and RMNCH+A counselor.

Training Need Gap

There is 100 per cent Emergency Obstetric Care. Training is required since no trained medical officers posted at the two designated First referral units. There is 60 per cent gap for Basic Emergency Obstetric Care training at PHC and 100 per cent gap at First Referral Units. Skill Birth Attendant training need is 60 per cent at the Sub center delivery points and 50 per cent at Non First Referral Unit, Primary Health Center and Community Health Center. There is 100 per cent Skill Birth Attendant training gap at Sub center. Gap for Integrated Management of Neonatal and child hood illness and Facility based-integrated Management of Neonatal and child hood illness training is very high at all level. Navjat Sishu suraksha karikaram training need is again very high at 100 per cent and 30 per cent at delivery points. Post partum insertion of uterine device training is another major gap in training, since there is 100 per cent training need in the district.

Infrastructure Gap:

(1) *Gaps in Basic Physical Infrastructure:* Building condition of 21 per cent of the PHC is not good and up gradation is required. Condition of labor room is not good at 21 per cent PHCs and 50 per cent FRU. Another major gap for functionality of delivery points is round the clock electricity and water. At 33 per cent of sub centers and 18 per cent PHCs there is no provision of round the clock electricity supply and round the clock water supply is not available at 33 per cent Sub-center and 29 per cent Level two facilities. Staff Quarter in not available at 67 per cent of the Sub-center and 82 per cent of the Primary Health Centers.

(2) *Gaps in Infrastructure for New-born care:* Newborn care corner is either not available or not functional at 100 per cent Sub-center and 30 per cent Level 2 delivery points and 50 per cent of FRUs.

There is no Sick Newborn Care Unit in district other than at district hospitals.

(3) *Blood Bank/Storage Unit:* Blood bank at district hospital is functional but there is no blood storage unit at other 2 designated centers.

(4) *Waste Management Mechanism:* Waste management mechanism is not satisfactory at 67 per cent Sub center and 54 per cent PHCs.

Essential Equipments Gaps

Complete set of Adult and Neo-natal resuscitation equipments are not available at seven percent Sub center and 39 per cent of the PHCs. Radiant warmer is not functional at 31 per cent L 2 delivery points. Suction apparatus and Manual Vacuum Aspiration is not available at 11 per cent and 82 per cent of the Level 2 and Level 3 delivery points. Operative equipments are available at only 1 First Referral Unit out of 2 designated.

Drugs and Supplies Gap

Supply of Oral Contraceptive Pills is not adequately available at sub-center, Emergency Contraceptive Pills and Sanitary napkin supply is also not adequate at 67 per cent and 21 per cent of the primary health centers respectively. At Primary Health centers Emergency Contraceptive Pills were not available at 21 per cent centers.

Additional Expenditure During Institutional Delivery

At 57 per cent of sub-centers and 50 per cent of PHCs mother had incurred extra cost for delivery services. Extra cost was either for travel or drugs or diagnostics.

Information Education and Communication Display:

IEC display is not satisfactory at 25 per cent Sub-center and 29 per cent PHC.

Gap in Knowledge, Attitude and Practice in Community

Mothers of 0 to 6 Years Baby:

Knowledge, awareness and practice among the mothers or caretaker of 0 to 6 years baby is another major issue for poor service utilisation in the district. Although the awareness about initiation and exclusive breast feeding is good but there is big gap in the practice of Breast feeding and complementary feeding? Correct knowledge and practice for home based diarrhea management is also poor in the districts. Knowledge regarding the danger signs of pneumonia and where to seek help in case of pneumonia is again a major gap identified in community gap assessment (Table.2).

Table- 2 : Knowledge and Awareness of Mothers or 0 to 6 Years Baby (n = 128)

Indicators	Knowledge and Awareness	Mother Knowledge & Awareness (%)
Breast Feeding	Awareness about Breast feeding (BF) initiation	64
	Initiation of Breast Feeding within one hour of birth	62
	Awareness about Exclusive Breast feeding and continued feeding	72
	Mothers Exclusively Breast fed her youngest child for Six months and continued BF till 2 years	66
Complementary Feedings	Awareness about initiating Complementary Feeding (CF)	61
	Practiced CF from 6 months onwards	60
Diarrhoea	Knowledge about ORS+ Zinc in case of Diarrhoea.	52
	Knowledge on availability of ORS+ Zinc with ASHAs	51
Pneumonia	Knowledge about at least two danger signs of pneumonia.	45
	Awareness about point of contact for recognizing the danger signs	41

Pregnant and High Risk Pregnant Women

Regular use of MCP card is very poor in the district with only 59 per cent of currently pregnant women having the card. Quality and regularity of ANC services also needs to be strengthened in the district.

Awareness about birth preparedness is also poor in the district. Knowledge about JSY and JSSK programme is although good but not universal. Distribution of safe motherhood booklet is also very poor it the district. Although 64 per cent of pregnant had necessary contact information about referral but still this need further emphasis to make it universal. 42 per cent of the pregnant women didn't have contact no. of ASHA and ANM. In the district majority of the high risk pregnant women were not guided on birth preparedness and referral (Table.3).

Table- 3: Knowledge and Awareness of Pregnant / High Risk Pregnant Women (n = 128)

Indicators	Women with correct Knowledge and Practice (%)
MCP card being regularly filled.	59
Adequacy of quality and regularity of ANC.	46
Awareness about birth preparedness	46
Knowledge of JSY and JSSK	64
Receiving safe motherhood booklet?	49
Pregnant woman having contact details for timely referral	61
Pregnant woman having telephone numbers of ASHA/ANM	59
Guidance on referral with birth preparedness for high risk pregnant woman	47

Conclusion

It can be concluded from the above study that delivery points are not distributed evenly in the district. There is a high and urgent need of trained and skilled professionals in the field.

Proper and Adequate supply of drugs is needed in the district. Equipment for newborn care needs to be updated in terms of quantity and quality. There is shortage of specialist Doctors, which should be improved in order to maintain and improve the health services in the district.

References

1. District Implementation Plan of Chhatarpur District by District Program Management Unit, 2014.

2. District Implementation Plan of Chhatarpur District, District Program Management Unit, 2013.
3. Quality Assurance Checklist by Government of India, April 2014.
4. Read more at http://www.brainyquote.com/quotes/topics/topic_women.html#6HH7shrLo0Ze1r31.99

16

Incorporating CCE at Pre-service Teacher Training Curriculum

Ms. Ritu Sharma & Sangeeta Solanki

"Women must tell men always that they are the strong ones. They are the big, the strong, the wonderful. In truth, women are the strong ones. It is just my opinion, I am not a professor."

— Coco Chanel

Introduction

The new system (continuous comprehensive evaluation) as compared to the previous system places lesser importance on written examination. Instead of evaluating the students based on marks scored, the new evaluation seeks to measure their abilities in different areas. Instead of evaluating the student based on final written test at the end of the academic year, the new system envisages continuous evaluation throughout the year. It tries to eliminate fear of examination from their minds. The students get opportunity to improve their performances without losing an academic year. The success of CCE system of evaluation will depend solely on the teachers to execute CBSE's plans effectively, because the destiny of India lies in its classroom. This has been rightly said by the education commission report, 1964-66. This implies that teacher, who is the organiser and controller of the classroom, is mostly responsible for the future of India. So the teachers must be properly equipped with necessary knowledge skills and abilities to deal with children. It is in this context that education of teachers becomes most important in any country.

The new curriculum envisages the implementation of CCE also. Deviating conventional written, term-end examinations, under their new evaluation policy non-terminal continuous comprehensive evaluation involving activities, project work and oral expression has been introduce of teachers were not familiar with the methods of continuous and comprehensive evaluation.

Need and Signature of the Study

Now a days evaluation is comprehensive, continuous & objective based, which helps to know the strengths, weakness, interests & attitudes of the pupil & also helps in the all-round development of the individual as education aims. To improve the learner's overall performance during school academic session and to groom his/her future career, there is an urgent need to adopt a new pattern of evaluation, i.e. continuous and comprehensive evaluation which is the latest in its origin. The teacher training institutes are in a way suppliers for the requirement of teachers in schools. The schools on the other hand have to engage teachers who are fully equipped with the latest trends so that when employed, they have no problem in discharging their duties and are able to meet the new challenge of implementing the new teaching/learning styles including CCE. So the curriculum planners should review the curriculum for teacher education periodically and minor additions matching with the latest trends and demands of society as well as the requirements of schools should be incorporated. The old dead wood from the curriculum should be removed to provide scope for some fresh as well as needed learning by the trainees.

Statement of the Problem

"Incorporating CCE at Pre-service Teacher Training Curriculum."

Operational Definitions of the Specific Terms

1. **CCE:** CCE is student's evaluation under the observation of teachers. In this evaluation all the activities of each student are observed by the teacher through out the year & the teacher will provide grades to the students based on this evaluation.
2. **Pre-Service Teacher Education :** Pre-service teacher education refers to the training in which the teacher is prepared for his profession prior to his entering into it, continuously in order to keep himself abreast with the latest developments in his subject areas and to acquire the communication skills for effective teaching.
3. **Curriculum:** Curriculum is considered as synonymous to syllabus, courses, etc. It is, in fact, an organised plan of course outlines along with the objectives, methods and strategies of transaction and learning experiences to be provided for the achievement of the desired outcomes.

Objectives of the Study

1. To study the need & significance of CCE.
2. To study the need for inclusion of CCE at pre-service level.
3. To suggest reformation in the curriculum of teacher education at pre-service level in the light of CCE.

Method of Research

Descriptive method has been used in the present study.

Conclusion

The Conclusion has been derived from the analysis of incorporating continuous comprehensive evaluation at Pre-service teacher training curriculum. The purpose of education generally of all levels of schooling and specifically at pre-service level should not just be to assess the level of growth, but more so to improve it.

Therefore CCE contributes a lot to our teaching learning process but unfortunately in the 21st century we are unable practice CCE in our class rooms. We should try our best to implement CCE whole heartedly with a missionary zeal. It will ultimately help us in moving from banal and hackneyed approach to evaluation to a more progressive and trendy approach.

CCE helps in improving student's performance by identifying the learning difficulties at regular time interval right from the beginning of academic session by employing action research and it followed by suitable remedial measures students learning and social skills can be enhanced among students. These skills should be developed in the students during formative years for their integrated and balanced personality.

It is in this context that researcher felt that the teacher trainees must be aware of the needs, the requirements as well as the latest introduction of continuous comprehensive evaluation. So the current models of teacher education offered by the DIETS (District Institute of Educational Training) such as D.ED (Deputy of Education) and the program of B.ED (Bachelor of Education) offered under the university system should incorporate the transactional concerns in teacher education enunciated in the NCFTE (National curriculum Framework for Teacher Education)

Educational Implications

Educational Research is a systematic attempt to gain a better understanding of educational process; generally with a view to improve its efficiency. Research is of no value until its findings are applied for anything which may have some practical importance. Certain educational implications can be derived from the findings of the present study, which are:

1. Teacher should pay individual attention to each student.
2. Teacher should encourage students to participate in co-curricular activities (scouting, guiding, cultural activities, sports, dance, drama, music, painting, debate, quiz, creative writing etc.) to their capacities to be more realists.
3. New Teaching techniques should be employed by the teacher for better adjustment of school in school.
4. For the success of foresaid suggestions, students should be praised and motivated.

5. Refreshes courses related CCE should be organized at pre-service teacher training level.

6. For success of CCE scheme in schools, it should be incorporate in teacher education.

7. There should be regular assessment of the students' activities of both scholastic and co-scholastic areas.

References

1. Carri, Remith George & Joseph, Asha, *Comprehensive evaluation & Quality Eduaction,* Edutracks Vol. 9- No.11, Neelkamal Pub. Hydrabad, July 2010, pp. 5-8.

2. Dixit, Akansha; *'Grading scores over making' Edutracks*, Vol. 4- No.10, Neelkamal Pub. Hydrabad, June 2005,

3. National Curriculum Frame work – 2005. National Council of Educational Research & Training, New Delhi: NCERT.

4. National Curriculum Frame work for Teacher Education – 2009. National Council of Educational Research & Training, New Delhi: NCERT.

5. Rajput, J.S.(2004), Quality of school Education , Encyclopedia of Indian education vol. II (L-Z) New Delhi : NCERT

6. Reddy, G.S, 'A revolution in education 'Edutrack Vol.8 – No.12, Neel Kamal Pub, Hydrabad, August,2009

7. Rout, Kumar Ranjan & Guru, Nibedita, "The Scenario of Continuous & comprehensive Evaluation in 21st Century," Edutrack Vol.10 – No.2, Neel Kamal Pub, Hydrabad, October, 2010, pp.19-20.

8. Kapur, Arun; 'CBSE proposal will spawn uniform mediocrity ' , Mail today, New Delhi, Wednesday , 9 Dec. 2009.

9. Pushkarna, Neha; 'Pvt Firms earn high Grades for CCE rollout', The Times of India, New Delhi, Monday, 6 september 2010.

10. Sibal, Kapil ; ' Grading System will be in class XII, Hindustan, Bareilly, Friday, 29 January 2010.

11. "Teacher learn how to make the grade," The Times of India, New Delhi, Wednesday Octuber 7, 2009.

12. www. cbse. nic.in/cce/cbse/.3.htm.

13. www.wikieducator.org/ continuous comprehensive evaluation

14. www./encyclopedia.jrank.org/articles/pages/6821/teacher education.html

15. Read more at http://www.brainyquote.com/quotes/topics/topic_women. html # 6HH7 shr Lo0 Ze1r31. 99

17

Quality of Life of Adolescent Girls (16-18 Yrs) and Its Associate Co-relates

Prof Farzana Alim and Moulaey Zainab

"Women have always been courageous... They are always fearless when protecting their children and in the last century they have been fearless in the fight for their rights."

—Isabel Allende

Introduction

Quality of Life is tied to perception of 'meaning'. The quest for meaning is central to the human condition, and we are brought in touch with a sense of meaning when we reflect on that which we have created, loved, believed in or left as a legacy. The term 'Quality of Life' is a recently developed concept which has been gaining recognition worldwide. It is a concept of multi-disciplinary discussion; gaining attention of researchers in different fields like education, psychology, medical science, geography, biology and sociology, first to count a few. It has been a widely used term because it evaluates the general well-being of individuals and societies. It is used in a wide range of contexts, including the fields of international development, healthcare, and politics. In the field of Economics and Geography also it has been a burning issue; however it should not be confused with the concept of standard of living, which is based primarily on income. Instead, standard indicators of the quality of life include not only wealth and employment, but also the built-up environment, physical and mental health, education, recreation and leisure time, and social belonging.

According to WHO – QOL is the individuals perception of their status in life according to the cultural and value systems the person lives in, considering their aims, expectations, standards and worries. The adolescence comes from the Latin word *adolescere,* meaning "to grow" or "to grow to maturity." It is customary to regard adolescence as beginning when children become sexually mature and ending when they reach the age of legal maturity. Adolescence is a transitional stage of physical and physiological human development that generally occurs during the period from puberty to legal adulthood. The period of adolescence is most closely associated with the teenage years, though its physical, psychological and cultural expressions may begin earlier and end later. For example, although puberty has been historically associated with the onset of adolescent development, it now typically begins prior to the teenage years and there have been a normative shift of it occurring in preadolescence, particularly in females.

Usually, adolescence is thought of as that period of life during which maturity is being attained; and especially this is true as far as maturity related to the development of the proactive power of an individual. This period also marks a time in individual's life when it is difficult to consider him as a child or an adult. Observation of, and experience with individuals during the "teens" reveal that there is a fairly distinct time during which the individual can't be treated as child, and actually resent such treatment. Yet this same individual by no means is fully mature, and can't be classed as an adult. During this transition from childhood to adulthood, therefore, the subject is referred to as an adolescent. G. Stanley Hall was the first to draw a vivid and striking picture of this stage of life, with all its specific characteristics, gradations and peculiarities. He cited the definition of the term from the dictionary as- *"(one) yet in the nest, and vainly attempting to fly while its wings have only pin feathers".*

Adolescence appears at the time when the surge of life reaches its highest peak. The adolescent's life is, or might be, full opportunity to enter into new experiences, to explore new relationships, to feel new resources of inner strength and abilities. Although adolescence is a time of great possibility, it is also a time when most young people must pay a price for the privilege of growing up. Their freedom to seize what life offers is curtailed both from within and from without. The outer restraints- the rules they must follow, the conditions they must confirm to are obvious and they are strong. Although these messages permeate the whole of society, including adolescent boys and girls, girls are often targeted by media and social body image ideals and are more likely to suffer negative health outcomes it they don't find their physical appearance to be up to the mark. This type of satisfaction or dissatisfaction related to ones physique will in turn affect their social and psychological needs especially among girls.

Studies of change in behaviour, attitudes and values throughout adolescence have revealed not only that these changes are more rapid in the early than in the latter part of adolescence but also that the behaviour, attitudes and values in the early part of the period are markedly different from those in the latter part. As a result it has become a widespread practice to divide adolescence into two subdivisions, *early* and *late* adolescence respectively. Early adolescence extends roughly from thirteen to sixteen or seventeen years, and late adolescence covers the period from then until eighteen, the age of legal maturity.

As adolescence is a period of great dilemma about whether an individual is a child or an adult and consequently it affects the quality of life of the adolescent girls to a large extent. Soon after the child enters this stage of life parents and teachers start expecting the child to behave like adults in one situation and like a child in other, on one hand and on the other hand these pubescent are under the peer pressure to stay up to their norms. Adolescents along with adjusting to the demands of parents, teachers, society, and peer group also have to adjust to the physical and physiological changes taking place within them. All these factors combined together have an effect on the Quality of Life of an adolescent. The individuals who adjust well to these demands and changes have a good QOL, in comparison to the ones who fail to do so.

Statement of the Problem

To study the QOL of the Adolescent Girls (16-18 yrs), difference in the QOL of the two age groups, and association between the physical, social and psychological correlates and QOL of the target group.

Aims and Objectives of the Study

1. To study the QOL of the Adolescent girls (16-18) years of age.
2. To study the difference between the QOL of early and late adolescent girls.
3. To study the relation between BMI (physical correlate) and QOL of the Adolescent girls.
4. To study the relation between social and psychological correlates and QOL of Adolescent girls.

Hypotheses

Following null hypotheses have been formulated for the present study.

1. There is significant difference in the QOL of the early and late adolescents.
2. There is significant relation between the physical correlate and the QOL of the adolescent girls.
3. There is significant relation between social correlates and QOL of the adolescent girls.
4. There is significant relation between psychological correlates and QOL of the adolescent girls.

Methodology

The method adopted for the present study was descriptive and statistical in nature.

Sample of the study

The sample of this study consists of 50 adolescent girls (16-18yrs). The study was conducted in Senior Secondary school for girls (+2) of A.M.U. Quality of Life was taken as the independent variable and co relates (physical, social and psychological) were taken as dependent variables.

Instrumentation

A standard questionnaire was used to conduct the study [A Quality of the Scale (Raphael, D. 1998, and The Quality of Life Profile: a generic measure of Health and Well Being. Toronto: University of Toronto Centre for Health Promotion)]. The target group was provided with the Questionnaire and told that the information provided by them will be kept confidential and will only be used for research purpose. BMI of the respondents was also taken to study the health domain. The body mass index (BMI) is a measure for human body shape based on an individual's mass and height.

$$\text{BMI} = \frac{\text{mass(kg)}}{(\text{height(m)})^2}$$

Statistical Techniques

After analysing the purpose of the study the most appropriate statistical techniques were used namely Mean (M), Standard Deviation (SD), Standard Error of difference between the Means (SEM), t-test was used to see the significance of the difference between two means.

Result and Discussion

The present study was intended to study the various dimensions of QOL. To see the relation between QOL and correlates associated with this age group (adolescence).

Table -1.1 Gives the Description about the QOL of the Two Age Groups (Early and Late Adolescents)

QOL of Sample	N	Mean	SD	t
Early Adolescents	25	40.87	54.685	1.39
Late Adolescents	25	49.34	61.403	

On applying t-test it was found that there is no significant difference between the QOL of two age groups as the calculated value of 't' was found to be less than the table value of 't'. Therefore we reject the null hypothesis. The extent of similarity between the QOL of the two samples may be attributed to the almost same age group. The age difference between the two samples is very less i.e. both are adolescents and thus have somewhat same kind of feelings and emotions about oneself and people around and surroundings.

Table 1.2 Gives the Description about the Relationship Between BMI and QOL of the Two Groups (Early and Late Adolescents)

Variables	N	Mean	SD	t
Adolescents (BMI)	50	27.6	6.540	2.78
QOL	50	230.45	38.403	

't' test was used to find the relation between BMI and QOL of the total sample and it was found that there is a significant relation between the two, as the calculated value of 't' is more than the table value of 't', therefore we accept the null hypothesis. This relation may be attributed to the fact that physical health is determined by the nutritional status of an individual and which in turn is calculated by BMI.

If a person is physically fit he is likely to have a good QOL. Social and psychological correlates were also taken in to consideration in relation to QOL, as there were sections in the questionnaire relating to self and relating to surroundings. It was found that there is a close relation between QOL and social and psychological correlates, because when a person is satisfied and happy with his/her self, he/she is likely to be happy with his surroundings which in turn affect the QOL.

Conclusion

It can be said that adolescent is the stage of life identified as 'identity v/s role confusion' (*Erik Erikson* in his psychosocial theory of development). The identity that adolescent seeks to clarify is who he is, what his role in society is to be...is he a child or an adult. This search for identity further affects life achievement of an adolescent. If they have a prolonged period of role confusion it will adversely affect their well being and on the whole their QOL. The adolescents who have well identified roles or are successful in identifying their roles in the world as a productive member, and stay happy which in turn affect their physical social and psychological health.

References

1. Baron, R.A., and Byrne,D. (2004), *Social Psychology*, tenth edition; Pearson Education (Singapore) Pvt. Ltd.
2. Beeelick, D.B. (1973), "Source of Student Satisfaction and dissatisfaction", *Journal of Educational Research,* pp.19-22, 28, 67.
3. Berk.E. Laura, (2003), *Child Development,* 6th edition, Tata McGraw Hill publishing company Ltd. New York.
4. Berlim, M.T. and Fleck, M.P.A. (2003), "Quality of life: a brand new concept for research and practice in psychiatry", Rev *Bras Psiquiatr,* Vol.25 No.4, pp.52-249.
5. Cummins, R. A (2000), Objective and subjective quality of life: an interactive model, *Social Indicators Research*, Vol. 52 No. 1,pp. 55-72.
6. Erikson, E.H. (1964), *Child and Society* (rev.ed.) Norton, New York.
7. Gill, T., and Feinstein, A. R. (1994), "A Critical Appraisal of the Quality of Quality of Life Measurements." *Journal of the American Medical Association,* Vol. 272: 619–626.
8. Hurlock, E.B. (1988). *Developmental Psychology- a life span approach*, 6th edition, Tata McGraw Hill publishing company Ltd. New Delhi.
9. Knox.P.L. Social Well being aspatial perspective, London, 1975.

10. Laird, B.R., Newcomb, A.F., and Bukowski, W. M. (1998), Preadolescent friendship and peer rejection as predictors of adult adjustment. *Child Development*. 69,104- 153.

11. Papalia, D.E., (1993), *A Child's World*, McGraw Hill Inc, New York.

12. Raeff. Catherine Janette B. Benson, (2003), Social and Cognitive Development in the Context of Individual, Social and Cultural Processes, Routledge. Place of Publication: New York.

13. Sandstorm, M. J., and Cillessen, A. H. N. (2003), *Sociometric status of children's peer experiences: Use of daily diary method*, Merrill – Palmer quarterly, 49, 427- 452.

14. Spilker, B., and Revicki, D. A. (1999) "Taxonomy of Quality of Life." *Quality of life and Pharmacoeconomics in Clinical Trials*. Philadelphia: Lippincott-Raven, pp. 25–32.

18

Rubber Plantation: A Way of Changing Livelihood of Tribals

B.K.Panda & Sukanta Sarkar

"Human progress is neither automatic nor inevitable... Every step toward the goal of justice requires sacrifice, suffering, and struggle; the tireless exertions and passionate concern of dedicated individuals."

— Martin Luther King, Jr.

Introduction

Plantation is a long, artificially-established forest, farm or estate, where crops are grown for sale, often in distant markets rather than for local on-site consumption. The term plantation is informal and not precisely defined. Plantations are developed on a large scale as the crops are grown for commercial purposes, not for local consumption. It has usually not included large orchards (except for banana plantations), but does include the planting of trees for lumber. A plantation is always a monoculture over a large area and does not include extensive naturally occurring stands of plants that have economic value.[1]

In forestry, plantations of trees are typically grown as an even-aged monoculture for timber production, as opposed to a natural forest, where the trees are usually of diverse species and diverse ages. A plantation is not a natural ecosystem. Plantations are also sometimes known as "man-made forests" or "tree farms", though this latter term more typically refers to specialist tree nurseries which produce the seedling trees used to create plantations. A plantation is usually made up of fast-growing trees planted either to replace already-logged forests or to substitute for their absence. Plantations differ from natural forests in several ways: Plantations are usually monocultures. That is, the same species of tree is planted in rows across a given area, whereas a conventional forest would contain far more diverse tree species. Plantations are always young forests. Typically, trees grown in plantations are harvested after 10 to 60 years, rarely up to 120 years. This means that the forests produced by plantations do not contain the type of growth, soil or wildlife typical of old-growth natural forest ecosystems. Most conspicuous is the absence of decaying dead wood, a very important part of natural forest ecosystems.[2]

Plantation is an economic unit producing agricultural commodities (field crops or horticultural products, but not livestock) for sale and employing a relatively large number of unskilled laborers whose activities are closely supervised. Plantations usually employ a year-round labor crew of some size, and they usually specialise in the production of only one or two marketable products. Plantation organisation of agricultural production is not a necessary consequence of large ownership units, nor does it require large land ownership. Another characteristic frequently associated with plantations is a relatively high degree of vertical integration, even of self-sufficiency. This may result when required inputs or processing facilities are not available locally and hence must be supplied by the plantation itself; or when processing plants built to supply an international market establish their own plantations in order to insure an adequate supply of raw-material inputs. Private plantations were the principal source of increasing supplies of tropical agricultural commodities throughout the seventeenth, eighteenth, and nineteenth centuries. The early twentieth century brought a great expansion of tropical plantations to supply European and American demand for such exotic commodities as coffee, tea, cocoa, bananas, palm and coconut oil, and rubber. The private plantation was still a major source of tropical commodities in the 1950s, especially in Asia and Latin America.[3]

What is Rubber Plantation?

The rubber plantations are exposed to perils like fire, lightning, forest fire, bush fire, flood, storm, tempest, inundation, land slide, rock slide, earthquake, drought etc. The peculiarity of rubber plantations is that if a few trees in a holding is damaged or perished, that particular patch of land cannot be used till the time the entire trees are cut and the area replanted.[4] It requires deep and lateritic fertile soil with an acidic pH of 4.5 to 6.0 and highly deficient in available phosphorous. Tropical climate with annual rainfall of 2000 – 4500 mm is suited for cultivation. Minimum and maximum temperature should be ranged from 25 to 34°C with 80 per cent relative humidity is ideal for cultivation. Regions prone to heavy winds should be avoided.[5]

Origin of Rubber Plantation

Rubber is a prominent plantation crop of considerable significance to the Indian economy. A native to Brazil, rubber was introduced to India in 1873 and its commercial cultivation started in 1902. This industrial crop has since emerged as an icon of small holders' stake in the plantation sector of our country. Natural Rubber tapped from the bark of the tree *Hevea brasiliensis*is the raw material for an industry manufacturing about 50,000 products. The consumption pattern of rubber in our country is highly in favour of natural rubber (76 per cent), quite contrary to the synthetic rubber's global consumption of about 53 per cent. The global area under rubber is estimated to be around 103 lakh ha. The present global rubber production is to the tune of 97.3 lakh MT (2007) mostly contributed by about 15 countries.[6] Plantation sector is not just a foreign exchange earner but a Key Sector.

In India's Inclusive Growth Strategy because of its role in employment generation, (especially women labour) livelihood of small and marginal growers, backward communities, balanced regional development and addressing environmental issues. Further it is, perhaps, the only sector where competitiveness determines decisively the ability to foster inclusive growth as the competing countries are desperate exporters with hardlyany domestic market.[7] The rubber plantation industry in India was started about seven or eight decades ago, the rubber manufacturing industry is comparatively of recent origin. It started only in the 1920's but has acquired power and strength within a very short time. World War II generated some favourable conditions for its growth. But substantial progress occurred only after independence. The post independent era is noted for the remarkable growth of rubber manufacturing industry.[8] In tropical and subtropical areas, tree plantations are being established for different land use systems viz. shift in timber production from native forests to plantation, restoration of degraded lands, catalysts of forest succession and also as buffer zones for biodiversity conservation.[9]

Rubber Plantation in India

Thailand is the world's largest producer of natural rubber. It produced 3,394 thousand tones in 2011. Indonesia is the second largest producer contributing around 27 per cent of the world's total natural rubber production. Malaysia produced 996 thousand tonnes and occupies the third rank in terms of production. India is the fourth largest producer of natural rubber in the world. In the year 2011, India produced 890 thousand tonnes of natural rubber, up from 851 thousand tonnesin the previous year. India contributes eight percent of the world natural rubber production. Other major producers include Vietnam and China contributing seven percenteach to the world production. Rubber plantations give yield only after six years of being planted and are productive for about 25 years. Indonesia, the second largest producer has 3,435 thousand hectares under rubber. While, Thailand which is the largest producer has 2,756 thousand hectares planted with rubber. This implies that Thailand has greater yield than Indonesia. China being the fastest growing economy of the world is also the world's largest natural rubber consuming country. At 3,603 thousand tone sit consumes 33 per cent of the total rubber consumed over the world.

India's natural rubber production has been increasing steadily over the past decade. The production grew at the rate of 4.8 per cent in the year 2011-12. India produced 904 thousand tonnes in 2011-12 compared to 862 thousand tones in 2010-11. Consumption too has been rising steadily. It grew at the rate of 1.8 per cent in 2011-12 and more than 6.8 per cent in 2009-10. Consumption grew from 525 thousand tones in 1995-96 to 964 thousand tones in 2011-12. The rubber growing regions in India can be classified under two major zones, traditional and nontraditional, on the basis of agroclimatic conditions. Rubber cultivation in India has been traditionally confined to hinterlands of southwest coast, mainly in Kanyakumari district of Tamil Nadu and Kerala. Kerala and Tamil Nadu together constitute the traditional rubber growing regions in the country. Kerala alone contributes 89 per cent of the total rubber produced in India and an area of 534,228 ha under rubber plantations. TamilNadu contributes another three percent of the total natural rubber production. NonTraditional Regions are hinterlands of coastal Karnataka, Goa, Konkan Region of Maharashtra, hinterlands of coastal Andhra Pradesh and Orissa, the northeastern states, Andaman and Nicobar Islands etc, where rubber is now being grown. In recent years among nontraditional region, Tripura has become one of the most thrust areas for Rubber growing because of its well acceptance worldwide. In fact, Tripura was declared the "Second Rubber Capital of India" by the Rubber Board. India has succeeded in Rubber cultivation due to research and extension work undertaken by the Rubber Board. The worldwide demand for natural rubber from Tripura is mainly because ofits elasticity.[10]

Traditionally, rubber trees are grown in the southern region of the Western Ghats in India, which accounts for over 90 per cent of its production in this country. However, the Brahmaputra valley region of India has become an alternate area for cultivating rubber trees since 1960s. The price of natural rubber remains high, which prompts farmers to take up rubber tree cultivation in Brahmaputra valley as a livelihood option. Rubber tree plantations provide valuable ecosystem services in the marginal and jhummed barren lands, where it is predominantly grown in the Brahmaputra valley.[11]

Plantation sector has an important role in the economic development of India as it provides some of the basic raw materials which are necessary for industrial development. As far as natural rubber is concerned, it is a strategic raw material. It caters to a wide range of industries manufacturing a variety or products. Rubber enjoys an important place among the commercial crops. India has only limited areas suitable for rubber plantation. The State of Kerala accounts for about 94 per cent of the land under rubber cultivation, the balance being distributed in Tamil Nadu, Karnataka, Goa, Assam, Tripura, Andaman & Nicobar Islands. Kerala, rubber cultivation covers a total area of 205,383 hectares. The rubber plantation industry in Kerala is composed of organised and unorganised sectors. Rubber plantation industry has recorded a phenomenal growth during the post independence period and is characterised by an upward trend in the production range from "import necessitating situation to the'exp0rtable surplus condition.[12]

Natural rubber occupies a dominant position among the plantation crops in Kerala. In Kerala more than nine lakh rubber growers are engaged directly in the production of natural rubber. The average size of holdings under rubber cultivation in Kerala is less than 0.5 hectares. Rubber covers a sizeable portion of the area in the plantation sector of Kerala. During 1980-81 the total cropped area in Kerala was 1717000 hectares, of which 396000 hectares (14.8 per cent) was under rubber. Subsequently the area under rubber increased and during 2001-02 it came to 475000 hectares (21.70 per cent). In Kerala natural rubber is the only crop which shows an increasing trencl both in the area and production. From 1989-90 onwards the total agricultural land in Kerala remains more or less fixed. But the area under rubber plantations is increasing year after year. One of the main reasons for such a change is the shift of farmers from other crops to rubber. Natural rubber is cultivated in all the districts in Kerala. But the area and production of natural rubber is unevenly distributed in Kerala. Rubber trees will not grow in places located above 1000 meters from the sea level. The coastal district, Alappuzha and hilly district Wyanad produce least quantity of natural rubber in Kerala. In Alappuzha, the density of population is highest and the scope of plantation crops is limited. Moreover the paddy fields are not suitable for rubber cultivation. Land above 1000 meters is not suitable for rubber cultivation. Hence the production of rubber is lower in Wayanad district.[13]

Kerala is one of the greatest producers of Natural rubber in India. Kottayam district stands top in the production of natural rubber. In Kerala production of Natural rubber has increased from 579866 tonnes in 2000-01 to 783485 tonnes in 2008-09. Production outside Kerala was at the same time 50539 tonnes and 81015 tonnes respectively. Total Natural rubber production in India was 630405 tonnes in 2000-01 which has increased to 864500 tonnes in 2008-09. Rubber is considered as a small grower s crop as it is a major source of income to the small agricultural holders of Kerala. Rubber cultivation requires utmost care and attention from planting to marketing. Rubber is considered as a small Growers crop due to various reasons.[14] As much as 45 per cent of the natural rubber plantations in India are in the low-yielding 'aged' category. Of this, one-fourth (11 per cent of the total) is over-aged, said an analysis of Rubber Board data on natural rubber plantations by the Automotive Tyre Manufacturers' Association (ATMA). According to ATMA, growers need to be encouraged to re-plant with higher re-plantation subsidies. Since natural rubber prices have come off from their peak levels right now, growers will be more receptive towards re-plantation initiatives of the Rubber Board. Any further delay will severely impact long-term interests of both the producing and consuming interests.[15]

A variety of taxes and duties to the Central and State governments are being paid by the plantation sector. The Central Sales Tax is levied under the Central Act and collected by the State Government. The entire amount comes to the State Treasury. A portion of the Central Income Tax and Excise duty also goes to the State Revenue. The most important areas of taxation of Kerala Government are (i) State Sales Tax/Purchase Tax (ii) Agricultural Income Tax and (iii) Plantation Tax. A striking characteristic of plantation agriculture is that it is labour intensive. In Kerala, rubber plantations employ the largest number of workers followed by tea, coffee and cardaniom.[16]

During 2006-07 a large quantity of Rubber was imported. 89,699 MT of natural rubber was imported by the user industry as the domestic prices had risen above the international prices. In 2007-08 the import figure remained almost steady at 86,394 MT, with the demand from the automotive industry remaining strong. India imports Natural Rubber on a regular basis from Malaysia since 1980-81. During 1984-85 to 1988-89 India's share of Natural Rubber Import from Malaysia was approximately 82 per cent of total imports. But from the year 2000-01 to 2003-04 shares of imports from Malaysia has slipped down to the ranges 15 per cent to 33 per cent of the total imported value of the year. In 2010-11, 5.09 per cent of the rubber was imported from Malaysia. Export of Indian natural rubber, which was little known in the overseas market until 2001-02, managed to get a break in the highly competitive global NR market. Export of natural rubber from India rose from the low level of 6,995 tonnes in 2001-02 to 55,311 tonnes during 2002-03 and 75,905 tonnes during 2003-04. The main factors contributing to the buoyancy in export were the export promotional measures adopted by the Government of India and the prevalence of relatively higher NR prices in the international market since June 2003.[17]

Rubber Plantation and Income Source

Since independence several steps have been taken up by the Tripura government and other organisations to rehabilitate the jhumias. In the state, two resettlement divisions for shifting cultivators were set up under the forest department. Subsequently, for successful implementation of different programmes a separate department named *"Tribal Rehabilitation in Plantation and Primitive Group Programme"* was created in October 1985. Several efforts from the Central government (through North Eastern Council), State government (agriculture, forest, animal husbandry, tribal welfare) departments, Indian Council of Agricultural Research (ICAR), nongovernmental organisations, etc. are also being made through implementation of various programmes. But, the progress in rehabilitation of the jhumias is very slow. One of the most important and recent strategies adopted for Jhumia rehabilitation in Tripura is the raising of rubber plantations. The rubber plantation project was conceived to provide a lucrative alternative to Jhum cultivation. By the time of the 9th five-year plan, the raising of rubber plantation had become one of the main strategies for rehabilitation of Jhumias through the World Bank Aided India rubber Project. Here the Central Government, Rubber Board and Bank had come together to aid the Tripura government to raise rubber plantations and development itself as the *"Second Rubber Capital of India"*[18]

The first attempts to settle the Jhumias were made by the Raja of Tripura who had taken a cue from the British government. He attempted to set up the Kalyanpur Reserve in 1931 and its area was extended in 1943. The reserve was situated in a fertile area outside forests and attempted induce the Jhumias to induce them to take to the plough. Tenancy Acts were enacted to protect tribal rights on land. The immigrants who moved were mainly non-tribals as such migration was encouraged by rulers to bring about prosperity in the state. Thereafter the post-independence period saw a spate of attempts to set up programmes to settle the Jhumias into occupations that were acceptable in the mainstream peasant economy. The Congress government attempted to set up colonies where the Jhumias were given land to carry out plough cultivation. The scheme that was entitled Shifting Cultivation Control Scheme was acentrally sponsored scheme where one family was to be granted a piece of cultivable land and Rs. 500.00 as initial capital.[19] The Tripura forest department has initiated a project for socio-economic uplift of the poor Jhumias (shifting cultivators) from International Tropical Timber Organisation (ITTO) of China. The state government had appointed a consultant to prepare a project for providing Jhumia rehabilitation through international funding. The main objective of the project was to reduce the number of shifting cultivators as well as to insist the tribal in eco-sustainable livelihood management.[20]

The Bulk Rubber Plantation Project (BRPP) taken up by the Rubber Board, Rampachodavaram, in collaboration with the Integrated Tribal Development Agency (ITDA) in three phases from 1994 in Maredumilli mandal has brought a significant change in the life style of tribal people, particularly primitive groups like Kondareddys.

Tribal people who were familiar only with podu and kondapodu cultivation from which they produced cereals are now talking about rubber products, marketing, prices, internet and other technologies. Devarapalli is the first village in this mandal where the Rubber Board took up 50 hectares of rubber plantation initially. It took seven years for the plants to mature and the officials had to take a lot of pains to make tribal people wait for such a long time. They formed Rubber Growers Tribal Welfare Society in 2001 and elected Pallala Venkat Reddy president and he is continuing in the position. Under the society we are total 35 families with 50 hectares of land. The rubber plantation is showing satisfactory growth in most of the areas of Maredumilli, Rampachodavaram, and Y. Ramavaram mandals. The income from rubber has uncovered new dimensions of economy, and explored new elements of development.[21]

Insurance Scheme for Rubber Plantations

The scheme is applicable to both mature and immature plantations. The policy is issued for a period of seven years from the last day of the month of planting for immature plants. Compensation will be available from the second year onwards, which is calculated on the basis of 'replacement cost of the plant plus present value of future returns arising out of the loss / death of the plant'. For mature plantations, cover will be provided for blocks of 3 / 2 / 1 year(s) from the 8th year of planting. Compensation is calculated the same way as for the immature plantations, i.e. taking into account the input cost and anticipated yield deducting there from recurring maintenance expenses. Fire, Lightning, Riot, Strike & Malicious Damage, Bush Fire, Forest Fire, Flood, Storm, Tempest, Inundation, Land Slide, Rock Slide, Earthquake and Drought provided the Block/Taluka concerned is declared as drought affected by the competent authority of the State Government. The policy is also extended to cover the loss or damage caused by road/rail/vehicles and wild animals. Losses due to diseases and insect-pest are excluded from the scope of cover. In the case of destruction of 75 per cent of trees and above per hectare, the loss will be treated as total and the insured will be paid compensation as per the policy.[22]

Rubber Board

From 1980, the Board has given equal importance to replanting and new planting and promoted both alike under common integrated schemes. These are called Rubber Plantation Development scheme. In the 10th plan, Rubber Plantation Development Scheme has been modified incorporating various components in addition to replanting and new planting. The scheme is implemented throughout India except the north eastern region (For north eastern region, a separate scheme, 'Rubber Development in the North East', has been approved by the Govt. of India). The Rubber Production Department has 4 zonal offices, 39 regional offices, and 166 field stations besides 21 Tappers' Training Schools, 15 regional nurseries, 4 District Development Centres and 2 Nucleus Rubber Estate and Training Centres. Extension officers are posted at all zonal/regional offices and field stations and they frequently visit estates and holdings for advisory purposes. Growers also can meet these officers at their offices. The Rubber Research Institute of India and the Department of Processing and Product Development also render free extension services to estates and holdings on matters requiring special attention.[23]

Conclusion

Plantation sector has an important role in the economic development of India as it provides some of the basic raw materials which are necessary for industrial development. As far as natural rubber is concerned, it is a strategic raw material. It caters to a wide range of industries manufacturing a variety or products. Since independence several steps have been taken up by the government and other organisations to rehabilitate the jhumias. In the state, two resettlement divisions for shifting cultivators were set up under the forest department. Traditionally, rubber trees are grown in the southern region of the Western Ghats in India, which accounts for over 90 per cent of its production in country. However, the Brahmaputra valley region of India has become an alternate area for cultivating rubber trees since 1960s. Since independence several steps have been taken up by the government and other organisations to rehabilitate the jhumias. In the state, two resettlement divisions for shifting cultivators were set up under the forest department. Subsequently, for successful implementation of different programmes a separate department named *"Tribal Rehabilitation in Plantation and Primitive Group Programme"* was created in October 1985.

References

1. *Plantation (2014),* Retrieved from http://en.wikipedia.org/wiki/Plantation
2. *Tree plantation,* Retrieved from http://www.bwna.org.in/TreePlantation.aspx
3. *Plantation,* Retrieved from http://www.encyclopedia.com/topic/Plantations.aspx
4. *Rubber Plantation Insurances*, Retrieved from http://www.aicofindia.com/AICEng/General_Documents/Product_Profiles/Rubber_Ins.pdf
5. *Rubber plantation*, See http://agritech.tnau.ac.in/horticulture/horti_plantation per cent20crops_rubber.html
6. *Rubber plantation*, Retrieved from https://www.nabard.org/english/plant_rubber.aspx
7. See http://cds.edu/wp-content/uploads/2013/01/Report_Structural Infirmities. pdf
8. See http://dyuthi.cusat.ac.in/xmlui/bitstream/handle/purl/3279/Dyuthi-T1253.pdf?sequence=1
9. P.S. Chaudhuri, Subhalaxmi Bhattacharjee, Animesh De, Impact of age of rubber (Hevea brasiliensis) plantation onearthworm communities of West Tripura (India), *Journal of Environmental Biology*, Retrieved from http://www.jeb.co.in/journal_issues/201301_jan13/paper_09.pdf
10. *Natural rubber 2012-13,* Retrieved from http://www.nmce.com/files/study/rubber.pdf
11. Debabrata Ray, M. D. Behera and James Jacob, *Indian Brahmaputra valley offers significant potential for cultivation of rubber trees under changed climate*, Retrieved from http://www.currentscience.ac.in/Volumes/107/03/0461.pdf
12. See http://dyuthi.cusat.ac.in/xmlui/bitstream/handle/purl/3279/Dyuthi-T1253.pdf?sequence=1

13. *Rubber Plantation in Kerala,* chapter 2, Retrieved from http://shodhganga.inflibnet.ac.in/bitstream/10603/6550/10/10_chapter per cent202.pdf

14. M.Shahul Hameedu, *Role of rubber producers societies in Kerala,* Retrieved from http://www.ijcrar.com/vol-2-2/M. Shahul per cent 20 Hameedu 2. pdf

15. *Business Standard (Aug 20, 2014),* 5 per cent of rubber plantations 'aged': Study, Retrieved from http://www.business-standard.com/article/markets/45-of-rubber-plantations-in-india-aged-atma-study-114082000574_1.html

16. See http://shodhganga.inflibnet.ac.in/bitstream/10603/547/12/13_chapter per cent203.pdf

17. *Natural rubber 2012-14,* Retrieved from http://www.nmce.com/files/study/rubber.pdf

18. Er.Sujit Das, Er.Subhrajyoti Choudhury, Ar.Arpita Roy, The Success Story of Rehabilitation of Jhumias in Tripura- A Study on Baramura-Deutamura Range, *Research Inventory: International Journal of Engineering and Science,* Vol. 1, Issue 10, (December 2012), PP 25-29.

19. *Archana Prasad, Forestry and tribal development: A Background Note for Tripura State Human Development Report,* Retrieved from http://planningtripura.nic.in/THDR/backgroundreport/Forestry per cent20& per cent20Tribal per cent20Development.pdf

20. See http://www.oneindia.com/2007/11/18/itto-to-support-tripura-for-jhumia-rehabilitation-1195372947.html

21. *The Hindu (Feb 15, 2013),* Rubber plantation project changes tribal people's lifestyle, Retrieved from http://www.thehindu.com/todays-paper/tp-national/tp-andhrapradesh/rubber-plantation-project-changes-tribal-peoples-lifestyle/article4417456.ece

22. *Rubber Plantation Insurances,* Retrieved from http://www.aicofindia.com/AICEng/General_Documents/Product_Profiles/Rubber_Ins.pdRubber plantation development scheme, Retrieved from http://rubberboard.org.in/acts/subsidy_schemes.pdf

23. See http://www.brainyquote.com/quotes/keywords/human.html

Bibliography

1. A. Venkat Raman, James Warner Bjorkman (2008), *Public-Private Partnerships in Health Care in India: Lessons for developing countries,* Taylor & Francis.
2. Akintola Akintoye, Matthias Beck, Cliff Hardcastle (2003), *Public-Private Partnerships: Managing Risks and Opportunities*, Wiley.
3. Albert N. Link (2006), *Public/Private Partnerships: Innovation Strategies and Policy Alternatives*, Springer.
4. Alberto Paloni, Maurizio Zanardi (2005), *The IMF, World Bank and Policy Reform,* Taylor & Francis.
5. Ambuj Gupta (2010), *Non-Performing Assets (Npas) in Indian Banks,* Lambert Academic Publishing.
6. Anders Åslund, George De Menil (2000), *Economic Reform in Ukraine: The Unfinished Agenda,* M.E. Sharpe.
7. Anne O. Krueger (2002), *Economic Policy Reforms and the Indian Economy,* University of Chicago Press.
8. Arpita Mukherjee, Nitisha Patel (2005), *FDI in Retail Sector, India,* Academic Foundation.
9. B. S. Bhatia, G. S. Batra (2006), *Management of Financial Services*, Deep and Deep Publications.
10. Bishwa Nath Singh, Mohan Prasad Shrivastava, Narendra Prasad (2003), *Economic Reforms in India,* APH Publishing.
11. C. H. Chai, K. C. Roy 2006), *Economic Reform in China and India: Development Experiences in a Comparative Perspective*, Edward Elgar Publishing.
12. Charles Gibson (2012), *Financial Reporting and Analysis*, Cengage Learning.

13. Dale R. Weigel (1997), *Foreign Direct Investment,* World Bank Publications.

14. Darrin Grimsey, Mervyn Lewis (2004), *Public Private Partnerships: The Worldwide Revolution in Infrastructure Provision and Project Finance*, Edward Elgar.

15. David Williams (1984), *Financial Astrology*, American Federation of Astr.

16. Debaprosanna Nandy (2010), *Banking Sector Reforms in India and Performance Evaluation of Commercial Banks,* Universal-Publishers.

17. Dr. Vibha Jain (2007), *Non-performing assets in commercial banks,* Regal Publications.

18. E S Savas (2000), *Privatization and Public-Private Partnerships*, CQ Press.

19. E. R. Yescombe (2011), *Public-Private Partnerships: Principles of Policy and Finance,* Butterworth-Heinemann.

20. Ellen Marie Pint (2001), *Public-private Partnerships: Background Papers for the U.S.-U.K. Conference on Military Installation Assets, Operations, and Services*, Issue 1309, Rand.

21. Ernest Aryeetey, Jane Harrigan, Machiko Nissanke (2000), *Economic Reforms in Ghana: The Miracle and the Mirage,* Africa World Press.

22. Eugene Brigham, Michael Ehrhardt (2010), *Financial Management: Theory & Practice*, Edition 13, Cengage Learning.

23. Franklin Allen, Douglas Gale (1994), *Financial Innovation and Risk Sharing,* MIT Press.

24. Gogula Parthasarathy (2003), *Economic Reforms and Rural Development in India,* Academic Foundation.

25. Graeme A. Hodge, Carsten Greve (2005), *The Challenge of Public-private Partnerships: Learning from International Experience*, Edward Elgar Publishing.

26. H. K. Yong (2010), *Public-private Partnerships Policy and Practice: A Reference Guide,* Commonwealth Secretariat.

27. Howard A. Frank (2006), *Public Financial Management,* CRC Press.

28. I.M. Pandey (2009), *Financial Management*, Vikas Publishing House Pvt Ltd.

29. Jae K. Shim, Joel G. Siegel (2000), *Financial Management*, Barron's Educational Series.

30. John Williamson (1994), *The Political Economy of Policy Reform,* Peterson Institute.

31. José María Fanelli, Lyn Squire (2008), *Economic Reform in Developing Countries: Reach, Range, Reason,* Edward Elgar.

32. Justin Nelson Michael (2011), *Non Performing Assets in Co-operative Banks*, LAP Lambert Acad. Publ.

33. Justin Yifu Lin, Fang Cai, Zhou Li (2003), *The China Miracle: Development Strategy and Economic Reform,* Hong Kong Centre for Economic Research and the International Center for Economic Growth.

34. K. Seeta Prabhu (2001), *Economic reform and social sector development: a study of two Indian states,* Sage Publications.

35. Kenneth A. Froot (2008), *Foreign Direct Investment*, University of Chicago Press.

36. Larry Jay Diamond, Marc F. Plattner (1995), *Economic reform and democracy*, Johns Hopkins University Press.

37. Manmohan Singh, Isher Judge Ahluwalia, Ian Malcolm David Little (1998), *India's economic reforms and development: essays for Manmohan Singh*, Oxford University Press.

38. Marco Neuhaus (2006), *The Impact of FDI on Economic Growth: An Analysis for the Transition Countries of Central and Eastern Europe,* Springer Science & Business Media.

39. Margaret M. Pearson (1997), *China's New Business Elite: The Political Consequences of Economic Reform,* University of California Press.

40. Menjor Singh (2001), *Economic Reforms in India: Problems & Prospects,* Mittal Publications.

41. Mirjam Bult-Spiering, Geert Dewulf (2007), *Strategic Issues in Public-Private Partnerships: An International Perspective,* Wiley.

42. Nicholas Avery et al. (2006), *Public-Private Partnerships: A Practical Analysis*, Globe Law and Business.

43. Organisation for Economic Co-Operation and Development (2002), *Foreign Direct Investment for Development: Maximising Benefits, Minimising Costs: Overview,* OECD.

44. Paolo Urio (2010), *Public-Private Partnerships: Success and Failure Factors for In-Transition Countries*, University Press of America.

45. Parmatam Parkash Arya, B. B. Tandon (2003), *Economic Reforms in India: From First to Second Generation and Beyond,* Deep and Deep Publications.

46. Pauline Vaillancourt Rosenau (2000), *Public-private Policy Partnerships*, MIT Press.

47. Philipp H. Pattberg (2012), *Public-private Partnerships for Sustainable Development: Emergence, Influence and Legitimacy*, Edward Elgar Publishing.

48. Philippa Dee (2012), *Economic Reform Processes in South Asia: Toward Policy Efficiency,* Routledge.

49. Pradip Baijal (2008), *Disinvestment in India: I Lose and You Gain*, Pearson Education India.

50. R. Charles Moyer, James McGuigan, Ramesh Rao, William Kretlow (2011), *Contemporary Financial Management*, Cengage Learning.

51. R. K. Mishra, Bulusu Navin (2002), *Restructuring Public Enterprises in India: Privatisation and Disinvestment*, Mittal Publications.

52. R. K. Uppal (2005), *Economic Reforms in India: A Sectoral Analysis,* New Century Publications.

53. Ricardo Ffrench-Davis (2002), Economic Reforms in Chile: From Dictatorship to Democracy, University of Michigan Press.

54. Ronald W. Melicher, Edgar A. Norton (2011), *Introduction to Finance: Markets, Investments, and Financial Management*, Edition 14, John Wiley & Sons.

55. Roy E. Bailey (2005), *The Economics of Financial Markets,* Cambridge University Press

56. S.N Bidani (2005), Managing *Non-Performing Assets in Banks,* Vision Books Private, Limited.

57. Stephen Osborne (2002), *Public-Private Partnerships: Theory and Practice in International Perspective*, Taylor & Francis.

58. Stephen W. Perl (2010), *Public-Private Partnerships: Costs, Benefits and Efficiencies,* Nova Science Publishers.

59. Steven Heydemann (2004), *Networks of Privilege in the Middle East: The Politics of Economic Reform Revisited,* Palgrave Macmillan.

60. Sudhindra Bhat (2008), *Financial Management*, Excel Books India.

61. Sudhir Naib (2004), *Disinvestment in India: Policies, Procedures, Practices*, SAGE Publications India.

62. Sultan Singh (2007), *Banking Sector Reforms in India*, Kanishka Publ.

63. Susan L. Shirk (1993), *The Political Logic of Economic Reform in China,* University of California Press.

64. Susan Robertson, Karen Mundy, Antoni Verger (2012), *Public Private Partnerships in Education: New Actors and Modes of Governance in a Globalizing World,* Edward Elgar Publishing.

65. T. V. Gopalakrishnan (2004), *Management of Non-performing Advances: A Study with Reference to Public Sector Banks*, Northern Book Centre.

66. Uma Kapila (1996), *India's Economic Reforms*, Academic Foundation.

67. World Bank. Independent Evaluation Group (2008), *Public Sector Reform: What Works and Why? : an IEG Evaluation of World Bank Support*, World Bank Publications.

Index